CHALLENGES TO POLICE, HUMAN RIGHTS AND NATIONAL SECURITY

CHALLENGES TO POLICE, HUMAN RIGHTS AND NATIONAL SECURITY

DR. KRISHNA MOHAN MATHUR

KALPAZ PUBLICATIONS
Delhi-110 052

Challenges to Police, Human Rights and National Security
(Human Rights, Police)

ISBN: 81-7835-182-X

Published in 2003 in India by
Kalpaz Publications
C-30, Satyawati Nagar
Delhi-110052
E-mail : Kalpaz@hotmail.com

Lasertypesetting by: Varsha Graphics, Delhi
Printed by: Mehra Offset Press, Delhi

Contents

Preface

The present book looks ahead to the various challenges to police, human rights and national security. The human tragedy and the legal, political and diplomatic questions raised by the U.S. invasion of Iraq in 2003 have generated heated debate around the world about human rights and national security of the states. We need to address these questions seriously. Our Indian Central Cabinet has asserted before Parliament that "Our freedom of action is not constrained in any manner by outside pressures" and claimed that the National Democratic Alliance Government will not compromise with "National Security Concerns". Since the issues of human rights and national security are multi-dimensional, an humble attempt has been made to understand the various challenges to human rights and National Security. While analysing the various challenges, I am reminded of what Emile-zola once remarked about the consequences of not facing the reality. He said, "While truth is buried underground, it grows, it chokes, it gathers such an explosive force that one day it bursts out, it blows everything up with it. In Gujarat, Kashmir, North-Eastern States and many other parts of the country, truth has been frequently been bursting in the face of India. Truth is easily visible to anyone, willing to see it. Nation needs to be warned that "Actions at later stages would be too late", and there is a need for immediate bold strategic planning and management, of various burning issues and challenges. Chapter 1 deals with challenges to Communal harmony and second chapter suggests various strategies for combating communalism. The recent tragic communal violence in Gujarat is distressing, indeed alarming. Establishment of a secular democratic polity is our ultimate objective and communalism has to be rooted out from the society.

Police professionalism has to be developed in India and police need to prepare itself for the challenges of 21st Century with a high professional ethos, sense of accountability and transparency in its functions. CRPF, as an armed force of the Union, has to meet various internal security challenges by equipping itself with modern weapons, high-tech equipment, high standard of training and morale. A dynamic society demands qualitatively and quantitatively modern police with democratic outlook, commitment to the duty and accountability to the Constitution. Chapter 5 analyses various low intensity conflicts which are bound to arise in a plural, secular, democratic and developing nation. Where nations can flounder through internal or external conflicts, they can also grow in strength and stature where there is suitable resolution of conflicts. Chapter 6 deals with organisational role stress in police work. Police organisations must not only recognise police stress and analyse its various causes, they must adopt proper stress–coping techniques at both organisational and individual levels. Chapter 7 highlights human rights in the context of internal security operations by the security forces of India. Police leadership must take care of the welfare, training, equipment, weaponry and morale of the security forces while operating in terrorism infested areas. Chapter 8 focuses on the obligations and responsibilities of the police leadership in protecting human rights of the people. Effective leadership and close supervision can definitely promote human rights even in disturbed areas like those prevailing in J&K and North-Eastern States. Ninth chapter brings out various challenges which police have likely to face in the 21st Century and also suggests a comprehensive agenda for police reforms which are overdue. Chapter 10 spells out various challenges to national security. Political leadership and all political parties have to develop a consensus approach to the national security problems. Chapter 11 brings out need for strategic management of national security. What is needed is a national debate based on a series of white papers on our national security threats, military and non-military measures to meet them and a clear enunciation of competing options for working out a long-term strategic management approach to the entire problem.

In the body of this book, I have only attempted to initiate a dialogue and offer my comments and viewpoints on various subjects. Conventional acknowledgements are really inadequate to express how much this book owes to all those authors whose views and comments have enriched my book. It is with great pleasure that I acknowledge my gratitude to all the authors and thinkers whose books, articles, and viewpoints have served as sources of reference to me. The book, I am sure, will be of immense utility to the police officers, administrators, security experts and national leaders. This book can be useful to the serving police officers, officers and men of security forces and Central Police Organisations/armed forces of India. Feedback and critical comments from the readers are most welcome. Suggestions for improvement will be gratefully acknowledged and considered for incorporation in the subsequent revised editions of the book.

I feel beholden to Swami Iswarananda Giri Ji Maharaj, of Samvit Sadhanayan, Sant Sarover, Mt Abu for his constant spiritual guidance, blessings and grace to me. My wife Prabha Mathur, my family members—Shikha, Niraj, Samvit, Shashvat, Pragya, Prakhar, Prabhav, Shiv Shubhang, Nandita and Yagnesh—all deserve my thanks for giving me various types of support and encouraging me by sparing from all domestic liabilities for devoting greater attention to complete the work. Thanks are due to Shri B.P. Garg and his dedicated band of staff for bringing out the book within a short time in such a good get up. This book is an oblation to my *Isht deva* - Lord Shiva whose divine grace and inspiration remained the blessed force behind this academic endeavour. Actually I am conscious of the fact that I am only an instrument in the hands of the Almighty for carrying out His designated task and deserve no credit at all being only "Nimmit Matra". My respectful surrender to His cosmic design is my duty and pleasure.

18 May 2003 **Krishna Mohan Mathur**

I feel beholden to Swami Sri Shivananda Giri Ji Maharaj, of Shree Siddhashram, Sant Sarovar, Mt Abu for his constant spiritual guidance, blessings and grace to me. My wife Prerna Mathur, my family members—Shikha, Niraj, Sanyut, Shashvat, Pragya, Prakhar, Prabhav, Shiv Shubhang, Nandita and Yogesh—all deserve my thanks for giving me various types of support and encouraging me by sparing from all domestic liabilities for devoting greater attention to complete the work. Thanks are due to Shri R.P. Goel and his dedicated band of staff for bringing out the book within a short time in such a good get up. This book is an oblation to my *Ishta deva* Lord Shiva whose divine grace and inspiration remained the blessed force behind this academic endeavour. Actually I am conscious of the fact that I am only an instrument in the hands of the Almighty for carrying out His designated task and deserve no credit at all being only "Nimitt Matra". My respectful surrender to His cosmic design is my duty and pleasure.

18 May 2001 **Mahendra Mohan Mathur**

1

Challenges of Communal Harmony

सं गच्छध्वं सं वदध्वं सं वो
मनांसि जानताम्,
देवा भागं यथा पूर्वे
संजानाना उपासते ।।
ऋग्वेद -१०/१९१/अथर्व वेद ६/६८/१-३.

(Move together, Speak together; May your minds understand together. Just as Gods of ancient times share the oblations offered to them, May you also share your wealth with Unity and Understanding). (R K Veda 10/191 Atha 6/64/1-3)

Time, Space and Causation of the objective universe is caused by the ignorance of its real nature and the knowledge of the real nature of the universe would help to lay the foundation of harmony in all the fields including the communal one.[1] Although the world is fundamentally a process of diversification yet it remains a universe according to Vedantic philosophy. Most of the communal thinking is based on the imagined reality of the community with its unique values, ethics, theology, religion, culture and communal collective living. "Communal harmony can be based metaphysically on the foundations of limitless consciousness of the Beautitude. God is thus non-dual reality. An octagon is not a contradiction of seven sides but is the harmony of all the eight sides. India can become a haven of communal harmony if its secularism is based on Vedanta."[2] Jung has even asserted that the domain of unconscious mind includes collective unconsciousness or social unconsciousness".[3] In India, all communities, Hindus, Muslims, Christians Parsis and tribal communities can live in harmony if they learn spirit of tolerance and respect for other religions and communities. This is a measure at once of the inherent beauty of the Indian psyche and the acquired ugliness of Indian Politics. It shows, yet again, that a country which has over the millennia absorbed, often welcomed, alien faiths and cultures cannot be seriously communal–minded. It may have a preponderant majority of people of one religion, but happily for everyone and the country as a whole. Hinduism is a way of life, an essentially tolerant faith and not an aggressive, hermetically sealed, proselytizing creed.[3(a)] Communal riots violate Human Rights of the common citizens.

Religions in India have been basically spiritual and non-dogmatic. Communal harmony in a plural, multi-religious and multi-ethnic society, is an essential requirement. Sociologically speaking, locality of residence and occupation are two crucial elements of a community's social structures. Since a plural society consists of a number of communities, these communities are expected to live in harmony, because inter-community conflict weakens and destroys the credibility of the state. In India even today, when you look at the rural people, there is a great deal of communal harmony and integration between various communities. In 2002, India had the horrific Godhra train massacre and the subsequent shameful communal riots in Gujarat.

India opted for a secular constitution after independence. This meant assigning religious or cultural differences to private spheres, attempting to unite them on a vaster scale, taking into consideration the social, economic or political demands of the people in general. Secularism is concerned with building social relations between the people on grounds of common interests and establishing communal harmony. Challenges of communal riots need to be analysed in terms of the concept and connotation of human rights. In India, communal riots and violence are the greatest challenges to the human rights of the ordinary citizens. Human Rights need to be preserved in a secular democratic society. Human rights as enumeriated in the Indian constitution are as under :

1. Right of Equality:
   - (i) Equality before Law; (Article 14)
   - (ii) Prohibition of discrimination on grounds of religion, race, caste, sex, or place of birth; (Article 15)
   - (iii) Equality of opportunity in matters of public employment; (Article 14)
   - (iv) Abolition of untouchability; (Article 17)
   - (v) Abolition of titles (Article 18)

2. Right to Freedom:
   - (i) Freedom of speech; etc.; (Article 19)
   - (ii) Protection in respect of conviction for offences;

(Article 20)

(iii) Protection of life and personal liberty; (Article 21)

(iv) Protection against detention in certain cases; (Article 22)

3. Right against Exploitation

(i) Prohibition of traffic in human beings and forced labour; (Article 23)

(ii) Prohibition of employment of children in factories etc.; (Article 24)

4. Right of freedom of Religion:

(i) Freedom of conscience and free pursuit of profession, practice and propagation of religion; (Article 25)

(ii) Freedom to manage religious affairs; (Article 16)

(iii) Freedom as to payment of taxes for promotion of any particular religion; (Article 27)

(iv) Freedom as to attendance at religious places or religious worship in certain educational institutions; (Article 28)

5. Cultural and Educational Rights:

(i) Protection of interests of minorities; (Article 29)

(ii) Right of minorities to establish and administer educational institutions. (Article 30)

6. Right to Constitutional remedies:

(i) Right to Constitutional remedies. (Article 32)

All public servants including members of the police organisations are duty bound to uphold the Constitution of India. Under Article 51 A, citizen of India have ten fundamental duties and the first duty is "to abide by the Constitution, respect its ideals and institutions, the National Flag and the National Anthem". The third fundamental duty of the citizens is "to uphold and protect the sovereignty, unity and integrity of the country." Human Rights jurisprudence has grown enormously over the last four decades and there is an urgent need to give training to all ranks of the police forces in human rights. Violations of human rights are committed on a large scale by the terrorists, secessionists, fundamentalists, extremists and criminals who have no regards for life and property of the people of the country. All over the world, democratic societies are threatened by violence which is practiced and exploited by secessionists, terrorists, fundamentalists, smugglers, drug traffickers and criminals. During the last ten years in Punjab, 12000 civilians and 17000 police personnel have been killed by the terrorists. In Kashmir during the last five years 4602 persons have been killed by the terrorists and there have been 14542 terrorists incidents of violence in the valley. Police has the face the eternal dilemma of Ends Vs Means in tackling various internal security problems.

India suffers from the malady of differences of the majority and the minorities, and thus institutionalized communal compartments–rather than for all legal, state and public purposes look upon all citizens as Indians, nothing less, nothing more. Also, in hailing to make at least primary schooling of fundamental right, in refraining from enacting a uniform civil code, and in ordaining reservation rather than free and compulsory education for the historically disadvantaged actions, the Constitution makers provided a fertile soil to unscrupulous politicians to saw their individious oats in.[3(b)] In a "pluralistic society" which has a plurality of cultures, institutions, communities and social systems, the communal riots are vexing and seemingly, hopeless problems which occur again and again.[4] Geographically, Hindu–Muslim conflicts have mainly affected in U.P., Assam, West Bengal, Bihar, Gujarat, M.P., Maharashtra, Karnataka, Kerala and Andhra Pradesh. Ethnic conflicts in Manipur, Assam, Nagaland and Tripura continues unabated. Plural societies have to carry out the difficult task of compromising and coalses many different and conflicting group interests within its broad national interest perspectives.[5] Caste-violences and atrocities on weaker sections of society have also posed serious challenges to the communal harmony of the society. Communal conflicts and riots create their repercussions in the following fields.[6]

1. Political field
2. Economic field
3. Social field
4. Religious field
5. International field
6. Crime area and Law and order situation
7. Human Misery areas
8. Cultural field
9. Faith in police and State authority
10. Constitutional and Legal dimensions.

Under the Constitution of India, the responsibility for law and order has been given to the State Government. The State Government will have to be the main agency to carry out routine law and order duties but Central Government should be able to act promptly and effectively where necessary.[7] It lies in the way our politicians have practice politics, the way the Constitution has been worked and used, the way religious freedom has been turned into communalism and narrow group mentalities with the sole aim of acquiring political power and patronage.[7] Even Kerala is not free of communal violence. On May 2, 2003, a 50 member armed gang hacked to death nine Hindus. A cadre of arms and explosives were recovered from the local mosque. Communal tension needs to the controlled by the state administration.

Samuel Huntington's thesis of forthcoming clashes of civilization has been a topic of extensive discussions among political and social scientists. He visualizes that the Western countries, whether Christian or otherwise, might come to clash with the Islamic thrust in future, while in Asia, the Hindu-Muslim conflict might accentuate drawing Pakistan into it.[8] From March 1991 to 1994, a total of 4158 communal incidents took place in the country in which 2866 persons were killed.[9] In many parts of the country particularly Bihar, Maharashtra and U.P., the neo-landlords such as Yadavs, Kurmis, Lodhs, etc. has become more aggressive in their attitude towards the Scheduled Castes when the BSP - SP combine came to power. The field surveys of the affected areas reveal that more than 90 per cent of the caste conflict have occurred between the backwards and the scheduled Castes. Communal clashes between Hindu-Muslim, Hindu-Harijans, Tribals-Non-Tribal, Sikh-Hindus and miscellaneous non-ethnic for the Period 1980-1988 are given in Table I. Ethnic clashes in the north eastern states can be regarded in broader sense as parts of communal disharmony. India provides all types of ethnic and communal groups and clearages are bound to disturb the communal harassment of the society. It was way back in 1968 that the National Integration Council (NIC) recommended amendment of Section 153-A of the Indian Penal Code to provide punishment for communal activities; the term being defined to mean any activity which promotes or attempts to promote on the grounds of religion, race, caste or community, or any other ground, whatsoever, feelings of enimity or hatred between different religions, or social groups, castes, or communities. This was done by the Amendment of the Criminal Law (Amendment) Act, 1972. Robert L Hardgrave (1934-35) points out that the complexity of Indian society is at once a cause of both conflict and stability. If we analyse the various challenges to communal harmony, we find a number of elements responsible for disharmony. The root cause of all kinds of disharmony or negative forces that give rise to various kinds of disharmony, is that man, is ignorant of his real identity and has identifies himself with his race, region, religion, community, castes, etc. Besides this spiritual aspect, there are other geo-political factors causing communal disharmony. Firstly, Pak inspired insurgency in Jammu and

Kashmir is creating serious challenges to communal harmony. The violent insurgency spear-headed by Islamabad aims at keeping India bogged down in Jammu and Kashmir with a view to fanning the flames of parochial passions.[10] It is abundantly clear that the solc purpose of the militants in perpetrating violence on the people belonging to a particular community on a Friday is to give communal colour to their nefarious designs. Secondly, we have seen demographic change with pre-dominant Muslim population adjoining Bangladesh starting from Murshidabad and going upto Kishanganj - Islampur sector in West Bengal and the border districts of Assam.[11] Some people even talk of likely emergence of a new Muslim state in the North East. The 1991 Census figures indicate the following percentage of Muslim population in the Assam border districts:-

Dhubri	-	7.45	per cent
Barpetta	-	56.07	,,
Goalpara	-	50.18	,,
Hailakandi	-	54.78	,,
Karimganj	-	49.17	,,
Cachar	-	34.4	,,
Nagaon	-	47.18	,,
Marigaom	-	45.95	,,
Darrang	-	31.97	,,

Communal harmony can be seriously threatened by the Bangladeshi migrants. A total of 2,68,231 refugees from four countries were residing in India–1,02,177 from Sri Lanka, 86,000 from Bangladesh, 80,000 from Tibet and 54 from Myanmar (Burma).[12]

Thirdly, recurrences of communal riots in India over years has not only tarnished the secular image of India but thrown a challenge to communal harmony. Fourthly, biased media projections and reports continues to disturb the peace and harmony of the Indian society at large. Fifthly, the long unsettled issues of Ayodhya, Varanasi and Mathur temples have been used by fundamentalists to disturb the peace and communal harmony of our plural - multi - religious society. Sixthly, political parties and their struggle for Minority vote has been used agains and again, to foment troubles. Political parties at times are responsible for communal dis–harmony. Seventhly, International atmosphere and outburst of communal frency in other parts of the world do have their repercussions in India.

Witness the inane but mandatory greetings from the highest political pedestals on all religious or sectorial occasions; witness presidents visiting temples on religious festivals; witness Prime Ministers placing Chaddars at dargahs; witness the rat race for hoisting Iftar parties (all this wirth Doordarshan cameras in attendance) and worst of all, come election time, witness the wooing and courting personally on the quiet or through secret emissaries, of priests and religious personages to seek the votes of their communities. There is no party of any consequence which does not works eloquent on secularism and at the same time align with communalists and casteists? On the other hand, show me more than one out of one hundred Indians who is a religious fanatic or even ordinarily communal minded - to whom her instance, it matters either way that a Sikh or a Muslim or a Hindu is the President of India or Chief Justice or Army Chief or cricket or hockey captain.[12(a)]

Injustice to minorities in Pakistan and Bangladesh and their immigration to India at times can disturb communal harmony in India. Pakistan, according to U.S. Intelligence officials, plans to conduct its first nuclear test blasts in the near future. Such reports are bound to create public opinion and probably demand for nuclear bomb in India. About, 5,316 Pakistan-trained terrorists had infiltrated into the Indian territory during 1995 and about 1275 foreign nationals were arrested during last one year. While crossing the international border.[13] The ISI based in Bangladesh was aiding and abetting terrorists and fundamentalist forces in the North East. The Government of India was aware of the sinister designs of the ISI of Pakistan to de-stabilise India by sponsoring terrorism and subversive activities in different parts of the country. Asghar Ali Engineer's main threat is towards providing an economic explanation as being the leading macro-cause of Hindu-Muslim riots and disharmony, communal riots are, according to Marxists are inevitable concomitant of the economic development process currently in progress in the country. Eighthly, role of fundamentalist and communal leaders/parties in fomenting communal disharmony cannot be exaggerated. The RSS, Jamat-e-Islam and other such communal organisations with the help of communal parties/ fronts creating an environment of communal disharmony. Recent incidents of Godhra and subsequent flare up in Gujarat have again drawn attention to the need for communal harmony. According to a rough estimate more than three thousand people lost their lives in Gujarat during the last 3 years. Let us face the hard reality and concede that the permanent obstacle in the path of a secular society in India is the same corrupt politics which has found its way into the social life of our country, as it is based on the divisions of caste, culture and religion. This is what is known as 'Vote bank politics'.[13(a)]

Ninthly, the Government policy of appeasement and discrimination to certain communities has created a feeling of injustice leading to communal disharmony. The implementation of the Religious Institutions (Prevention of Misuse) Act' 1988 provisions has been half hearted. Tenthly, the gory annals of communal violence over the last few decades are replete with instances of processions, triggering off mayhem. Lastly, but not the least, the absence of an effective intelligence system and the "fire brigade approach had resulted in communal flare ups occurring at the same time and place over and over again. Research surveys reveal that social, political, ethical, economic and demographic causes can also be traced back behind many communal riots. Over crowding, poverty, unemployment, social and communal prejudices are other factors behind communal violence in many cases.

The recent trends in communal riots can be briefly enumerated as under:-

1. Spread of communal riots from urban to rural areas although urban areas continue to be seriously affected.
2. Increase in the ferocity and higher quotient of violence and increased sense of insecurity amongst people.
3. Use of sophisticated fire-arms and explosive devices.
4. Attack on places of worship, woman and children.
5. Greater use of printed material and other means of communication for spreading rumours and fanning communal passions.
6. Increase in the level of religious intolerances and insensitivity towards the feeling of the other community.
7. Role of the hostile neighbouring country and its agencies in starting and perpetuating these riots.
8. Petty/Frivolous issues getting magnified by anti-social and other vested interests, thereby causing such riots.
9. Role of politicians and the present electoral system.
10. Nexus between the politician and the anti-social elements.
11. Collusion/inaction by law enforcing agencies both at the pre-riot and during riot stages.
12. Revival of fundamentalism, both in the majority community and the minority community leading to the mushrooms growth of pseudo-religious and communal organisations.
13. Spread of communal virus amongst the younger generations.
14. Demographic changes caused by influx of people from neighbouring countries affecting even uninfluenced areas.
15. Military in J&K and Punjab has lead to migration of population adding to communal tensions and creating rift in the

communities living with amity so far.

16. Police and district administration is slow in response and at times partial to certain communities.

Communalism in Gujarat

The recent tragic communal violence in Gujarat is distressing indeed alarming. Nearly 600 people have died in the recent Gujarat riots in 2002. On February 27, 2002, at about 8.03 a.m., incident at railway station Godhra claimed lives of 57 Kar Sevaks who were returning from Ayodhya. At 8.30 a.m. Chief Minister Narendra Modi was informed of the carnage. Gujarat Assembly was adjourned at 4.30 p.m. and Modi gifted Godhra railway station and the town and issued shoot at right orders to the police. At 10.30 p.m. Chief Minister held meetings with senior government officials at Gandhinagar and ordered curfew in sensitive places and pre-emptive arrests. On February 28, 2002, at 12 p.m. Modi informally Centre for calling in Army. Cabinet Secretary T.R. Prasad told Defence Secretary Y. Narain to mobilize the Army. At 4. p.m. Modi requested army deployment following consultation with Shri L.K. Advani. At 6.45 p.m. on 28 February 2002, cabinet committee on Security met under the Prime Minister's chairmanship and approved the immediate movement of troops to Ahmedabad and other parts of Gujarat Shri Vajpayee departed George Fernandes Defence Minister to supervise the deployment of troops. On March 1, 2002 after the arrival of a Brigade of 54th Division, troops took flag march in Ahmedabad at 9 a.m. to control the violence Communal Riots continued in Gujarat for next 72 days and the Union government appointed Shri K.P.S. Gill as security advisor to stern the tidal wave of hatred, communal frenzy and human rights violations. The number of seriously injured stood at approx 1420 and arson case stood at 22560. Nearly 42400 arrests were made and 1410 tear gas shells were fired and 10500 rounds of ammunition was spent in firing, killing 192 rioters and mischief mongers. More than 62000 strong Army and central para-military forces were deployed to assist the Gujarat administration to control communal violence. Amnesty International in its 2002 report has observed: "(1) Gujarat Govt. and the police took insufficient action to protect civilians, (2) state Govt. did not provide appropriate rehabilitation." Most of the recommendations of the National Human Rights Commission were ignored by the Govt. (*Times of India* 20 May 2003).

Secularism has become a tool to justify the wrongs done by the minorities: Islamic terrorism is glossed over, while Muslim obscurantism is encouraged, often by the state, as in the Shah Bano Case. From Hazrat Bal to Charar–e–Sharief, there is a continuity–of giving safe passage to the Muslim terrorists—a product of timid and be-fuddled mind and shows hesitancy and hollowness in action on the part of the government. Kashmir policy has failed to control Islamic terrorism and communal violence.

Gujarat has a long history of communal violence and riots. The state of Gujarat has sent over 20 saffron Members of Parliament to the Lok Sabha since 1991. The enigma of Gujarat can be traced back to the history. The historic Somnath temple was ravaged by Mahmud Ghazni almost a thousand years ago and reconstructed in 1950. The traumatic September 1969 Ahmedabad riots grievously damaged the Gujarati Psyche. Over 600 lives were lost in the holocaust spread over four to five days and subsequently Gujarat witnessed many Communal clashes. In Gujarat nine per cent of population is Muslim yet they have only four Muslim MLAs in a Vidhan Sabha of 182 members. The noted Indian American scholar of the University of Michigan–Ashutosh Varshney in his book Ethnic Conflict and Civic Life, looks at three pairs of cities, "Calicut and Aligarh", "Hyderabad and Lucknow", "Ahmedabad and Surat" to understand communal violence and the will springs of communal harmony. The tragic fact is that Gujarat diaspora is fulling more than diasporadic communal tension. In Gujarat Muslim madrassas are expanding, oiled by gulf money and political parties are playing the dirty game of minority vote bank politics.

Emerging Trends and Challenges to Communal Harmony

1. According to Ashis Nandy, Ultra Nationalism has come to India. It is a standardised version that has taken a toll of more than 100 million lives during the 20th Century. It is the nationalism in which Europe has traditionally specialised.
2. Infiltration of Pakistani trained terrorists and insurgents. The gruesome massacre of the innocent residents of Doda by armed miscreants early in 1966 is too patent to be taken lightly. The violent insurgency spearheaded by Islamabad obviously aims at keeping India bogged down in Jammu and Kashmir with a view to fanning the flames of parochial passions. [14]
3. Sinister designs of ISI of Pakistan to destabilize India is a most noticeable phenomena. The Hazartbal incident and infiltration of Pak-trained infiltrators are clear indicators.
4. Series of bombing in cities like Mumbai and its after affects by organised criminal gangs can be regarded as one of the noticeable trend.
5. Election time—use by politicians to create communal disharmony. For wooing minority communities, political parties

try to foment communal disharmony.

6. Increasing empowerment of certain communities resulting in their violent struggle with other communities–Prospects of weaker sections of the society and backlash in other places.
7. Use of RDX and sophisticated weapons is another noticeable trend.
8. Nexus between Pak-inspired conspirators and Government officials–According to one modest estimate by Himanshu Shekhar Jha, atleast ten per cent of the officials of Jammu & Kashmir have vital links with Pak sponsored terrorists. Such anti-national and anti-social elements must be weeded out and only then communal harmony can be established in J&K.
9. Heightening of Communalism– "The heightening of Communalism today is simultaneously the product of social, moral and political crisis in society and the reaction of the ruling to this crisis.[15]
10. Shifting of people from Kashmir and getting refuge status. Due to Pak-inspired violence and insurgency in Kashmir, many people have been uprooted from the Valley. "They have already achieved spectacular success in uprooting 78,000 families from the valley. More than 3,00,000 (3 lakh) Kashmiri Pandits and others belonging to the indigenous population are now camping in Delhi, Chandigarh, Amritsar and other parts of India as refugees. In addition to these Hindu exiles over 1,00,000 (one lakh) Muslims opposed to terrorism have also been turned out of their homeland.
11. Quagmire of Quota—The Constitution of India has provided a number of safeguards to certain communities of India particularly the Scheduled Castes and Scheduled Tribes for a specific period with the object of removing their social disabilities and promoting their varied interest. In recent years, the disastrous consequence of mandalisation has not only been the hike in the reservation quotas but the scramble for quotas even among the communities that are far from socially disadvantaged. The process has largely been aided by the race among political parties to carve out assured vote banks. The result is that more and more clamouring to be categorised as backward or put in the Schedule Castes and Scheduled Tribes

needing special protection, the quota system has come to acquire a self-perpetuating character.

Government of India Guidance to Promote Communal Harmony

Government of India, Ministry of Home Affairs have issued guidelines to all the Chief Ministers and Governors on 23rd April, 1990. Some of the important guidelines are reproduced below:-

1. Intelligence

Intelligence is the eyes and ears of any administration. The organisational aspect of intelligence, with special reference to its adequacy, scope and efficacy, both at the State level and in the Districts/Towns/ Areas identified as sensitive/hyper-sensitive should be thoroughly reviewed on a priority basis. Emphasis should be laid on the setting up of special intelligences units for tackling communal problems. Special training should be imparted to be personnel manning these units so as to ensure proper, systematic and timely feed back of the requisite information to the concerned authorities. This should be made an integral part of the assessment exercise which would be beneficial to the District Authorities while making contingency plans, especially when major festivals are found the corner. Organisations collecting intelligence/information should keep a close watch on the activities of the organised communal groups with special reference to their propaganda and publications. There is an urgent need to make use of the intelligence feedback so gleaned from the ground level. To ensure this, there must be atleast a monthly review of intelligence at the district level by the District Magistrate, Superintendent of police and the Head of District Intelligence.

2. Preventive Action (Non Official Participation)

The working of the District Integration Committees/Ekta Samities should be energized. Their working should be closely monitored by the District Magistrate. Deliberations of these meetings should be communicated atleast once a month to the state Government. Similarly, the state level Integration Committees headed by the Chief Ministers, should review the situation atleast once a quarter and keep the Central Government posted with their parleys. Search parties in the communal riot areas should be accompanied by the prominent persons of the locality. Police officials should not conduct the searches alone. Industrial areas may be prone to the communal flare-ups. Tripartite Committees comprising representatives of State Government employees and the labour should be set up.

3. Immobilization of Anti-Social Elements

The Police, the local intelligence and the local bodies best know the elements, who have the capacity to create possible communal rifts, directly or indirectly. An up-date of these persons should be readily available in all police stations and the district headquarters. Whenever a festival, religious procession etc. is about to occur the District Administration should take timely advance action to immobilize these elements through preventive arrests. Organisations which foment trouble can be either openly communal or covertly so. In either case, these should be under the constant watch of intelligence/police authorities. Effective will needs to be displayed by the District authorities in the management of such situations so that ugly incidents do not occur. Adequate power under Sections 153(A), 295 and 295-A of the IPC are available which can be made use of by the District authorities.

4. Processions

The recent past shows that processions have been the single largest cause of communal conflagrations. As far as possible, no new processions, as did not exist before 1.1.90, should normally be allowed. Only traditional religious processions should be permitted in sensitive areas. These should be accompanied by adequately armed police 'Bandobust' commensurate with the estimated strength of the participants. Only traditional slogans should be permitted and in the event that slogans offensive to other communities are shouted, the organisers of the procession should be made to pay a heavy fine. In any case, the organisers should be asked to guarantee good behaviour, a breach of which should attract a collective fine, heavy enough to be deterrent.

5. Use of Loud-Speakers

Police Act or similar local legislations should be effectively used while granting permission for the use of loudspeakers. Care should generally be taken not to permit use of loudspeakers between 11-00 p.m. and 5-00 a.m.

6. Removal of Irritants, Objectionable Acts

Advance warning should be given that strict action will be taken against those who violate the norms of good behaviour while celebrating festivals. Slaughtering of animals in public places and near places of worship should be avoided.

7. Places of Worship

Any construction of religious place should be made only with the prior approval of the District authorities and at the earmarked place. Cases of construction of unauthorized religious places should be dealt with severely under existing laws. Negligence on the part of the District Administration in implementing this direction should be seriously viewed and the guilty dealt with. Though the enabling provisions of the Religious Institutions (Prevention of Misuse) Act, 1988, it should be ensured that no storage of arms and ammunition takes place inside any place of worship.

8. Press

It is the responsibility of the press to report incidents factually without, imparting a communal colour to them. It should not sensationalize the prevalent situation and should only publish the facts after checking their veracity. There should be a coordinated interaction between the Magistracy, the police and the publicity set up at the District level for the proper use of the media to create public opinion against such incidents.

9. Administrative Measures

Communally sensitive places have been identified in the riot-prone States. This has been done to help the States in making administrative arrangements for these areas. As such, manpower requirements for these areas should be realistically assessed. It should be ensured that all vacancies are filled up and manned. Police Stations/Posts should be set up in all sensitive/trouble-prone areas. These should be provided with adequate personnel, weaponry, communication links, equipment, vehicles etc. These administrative measures should be constantly reviewed. Having identified communally sensitive places/pockets, it should be ensured that a Control Room at the district level is permanently set up, which should be adequately manned by competent personnel. At the slightest indication of communal trouble, the contingency plans should be put to use without the least hesitation. As soon as a communal incident occurs, a report should be sent thereon to the Ministry of Home Affairs immediately which should be followed with a detailed report within 10 days of the occurrence of the said incident, mentioning, *interalia,* the grant of awards for good work or punishments for showing laxity to the district officers connected with the incidents. A mention should be made in the ACRs of DMs/SSsP which should reflect their capability in managing communal situation.

District Level Screening Committees be set up with the District Collector as its Chairman. These would review all arrests and detentions– both preventive and in the wake of communal riots - to ensure that the elements responsible for instigation and committing violence do not go free. These Committees should have representation of prominent and fair-minded citizens known for their integrity.

10. Medical Relief

It should be ensured that proper medical care units exist in all the sensitive places/pockets, which can handle emergencies.

11. Illegal Possession of Arms

It has been the recent experience that illegal lethal weapons are used quite widely in communal riots. A campaign to detect and unearth such arms, raid places of manufacture should be launched by the District Authorities immediately. A special review of arms licences issued should be done and in the case of inadequate justification, licences should be cancelled.

12. The Role of Police

Police is the Chief image-maker of any District Administration. Great care and attention should be paid towards providing proper leadership and suitable motivation to the police force. The emphasis should be on keeping their morale high. There should be a review of the training programmes for the police forces with a view to inculcating in them the attitudes of secularism and communal harmony. It has been commonly observed that the presence of minority community members in the police force deployed in communally sensitive areas goes a long way in winning the confidence of the minority communities. This is of vital importance. The following steps should be undertaken without any loss of time:-

(a) Launching of Special Campaigns to recruit more members of minorities in the State Police Forces.

(b) Creation of composite battalions of armed police which should include members of all religious communities including SCs/STs for exclusive use in maintaining communal peace and amity in the sensitive areas.

(c) Starting of special training/orientation programmes for State Police Force with a view to maintaining communal harmony.

The positioning and placement of the Armed police should be done in such a manner as to ensure their quick and easy movement to trouble spots. In case the armed police is deployed to assist the civil police, at no time it should remain leaderless. Steps should also be taken to ensure smooth functioning between the civil administration and the Army.

13. Essential Services Management

In many riot situations, people suffer on account of delayed/non-provision of essential supplies such as food, milk, water, electricity and medicines. By ensuring their timely provision, it is felt that the District Administration would be removing major irritant.

14. Punitive Action

Laws relating to collective fines should be used without fear or favour, whenever the situations warrants. Special Courts should be set up for the expeditious trial and disposal of communal riot cases. When a communal riot takes place and Enquiry Committee/Commission is set up, it should be given a time-specific mandate for completion of its inquiry. Its recommendations should be expeditiously implemented, say within 3 months, and the Central Government should be kept informed.

15. Personnel Policy

It should be ensured that officers, who are honest, upright and whose integrity is beyond doubt, are posted to the communally sensitive districts. The same consideration should also be applied to the other personnel in such areas. It should be ensured that no time gap is allowed between their transfer out of and posting to these areas. Due recognition needs to be paid to the services rendered by the personnel in preventing and dealing with communal disturbances. A scheme of granting suitable awards in the form of promotion/commendation certificates/cash awards should be considered. A similar system of award can be envisaged for the public also.

16. Rehabilitation

A revised scale of payment of relief to riot victims has been drawn up. The amount of exgratia relief grant for cases of death or permanent incapacitation has now been fixed at Rs. 50,000. A pension of Rs. 500 per month will also be given to the widows of the victims of riots belonging to the low income group. These will become effective for cases occurring from Ist April, 1990. Lot of resentment is generated on account of non-payment of timely relief/compensation to the riot victims. A system of expeditious disbursement of the scale of relief should, therefore, be devised.

17. Documentation

The documentation of information, in its entirety, should be completed in the minimum period of time at the cessation of every communal riot.

18. Role of Ministers/ Office Bearers of Political Parties

Ministers and office bearers of political parties should exercise maximum restraint and self-discipline in making public utterances on any issue concerning the communal disturbances. No minister or an office bearer of any political party should participate in a function or a meeting or a procession, which may have a bearing on religious or communal issues. It would be best if the District Magistrate is consulted before participating therein.

Action Plan for Bringing Communal Harmony

We, in India are secular by intention, but communal and casteist by our behaviour. Ideals are stated to indicate our intentions but the world in far too complex to be contained within our moral and ideal paradigms.[16] There are no easy formulations of the problem, no easy solutions and no easy way out of the existential predicaments for combating communalism in a multi-religious, pluralistic, developing and democratic society.

Need for National Efforts for Bringing Communal Harmony

Communal harmony is a sort of surrogate ideological war which is increasingly guided by many psychological factors like communal prejudices, communal bias, discrimination, alienation, assertion, aggression, communal aspirations and anonymity at time by remote control. Separation of religion from politics, ban on private/communal organisation, which propagate communal mobilization, economic development and efforts to bring communal harmony are areas, which demand very delicate handling of the problem.

Need for Renovating Polity for Bringing Communal Harmony

Indian polity should be renovated and revamped with high ideals and practices of secularism, democracy and social justice at its care. Randhir Singh has rightly held that "the spread of communal strife is in direct proportion to the depth of the crisis in Indian policy and politics of the ruling classes on the one hand and in inverse proportion to the presence or power of the left class based politics of the people on the other hand.[17]

Ban on Communal Parties and Effective Check on External Interfence

The Indo-Pak borders are porous and that is why both Sikh and Kashmiri militants can go to Pakistan and return after getting training, arms and some more. It is, therefore, necessary that we should seal our borders and ensure that no foreign power interferes in the internal affairs of the country.

Constitutional Recognition to Minority Commission and Need to Modernize Minorities

The Muslims must realize that their future is bound-up with the future of secularism and they should support and strengthen the Hindus and others who have launched a crusade against communalism. Without the minorities support this crusade may not succeed.

A secular and pluralistic society, in a democratic model of nation building, has to resolve its inner contradictions by the show processes of economic and political developments. Maintenance of communal harmony is as much the responsibility of minorities as it is of the majority community.

Protection of Minorities Particularly Refugees who had to Flee from their Homes to Save their Lives

For combating communalism, protection of minorities and rehabilitation of refugees who have fled away from their homes of Punjab and Kashmir must get priority.

It is the compulsion of history and geography that the various communities in the country must have peaceful co-existence and work in harmony to make India strong. The majority of the people in all communities of India are peace-loving and wish to abide by the rule of law. We had a rich tradition of community concern and mutual assistance.[18]

Need to Decommunalise the Present and Future Citizens by Bringing Changes in their Behaviour Pattern and Making them Secular

Positive efforts towards de-communalisation or genuine secularisation of the present and future citizens behaviour is a matter of primary socialisation, beginning from family, school and the place of worship, to which secondary factors like poverty, historical cognitions, peer group, behaviour and the democratic vote have added its own rabidity.[19]

The Indian version of secularism signifies the peaceful co-existence of religious communities and a creative interaction between various traditions. This needs to be reconstructed and evolved in order to deal with the religious aspects of disrupted social and political relations in the current crisis. The secularism must be built on amity between different communities and understanding of other's viewpoint.

Special Courts for Riot Cases and Reforms in Criminal Justice System

It is high time we revamped and remedied the basic weaknesses in our criminal justice system. For expeditious disposal of communal riot cases special courts can be constituted.

The success of law enforcement agencies lies in not merely quelling the riots but recognizing the problems in embryonic stage and averting it. Timely and accurate intelligence can provide assistance to law enforcing agencies in making decisions and directing actions that will thwart, suppress or prevent a riot.

Need to Evolve a Uniform Civil Code

Communalism in India cannot be eradicated unless Uniform Civil Code for all people living in a secular country like India is effectively enforced after enactment. Article 44 of the Indian Constitution reads as follows: "The state shall endeavour to secure for the citizens a uniform civil code throughout the territory of India".

The failure to introduce a uniform civil code, as stipulated in the Constitution, is one of the most telling examples of the failure of our non-discriminatory secularism. Not satisfied with this failure, the state has followed policies which have been perceived to now favour one community and now another community.[20]

The Supreme Court has observed in Shah Ban Judgement case as under: "It is a matter of regret that Article 44 of our Constitution has remained a dead latter. There is no evidence of any official activity for framing a common civil code for the country - a beginning has to be made if the Constitution is to have any meaning."

Prompt Action at Various Levels to Bring Communal Harmony

Whenever communal tension shows a tendency to mount, prompt action at various levels should be taken immediately to control it before it erupts into an actual riot.

Protection of Administrators and Police Officers from Communal Virus

During the last fifty-three years, Indian politics has been highly communalized with the result that no wing of the State apparatus could escape from the virus of communalism. It is therefore necessary that administrators and police officers should be kept immune from communal virus. Recruitment, training and professionalism are some of the key areas by which protection can be ensured for administrators and police officers from communal cancer.

Strengthening of Intelligence System and Identification of Communally Sensitive Areas/Districts

A place where communal riots occur or tension between different communities prevails is considered by the authorities as a communally sensitive spot, communal tension does not spring up overnight. It is built up over a period of time. Suckled on communal propaganda, nursed on communal incidents and fed on rumours, until men's hearts are filled with hatred and their thoughts turn to violence.[21]

Reforms in Education System to Evolve Secular Education

The real remedy is political education, national education, health education of people's minds. Education from the primary to the post-graduate stage should be reoriented:-

(i) To serve the purpose of creating a sense of Indianness, Unity and Solidarity;

(ii) To inculcate faith in the postulates of Indian democracy; and
(iii) To help the nation to create a modern society out of the present traditional one.

The role of teachers in combating communalism is particularly important since anything they do will soon percolate to the minds of their students thereby helping the idea to blossom into a national ethos.

Ghetto Psychology of Minorities Encouraging Fundamentalism Needs to be Replaced by a Nationalistic Psychology and Inculcation of Scientific Temper

There is an urgent need to bring a psychological orientation in the masses to accept 'Unity in Diversity' and 'Respect for all religions'. What is needed is a serious and deeper understanding of our classical and positive concept of secularism in these sense of Sarva Dharma Sambhawa and its dynamic interpretations as to ensure creative, constructive and dignified co-existence of all religions in our democratic republic. A secular state has to wage a resolute struggle against all forms of intolerance, credulity, superstition, emotionalism and irrationalism.

Encouragement to Inter-Religious and Inter-Community Harmony and Understanding

There is an urgent need for social mobilization to combat communalism. Karl W. Dentsch formulated the concept of social mobilization which, according to him, is "the process in which major clusters of old social-economic and psychological commitments are eroded or broken and people become available for new pattern of socializations and behaviour". The anointment of Aneesa Mirza as the first woman muslim mayor of Ahmedabad in Gujarat on April 16, 2003, is a reinstatement of true secularism in our plural society.

Censure or Ban on Communal Writings and Speeches

D.P. Madan Commission report on communal disturbances at Bhiwandi, Jalgaon and Mahad (Maharashtra) in 1970 has recommended pre-censorship of news relating to communal disturbances before it is published in the newspapers. District authorities should themselves issue news bulletins for publication.

Effective Role of Peace Committees and Citizens Vigilance Committees

The National Integration Council at the Srinagar Conference in 1968 recommended among other suggestions:- "The constitution of citizen's committees as consultative bodies at the state and district levels to promote and maintain communal harmony, their functions being the holding of advance consultations with leaders of religious groups to ensure peaceful celebrations of festivals and to endeavour to promote joint participation by all communities in the festivals."

Qualitative and Quantitative Reforms in Police and Other Law Enforcement Agencies

For combating communalism the police organisation will have to be revamped both in terms of quantity and quality and modernisation of police has to be carried out as a national priority.

Establishment of a Secular Democratic Polity, An Operative Ideal

Secularism is an operative ideal which must be achieved in India if communalism is to be rooted out from the society. Secularism or SARVA DHARMA SAMBHAVA has been defined by Vinobaji as follows:- "There are four essential ingredients of Sarv Dharma Sambhava - the feeling of equality of all religions. One of them is the faith in one's own religion, the second is the respect for all religions, the third is the reformation of one's religion and the fourth one is opposition to irreligiousness". Establishment of a truly secular and democratic polity is indeed a stupendous task and it adds to the magnitude of the problem if the society is multi-religious and multi-ethnic as our Indian society is to establish a truly secular state, one must understand in all earnestness the psyche of Indian people and their religious-cultural traditions.

Why Communalism Could not be Controlled and Eradicated so Far?

Ineffective police response, lack of timely intelligence, lack of political will and delays and distortions in the criminal justice system are partly responsible for failure in combating communalism.

Generally, communal riots could not be effectively controlled because there is lack of sincerity on the part of the political masters and each occasion is calculated in terms of election politics.

Concluding Remarks

It is appropriate to refer to Gurudev Rabindra Nath Tagore's vision of the India of tomorrow, which in his inspiring language, symbolizes the philosophy of communal harmony in following poetic terms:-

"Day and night thy voice goes out from land, calling Hindus, Buddhists, Sikhs and Jains round the throne and Parsee, Musalmans and Christians, offerings are brought to thy shrine by the East and the West to be woven in a garland of love, thou bringest the hearts of all people, into the harmony of one life. Thou dispenser of India's destiny, Victory, Victory, Victory to thee.''

Social Conflicts in India (Period covers - 1980 - 1988)

State/Territory	*Hindu Muslim*	*Hindu Harijan*	*Tribals Non-Tribals*	*Sikh Hindu*	*Other Ethnic*	*Non-Ethnic*	*Total*
States							
Andhra Pradesh	4	1	3	-	-	4	12
Arunachal Pradesh	-	-	1	-	1	-	2
Assam	1	-	2	-	22	1	26
Bihar	2	7	7	1	5	5	27
Goa	-	-	-	-	1	-	1
Gujarat	8	3	1	-	8	-	20
Haryana	-	-	-	-	-	-	-
Himachal Pradesh	-	-	-	-	-	-	-
Jammu & Kashmir	2	-	-	-	2	-	4
Karnataka	-	1	-	-	1	-	2
Kerala	1	-	-	-	-	4	5
Madhya Pradesh	-	-	-	1	1	4	6
Maharasthra	3	2	1	1	-	2	9
Manipur	-	-	12	-	-	-	12
Meghalaya	-	-	4	-	-	-	4
Mizoram	-	-	17	-	-	-	17
Nagaland	-	-	8	-	-	-	8
Orissa	-	-	2	-	-	-	2
Punjab	-	-	-	78	-	-	78
Rajasthan	-	-	-	-	-	-	-
Sikkim	-	-	-	-	-	-	-
Tamil Nadu	1	2	-	-	1	-	4
Tripura	-	-	14	-	-	-	14
Uttar Pradesh	13	3	-	1	-	2	19
West Bangal	1	-	13	-	-	3	17
Union Territories							
Andaman & Nicobar(Island)	-	-	-	-	-	-	-
Chandigarh	-	-	1	-	1	-	2
Dadar & Nagar Haveli	-	-	-	-	-	-	-
Delhi	-	-	-	4	-	-	4
Lakshdweep	-	-	-	-	-	-	-
Pondicherry	-	-	-	-	-	-	-
Total	36	19	85	86	42	25	293

In 2001, 617 incidents of communal violence were registered in which 199 people were killed and 2066 injured. Nearly 90 per cent of the incidents were reported from Maharashthra, Uttar Pradesh, Gujarat, Rajasthan, Karnataka, M.P., Bihar, West Bengal and Tamil Nadu. So far communal stripe had already claimed around 760 lives in Gujarat alone and rendered 98000 people homeless. 25 These communal clashes violate human rights of the citizens, to whatever community they belong to. In his book, Anti-memoire, the well-known French thinker—Andre Malraus, writes that he once put this question to Pandit Nehru, the then Prime Minister of India, "What is the most difficult problem facing you as Prime Minister?". Nehru replied, "To build a secular state in a religious society." Now the final hour has come to adopt constructive politics in which the people's support is secured on the basis of the genuine interests of the country. Destructive politics, which seeks to secure the vote of one group by awakening hatred for another must be totally abandoned.[26]

References

1. H.H. Swami Maheshanand Giriji Maharaj on Vedanta and Communal Harmony - Bhartiya Sanskrit Samaj, Delhi, 1991.
2. Maheswaranand Giri - Vedanta and Communal Harmony, 1991.
3. Carl Jung - The Integration of Personality - 1940., p. 58.

3(a) Sumer Kaul on Communal Politics - Divide and Reap- *Hindustan Times*, New Delhi, Saturday April 20, 1996.

3(b) -do-

4. Krishna Mohan Mathur - *Indian Police - Role and Challenges* - Gyan Publishing House, New Delhi, 1994 - p. 73.
5. Krishna Mohan Mathur - *Management of Internal Security* and Related Issues - Gyan Publishing House, New Delhi. 1995 p./143.
6. For various dimensions of the Ayodhya Fall-out for internal security please see K.M. Mathur - *Police Law and Internal Security* - Gyan Publishing House, New Delhi, 1994 - pp. 343-346.
7. K.M. Mathur - *Concerns and Constraints in Administration*, RBSA Publishers, SMS Highways, Jaipur,1991 - p. 14.
7. Sumer Kaul on Communal politics - Divide and reap - *Hindustan Times*, New Delhi, Saturday 20 April, 1996.
8. Samuel Huntington. Clashes of Civilization
9. Rajya Sabha Questions - Reply given on 9th March, 1994 - See *Indian Express,* 10 March, 1994.
10. Himanshu Shekhar Jha - Pak-Inspired violence in Doda, The *Hindustan Times*, 21 March, 1996.
11. For similar views see T.V. Rajeswar "On Bangladesh - History Lessons unlearnt". *The Hindustan Times*, 18 March, 1996.
12. Rajya Sabha questions - Reply given on 9th March, 1994-*Indian Express*, 10 March 1994.

12(a) Sumer Kaul on communal politics - Divide and Reap *Hindustan Times*, New Delhi, Saturday April 20, 1996.

13. *The Times of India* - New Delhi, March 7, 1996. Border Fencing may be completed by 1997 - Minister of State for Home Sibtey Razi told the Rajya Sabha on March 5, 1996.
14. Himanshu Shekhar Jha - Pak-Inspired Violence in Doda - *The Hindustan Times* 21.3.1996.

15. Randhir Singh - Theorizing Communalism A Fragmentary Note in the Marxist Model - *Economic and Political Weekly*, July 23, 1988.
16. Inderjit - *Double Talk on Communalism* - May 9, 1989.
17. Randhir Singh - Theorising Communalism - An Explanatory Note in the Marxist Mode - *Economic and Political Weekly,* July 23, 1988, p. 154.
18. S.S. Gill - Rich Government Poor people - *Indian Express,* 5th April, 1988.
19. Ashis Nandi - New Ideology of Religious Tolerance - *The Times of India*, Delhi, January 21, 1981.
20. A.R. Saiyed - *Secularism in Retreat - The Communal Secular Paradox in India - Secularism and Indian Politics* - Edited Bidyut Chakrabarty - 1990. p. 148.
21. S.C. Misra - *Communal Riots in India*, p. 195.
22. Nikhil Chakravarty - *Mainstream* - 26th January, 1991.
23. A.S. Abraham - Cars for active Secularism - Leading Role of the State - *The Times of India* - 15th October, 1990.
24. The state against the Nation-*Mainstream* - June 27, 1987 p. 22.
25. *Time of India* - 17th April 2002.
26. Maulana Wahiduddin Khan - The Future of Secularism - *Hindustan Times*, 25th April, 1996.

2

Combating Communalism

The situation of our time
Surrounds us like a baffling crime,
There lies the body half-dressed,
We all had reason to detest,
And all are suspects and involved
Until the mystery is solved
And under lock and key the cause
That makes a non-sense of our laws

(W.H. Auden – (New Year letter 1940)

The tragic failure of Indian polity in combating communalism makes every enlightened citizen think why and how we have failed so far in establishing our secular credentials in the community of nations. In words of Randhir Singh, "the heightening of communalism today is simultaneously the product of social, moral and political crisis in society, and the reaction of the ruling to this crisis. With the older basis of their power and hegemony weakening, they are increasingly turning to communalism in particular, to win votes, fragment and divide the people and above all, secure their continued political and ideological dominance over them.[1] Communalism refers to an attitude of an allegiance to one's community and is generally associated with a narrow, selfish, divisive and aggressive attitude on the part of a particular community. Communalism is a pre-disposition (state of mind) of a person or a group belonging to a particular religion (or caste/ community/sect within it) arising out of a feeling that a threat real or imaginary exists in his/their faith which should be combined by the collective action of the members of the religion (or caste, community or sect).[2] According to Bipin Chandra simply put, communalism is the belief that because a group follows a particular religion they have, as a result, common social, political and economic interest. Rajni Kothari does not regard communalism as an aberration but something that is a part of system in which changing social and political ethos of the country gives raise to the growth in rapidity and veridity of the communal spirit, and of communal violence. It is a consequence of "secular politics reduced of all normative content, majoritisation and increasing erosion of institution, peoples' participation and discussion.[3] Communalism in the Indian sense is a consciousness, which draws on a supposed religious identity and uses this as the basis for an ideology. It then demands, according to Romilla Thaper, political allegiance to a religious community and supports a programme of political actions designed to further the interest of that religious community". Lala Lajpat Rai in1924 wrote "The communal problem in India is no more a Hindu-Muslim problem. It is becoming a Hindu-Muslim-Sikh-Christian-Parsee-Buddhist-Jain problem." Never was the communal consciousness so keen so assertive. Nay so aggressive as within the last 50 years. There is growing dissensions between the Shias and Sunnis which end in rioting frequently particularly during Moharram festival in Lucknow where Shias are concentrated in large number. Similarly Sikhs in Punjab we fighting for "Khalistan". Today communal disharmony between Hindus and Muslim and Hindus and Sikhs is threatening to unfold new season of militancy. Communalism has become a bone of contention in the struggle for power through the electoral process. Mutual recrimination and allegations by each community that the other started the riot come to dominate communal polemics and the real damage arising out of communal outbreak is sidestepped.[4] Gandhiji has emphasised that "communal harmony could not be permanently established in our country so long as highly distorted versions of history were being taught in her schools and colleges through the history text books."[5] The deprived community likes to overcome the sense of insecurity by getting political power. Instead of anticipating their grievances in a secular way they resort to communal politics. Thus, a nexus starts between the political leaders, religious leaders and the capitalists which leads to communal tensions. Stresses of urban life, strains of competitive economic model, rivalry among anti-social group, political contests, increasing degree of unemployment among large sections of population, rivalry among intra-communal, religious and secular leadership play their role in exacerbating communal situation.[6] During the last two decades, Indian society has changed beyond recognisation. May be something was happening imperceptibly. May be all that has happened now was bottled up from the days of partition or even before. "The Indian society has never been so polarized and fragmented as it is today. Some newspapers and Video cassettes which have sold more than 1.5 millions have further distanced the people from one another through exaggerated accounts and communal exhortations. Tension even in the deep countryside is raw, one can taste it.[7] In Kashmir, there is bitterness, there is anger, there is anguish because communal politics is getting direct support from across the border. According to Arun Shourie, "we are regressing back to our religious identities–more and more of us are once again looking upon, ourselves as 'Sikhs' or 'Muslims' or 'Hindus' rather than as Indians,"

Communalism at the Cross-Road

Communalism is the result of communal prejudices discrimination, social tension and social violence. 60 per cent of the communal riots have risen from petty causes and quarrels and another 25 per cent have been caused by provocation of a religious nature indicating socio-cultural alienation between communities.[8] Why secularism has not been firmly rooted in Indian masses? How far universalisation of education modernization of traditional societies, the erection accessible avenues for skill acquisition and the amelioration of the living conditions of the poverty striken colonies can be of some relevance in defusing communal tensions. These are the questions to be solved by the nations. "In a culturally plural society like Indian social mobilization engenders competition among different communities and citizens tend to see through a communal prism and to be responsive to appeal communalism has become a matter of opportunism. Communalism has other dimensions too. More important among them are (1) the differential rate of mobilization; (2) institutional assimilation; and (3) the nature and pattern of political institutions.[9] Communalism stems for deprivation, a sense of exclusiveness, insecurity and alienation. Communalism is a political concept par excellence. To correlate religion with communalism is to ignore the essential nature of communalism. India is facing communalism and secessionism, fed by religious abscurantism and fundamentalism which has threatened the vitals of Indian society. Communalism has taken a vicious grip of large sections of society. This is in part the result of permissive communalism practised in the name of liberal secularism.[10] The year 1984 witnessed 184 communal incidents, 1985 was worse with 580 incidents, 1986 growing gloom with 672 incidents in which 400 persons died and 5000 were injured and following years have shown greater frequency and intensity of communal violence.[11] Never before has country been so infected by communal virus. Religious places have become the centre for spreading hatred and religious issues have come to limelight due to Muslim Womens Bill. All India Gurudwara Act, Sati Prevention Act and most of all due to Ramjanam

Bhumi–Babri Masjid issue. Kuldip Nayar has observed, "I can understand a certain type of frenzy overtaking some, who do not appreciate the ethos of national movement, or for that matter Hinduism, but the contamination of intellectuals, technocrats and bureaucrats is beyond me. Even the most liberal have been swept off their feet. They do not seem to realise, even from their selfish point of view that a disturbed and divided India would harm the Hindus more because they constitute 80 per cent of the population."[12] All the about pseudo secularism has added to the will of those who are wielding the long knife in the darknight that descended over a large stretch of our land.[13] During communal riots all communities suffer and ultimately it is the mankind which becomes the victims of the communal wrath. Number of persons killed during riots from 1981 to 1986 are given below:

Table Showing Persons Killed During Riots

Year	*No. of incidents*	*Hindus*	*Muslims*	*Others*	*Police*	*Total*
1981	319	67	127	2	-	196
1982	474	83	152	3	-	238
1983	500	168	858	125	2	1143
1984	476	131	284	45	7	467
1985	553	145	185	-	2	332
1986	611	159	236	-	1	396

**Source* - The Telegraph, Calcutta - 1988.

From October 30, 1990 onwards the country has witnessed unprecedented communal violence. It was not only the scale and intensity but also cruelties committed during the current wave of communal violence were unprecedented. The intensity and spread of violence was such that it shook the nation and that after 1947 such violence was not witnessed in the country. Since the end of October 1990 Uttar Pradesh has become a virtual battle field. As many as 40 out of the 63 districts of Uttar Pradesh have been under curfew at the same time. Curfew had to be imposed at regular intervals in 27 towns.[14] Between 1968 to 1978 there were 3281 incidents in which 6410 Hindus, 5789 Muslims and 2366 other community members and 1566 police personnel were injured. In Gujarat, the toll of communal violence in 2002 was 678 innocent people inducing 58 people at Godra.

Why Combat Communalism?

Communalism results in communal tension, communal hatred, communal prejudices, communal riots and destruction of life and property and is thus greatly harmful to any multi-religious society or secular nation as a whole.[15] The incidence of communalism is an alarming phenomenon which seems to have become an integral socio-political life of India. We are moving into an extremely dangerous phase to find that communalism has spread its tentacles into the state apparatus contaminating the working of administration, and police which have openly or secretly compromised with or supported communal forces or practised communalism. "Communal riots are shame of the nation" says Asgar Ali Engineer. They bring out the barbarism and monstrocity putting even Hitler's acts to shame.[16] The need for combating communalism arises because of the damage it does not merely to life and property buts to our psyche and belief system. It releases a poison of hatred which spreads like fire at the slightest spark. Such sparks are many due to the tension which exists in our polity due to selfish pursuits of politicians, socio-economic disparity and discrimination as well as psychological and emotional stresses of modern life. We have begun to take communal violence in our stride, something of a normal occurrence which can be connived at. We have stopped resisting and challenging the monster which is swallowing, day by day, all our human values and national ideals. We have surrendered to it and learnt to live with it.[17] Communal riots spoil the country's image in the world and give a handle to Pakistan to malign us. Communal riots set a chain of retaliation and counter retaliation. Communalism also harms our secular image. The term, communalism, does not convey the gravity of the crisis that confronts us today. The map of India today, is dotted with blood stains, blood stains of brothers fighting brothers, Bhagalpur, Bijnor, Hyderabad, Aligarh and Kanpur have today turned into not only the disgrace points but danger signals for India's nationhood. During the last 43 years little has been done to tackle the basic malady. "Shamefully we have continued to indulge in double talk and deception. We have still to implement the unanimous resolution adopted by the Constituent Assembly (Legislative). Way back on April 3, 1948, to eliminate communalism from India's body politic the resolution which was passed against the background of Mahatma Gandhi's assassination, called upon the Government to take legislation and administrative measures to eliminate communalism so as to ensure proper functioning of democracy and the growth of national unity and solidarity. Specifically, it demanded action to prevent communal organisations from engaging in politics any activity other than those essential for the bonafide religious, cultural, social and educational needs of the community.[18] The problem of communalism basically has to do with the structure of our society and the transition to modernisation.

Action Plan for Combating Communalism

Combating communalism in a multi-religious democratic society is an exremely difficult and complicated task because "We, in India, are secular by intention but communal and casteist by our behaviour. Ideals are stated to indicate our intentions but the world is far too complex to be contained within our moral and ideal paradigms.[19] There are no easy formulations of the problem, no easy solutions and no easy way out of the existential predicaments for combating communalism in a multi-religious, pluralistic, developing and democratic society.

Need for National Efforts in Management and Control of Communalism

Communalism is a sort of surrogate ideological war which is increasingly guided by many psychological factors like communal prejudices, communal bias, discrimination, alienation, assertion, aggression, communal aspirations and anonymity at time by remote control. Communalism grows and develops in a society gradually through feelings of prejudices, bias, discrimination, distrust and ultimately a sense of insecurity between communities. Gradually a hostile belief system develops in the communities which is strengthened by communal propoganda, relative deprivation and discrimination. Communal speeches, writings, processions and petty quarrels build up mobilisation–communal explosion in the form of violence take place when Social Control forces are unable to promptly act to manage the explosion. A Holistic analysis of the communalism and communal violence can be made through following matrix (see next page).

Due to paucity of space, various variables of the matrix of communalism have not been discussed in the present chapter. Combating communalism is a very challenging task and require full utilization of all resources of the society. While communal violence has to be dealt by forces of order, communalism at psychological and social level has to be dealt by very well organised psychological operations by mass media like TV, radio, cinema and the printed media. Separation of religion from politics, ban on private/communal organisation which propogate communal mobilisation, economic development and efforts to bring communal harmony are areas which demand very delicate handling of the problem. Parents, teachers religious leaders and the community at large have their own roles to play in effective management of communalism and spread of secular values. Economic development of the poorer sections of the society is necessary because as long as economic problems exists, people would fall prey to communal propoganda. Intellectuals, leaders of the

Matrix of Communalism and Communal Violence/ Action Plan for Combating Communalism

Social System	Economic System	Constitution of India	Psychological factors causing communal feelings	Religion
Communal tension and discontent	Acquisitiveness; Relative deprivation	Election; Political System	Petty quarrels; Competition; Provocation; Distrest; Discrimination; Blames; Prejudice	Religious Teachings & Rituals
Communal disharmony	Aggression; Assertion	Relatively Deprivation; Communal Organisation	Communal Organisation; Communal Turbulance and security; Communal Testivism	Religious propaganda
Social boycott and segregation	Economic competition	Political rivalry	Disorder; Propaganda for Mobilestation of Communal disharmony	Foremixing of Religion with politics
Class social interaction	Economic Development of poorer sections	Mass social education against communalisation	Ban on Communal Organisation; Psychological OPS through mass media and Education	Separation of Religion from Politics
Social reformers	Economic Reforms	Communal understanding and modernisation	Tolerance; Communal understanding; Communal harmony	Religious Tolerances
Management of Communal violence through systems approach			Control and Preservation of Communal violence and prejudices	Secularism and Modernisation

society and agencies and the Government have an important role to play by not allowing foreign powers to destabilize the country by encouraging anti-national forces. The national majority community has a very significant role to perform towards the minorities. The political leaders, bureaucrats, educationists and police personnel have to adhere to the secular values and ensure communal harmony in the society. Criminal Justice system needs to play its effective role in diffusing communal tensions by quick judicial announcement. Legislators have to ensure that uniform civil code is enacted at the earliest possible. The whole nation has to put all possible efforts to combat communalism and modernisation alone will open up new opportunities.

Need for Renovating Polity

If communalism is to be fought successfully the secular polity of India will have to be renovated and secularised in a true sense. Communalism can be fought by rapid industrialisation, equitable distribution of wealth and power, when the Indian polity is liberated from the shackles of pervasive illiteracy, poverty and back wardness. Communal elements have to be shunned and communal parties have to be isolated and exposed. The leadership of political parties should evolove a code of conduct not to allow religion to be used for electioneering. Religious propoganda has to be banned. Instead of leading organising religious processions and issuing greetings to the people on various religious occassions, the leaders and politicians should mobilise, organise and unite people keeping in view "composite cultural ethos and secular traditions of India."[19]

Ruling parties must instil a feeling of confidence and security among the minorities who fear being overwhelmed by the majority and losing their respective identity. Paradoxically, minorities complain of insecurity and discrimination while the majority feel that they are being neglected in their own home. Such feelings reveal themselves through communal conflicts. The leading political party in power has to strike a delicate balance when framing its policies, so as to satisfy the minority without displeasing the majority. Unfortunately today, the growth and rise of many Hindu, Muslim and Sikh militant organisations has resulted in aggressive communalism and most of the politicians irrespective of their political parties, give the pretention of being secular but "could be tactically communal when the situation so demanded".[20] The remedy lies in banning such organisations and communal parties. Canvassing for votes on the basis of religion and caste for election to any office must be stopped. The arrest and detention under N.S.A of those communal leaders who provoke and incite their communities against others can prove effective.[21] Kuldip Nayar has observed– "My expectation from the politicians has never been high. They first criminalised politics; they have now communalised it. And I have not found any party or leader rising above the consideration of electoral prospects."[22] Religion is used as a vehicle for serving their political interests. K.M. Ashraf has aptly described this as "political trade in religion." It is therefore imperative that Indian polity should be renovated and revamped with high ideals and practices of secularism, democracy and social justice at its core. Randhir Singh has rightly held that" the spread of communal strife is in direct proportion to the depth of the crisis in Indian policy and politics of the ruling classes on the one hand and in inverse proportion to the presence or power of the left class based politics of the people on the other hand.[23]

Ban on Communal Parties and Effective Check on External Interference

Between 1985-87 nearly 2200 Pakistan infiltrators were apprehended in the western border of whom 2050 were pushed back and the remaining were handed over to the Punjab Police. In 1985 approximately 30,000 Bangladesh infiltrators were pushed back by BSF on the west Bengal border alone. According to Sri N.S. Saxena- "The Indo-Pak borders are porous and that is why both Sikh militants and Kashmiri militants can go to Pakistan and return after getting training, arms and some money. It is therefore necessary that we should seal our borders and ensure that no foreign power interferes in the internal affairs of the country. Similarly it is necessary that we should through enactment of effective laws/communal parties. The real remedy however is political education of the masses about the need to dissociate themselves from such communal parties. Raghubir Dayal Commission Report has held that genuine improvement of relations between Pakistan and India may go a long way in allaying apprehensions and removing mistrust. There were only 12 communal organisations in the country till 1947. But now there are 500 communal bodies. The R.S.S, Jamaat-Ulma-i-Hind, Dal Khalsa, Hindu Suraksha Samiti, Talaligue, Jamat, Majlis-Ittabadul, Muslim League, Haji Mastan and Dalit Muslim Minority, Suraksha Mahasangh, RSS BJP, Viswa Hindu Parishad-Shiv Sena, Trishul Sena, Bajrang Dal, Jamaat-e-Islam are communal bodies. There should be specific provisions in the constitution which should ban all communal organisations which lead to the emergence of fundamentalism, obscurantism and orthodoxy constitutional amendment alone will not do. If the communal groups do not desist from mutually fuelling each others communalism on the lines that have been witnessed in the recent past, the country will be set on the high road to communal conflict, the dimension and diabolism of which will make the past riots seem like trivial incidents.

Constitutional Recognition to Minority Commission and Need to Modernise Minorities

Progressive Muslim intellectuals must educate their community and persuade it to accept the necessity of reforming the Muslim law in regard to marriage and divorce. The need to reform Muslim personal laws of marriage and divorce is based primarily on consideration of fairness and justice to Muslim women. As Zafar Imam has observed. "The task of creating a social base for modernisation must exclusively rest on the Indian Muslims themselves" Richard A. Seherrhorn has rightly said, "The Muslims must realize that their future is bound up with the future of secularism and they should support and strengthen the Hindu and others who have launched a crusade against communalism. Without the minorities support this crusade may not succeed." Constitutional recognition should be given to the Minorities Commission which was established in 1978. Actually Ramjanam Bhoomi and Babri Masjid are not substantive but symbolic issues. Through them the two partners in the nation-building process are fighting for political and economic space"[24] A secular and pluralistic society, in a democratic model of nation building, has to resolve its inner contradiction by the slow processes of economic and political developments. Maintenance of communal harmony is as much the responsibility of minorities as it is of the majority community.

Protection of Minorities Particularly Refugees who had to Flee from their Homes to Save Their Lives

For combating communalism, protection of minorities and rehabilitation of refugees who have fled away from their home of Kashmir must get priority. Their sense of insecurity and frustration makes the minorities easily available pawns to the active communal forces who exploit them for selfish purposes and, therefore a sense of security and confidence has to be instilled in the minorities. Hindus are considered minorities in Kashmir and have undergone lot of hardship for their rehabilitation as an uprooted community need to be made. The safety of the nation and of the minorities must be our primary concern particularly when we have seen the damage that communal politics has done in the past."[24a] One of the most important remedies of communalism lies not in blaming the minorities, but in providing opportunities and creating an environment where they have feeling of security and faith in the justness of the system.[25] It is the compulsion of history and geography that the various communities in the country must have peaceful co-existence and work in harmony to make India strong.

The majority of the people in all the communities of India are peace loving and wish to abide by the rule of law." We had a rich tradition of community concern and mutual assistance"[26]

Need to Decommunalise the Present and Future Citizens by Bringing Changes in their Behaviour Pattern and Making them Secular

Positive efforts towards de-communalisation or genuine secularisation of the present and future citizens' behaviour is matter of primary socialisation, beginning from family, school and the place of worship, to which secondary factors like poverty, historical cognitions peer group behaviours and now the democratic vote have added its own rabidity.[27] The de-communalisation process should represent a collective attempt on the part of the individual, the society and the state to help each other evolving the value norms of universalism, pluralism, and liberalism respectively. At individual level, efforts must be made to develop rationality, tolerance, humanism, culture of mind, empathy and pride and courage of conviction while at the societal level, enlightened social pluralism, co-existence of non-parochial groups flexible order of liberal faiths, respect for all religious groups and truly non-discriminatory behaviour on the basis of religion are the value norms to be developed. There is no going away from the fact that secularism or whichever other word one may use, is whàt holds the variety of religions, cultures and traditions that India is together. May be secularism was hijacked by the fundamentalist and the hardliners who dominated or dictated in the name of religion. The remedy is to retrieve it, not to substitute it.[28] During the last ten years, there seems to be great panic in the ranks of the secularists. Modern Indians who are truly concerned about the secular value nature of Indian polity and who are a minority today need to assert themselves and understand the dangerous political economy of communalism." We live in an India where more than 80 per cent of the communal clashes and riots still take place among the less then 20 per cent of Indians who stay in cities are increasingly disconnected from their traditional community ties and consciousness . . . A vague generalized political commitment to faith is all they are left with by way of their roots in the traditional moral order that is what they try to aggressively defend.[29] It is necessary that we believe in a truly democratic polity which is plural in nature and allows different living cultures to flourish and bloom. There is no reason why one cannot be first a an Indian, as long as one is willing to give the same right to others. M.N.Roy had once pointed out "Secularism is not a political institution, it is a cultural atmosphere, which cannot be created by proclamation of individuals however highly placed and intensely sincere." The Indian version of secularism signifies the peaceful co-existence of religious communities and a creative inter-action between various traditions. This needs to be reconstructed and evolved in order to deal with the religious aspects of disrupted social and political relations in the current crisis. The secularism must be built on amity between different communities and understanding of other's viewpoint.

Special Courses for Riot Cases and Reforms in Criminal Justice System

For effectively combating communalism reforms in Criminal Justice System have to be carried out on priority basis and special courts can be established for expeditious disposal of communal riot cases. "Now an average case takes several years while the murderers, arsonists, rapists are out on bail. This has shaken the faith of the common man in the legal process. Its place has been taken by fake encounters and revenge killings."[30] It is high time we revamped and remedied the basic weakness in our Criminal Justice System. For expeditious disposal of communal riot cases special courts can be constituted. In communal riots, the conviction rate is hardly 2 per cent. This is not irremediable. But it needs revamping of both the police and the judiciary. Communal riots are not checked by flying in empty balloons or by giving moral lectures. The majority of communal riots are partly caused by the "laxity of the administration".[31] If the communal riots are to be curbed, effective criminal justice system has to be evolved in the country. The existing legal provisions both preventive and punitive are adequate for prevention and suppression of communal riots.[32] Even if laws are good, unless they are effectively implemented they serve no useful purpose. Increasingly people have begun to question the very effectiveness of the legal provisions mainly because of laxity in their implementation. The way out is to redesign the instruments, to reeducate the operators and to recondition the climate. They have to pay greater attention to protection minorities and weaker sections and redress their grievances on a priority basis. The success of law enforcement agencies lies in not merely quelling the riots but recognising the problems in embryonic stage and averting it. Timely and accurate intelligence can provide assistance to law enforcing agencies in making decisions and directing actions that will thwart, suppress or prevent a riot. Rumours must be prevented from stirring the trouble. Preventive legislation is provided under (1) Code of Criminal Procedure 1973 (ii) Indian Penal Code providing for private defence, (iii) Police Act 1861 (iv) Regulation of Public assemblies and processions and licensing the same (v) externment of anti-social and communal elements from disturbed areas (vi) powers to control prejudicial publication likely to incite communal feelings (vii) Indian

Arms Act, 1959 Explosives Act 1884 and Explosive Substance Act 1908.

Need to Evolve a Uniform Civil Code

Communalism in India cannot be eradicated unless uniform civil code for all people living in a secular country like India is effectively enforced after enactment. Article 44 of the Indian Constitution reads as follows: " The state shall endeavour to secure for the citizens a uniform civil code throughout the territory of India". Personal Laws need to be delinked from religion and the party in power cannot wait for the day when the Muslim community on their own would demand uniform civil code. The Muslim women (Protection of Rights on Divorce) Act enacted in May 1986 was a step in the retrogressive direction. The most point for consideration is whether progress in a changing society is compatible with static social laws. In words of A.R. Saiyed, "The failure to introduce a uniform civil code, as stipulated in the constitution, is one of the most telling examples of the failure of our non-discriminatory secularism. Not satisfied with the failure, the state has followed policies which have been perceived to now favour one community and now another community. [33]" The Supreme Court has observed in Shah Bano Judgement case as under. "It is a matter of regret that Article 44 of our Constitution has remained a dead letter ... There is no evidence of any official activity for framing a common civil code for the country ... a beginning has to be made if the constitution is to have any meaning. Inevitably, the role of the reformer has to be assumed by the courts because it is beyond the endurance of sensitive minds to allow injustice to be suffered when it is so palpable" (Mohammed Ahmed Khan Vs Shah Bano Begum AIR 1985, (/945).

Prompt Action at Various Levels to Control Communal Riots and Tensions

The Ministry of Home Affairs, Government of India, had identified 186 trouble-prone districts categorizing eight communally hypersensitive.[34] These sensitive areas require prompt action at local levels to keep off communal tension. It is imperative to immediately settle Ramjanam Bhoomi/Babri Masjid issue. Muslim community can play a vital role by exhibiting its magnaminity by voluntarily gifting the Mosque to Hindu community and building another mosque in newly locality. Whenever, communal tension shows a tendency to mount, district and local authorities should immediately try to control it before it erupts into an actual riots. Prompt action at various levels should be taken and adequate preventive measures should be taken against those who try to create ill-feeling or hatred between the communities. Possession of arms such as daggers, knifes, spears, swords, etc. in areas prone to communal trouble should be banned under Arms Act. District level officers should be fully conversant with the Emergency Scheme for dealing riots and Internal Security Scheme should be rehearsed from time to time. All measures of preventive nature like arresting of goondas and anti-social elements should be taken on the apprehension of a communal disturbance. All measures to contradict false rumours must be taken at the earliest opportunity when prevails. Patrolling by police, and paramilitary organisations must be made more effective. Ample use should be made of preventive sections of Criminal Procedure Code to curb tendencies of people to commit breach of peace. Severe action should be taken against administrative officers who fail to take preventive measures against occurrence of communal riots and when such failure indicates negligence on their parts. Probe into many communal riots have shown that "Ineffective administrative system" especially where there is a nexus between politicians, bureaucrats, police and criminals and anti-social elements, the communal violence spreads like a conflagration destroying many precious lives and property. There seems to be no check on anti-social elements who make hay while the administration turns a blind eye towards them. It is imperative that adequate and effective administrative machinery which is responsive to the prevailing situation always stands alert. Adequate representation should be given to various communities so that the public at large has faith in the impartiality and secular nature of the administration and police, so that they turn towards it for help in case of a riot or violent upheaval instead of taking the law in its own hands. It has been observed during recent communal riots in the U.P. that P.A.C. was partial, harsh, communal and biased against the minority community. The officials like District Magistrate and Superintendent of Police must be held responsible for their inaction. Generally, the administrators, particularly the police are not evidently sure of what is expected of them by their political masters. While all political parties have to declare their secular credentials if they want to contest the elections yet the government has admitted in Delhi High Court that this was not obligatory. No district police or a superintendent or a district collector is sure of how to deal with the communal situation because the preferences of political masters can change at the end of the day.[35] The government should issue instructions that in communal violence prone areas the secular minded personnel should be appointed in administrative set up. At times, Army has to be called for combating communalism when civil administration fails to tide over the explosive communal situation.

Protection of Administrators and Police Officers from Communal Virus

During the last fifty-three years, Indian politics has been highly communalized with the result that no wing of the State apparatus could escape from the virus of communalism. It is therefore necessary that administrators and police officers should be kept immune from communal virus. Recruitment, training and professionalism are some of the key areas by which protection can be ensured for administrators and police officers from communal cancer. High standards of professional training after proper recruitment can alone create a special bread of super-nationalist human beings who can be systematically be cultured and immunized to stay professionally healthy in the midst of recurring cancer of communalism in Indian polity. Administrators and police officers as social surgeons should immunize themselves too strongly to catch any communal infection. To avoid germs of communalism, administrators and police officers have to be given very high level of motivation, professional pride and appropriate value-system during their training. They have to midwive the secular character of Indian society and to avoid a fatal miscarriage, they should possess high professional insights in antenatal and postnatal profiles of the Indian society. Great organisational efforts are needed to minimise the complaints of police communalism and foster secular behaviours among police leaders in general and constabulary in particular. Central Police organisations like BSF and CRP must be kept immunized from communal virus by providing them effective training in value system of secularism and nationalism. Value norms like religious tolerance, humanism, rationality and secularism have to be inculcated in the administrators and police officers of the country so that they may keep secular flag flying high. A radical break-through in the administrative culture of the country is more than overdue. The author is however conscious of the fact that these higher values of life and of the profession are too easy to preach but too hazardous to practice just by doning the uniform or joining the administrative services of the country.

Strengthening of Intelligence System and Identification of Communally Sensitive Areas/ Districts

A place where communal riots occur or tension between different communities prevails is considered by the authorities as a communally sensitive spot, communal tension does not spring up overnight. It is built up over a period of time, suckled on communal propaganda, nursed on communal incidents and fed on rumours, until men's hearts are filled with hatred and their thoughts turn to violence.[36] Communal writings and speeches are the two main vehicles of communal propaganda. It is therefore utmost important that intelligence system should be strengthened and revamped so as to give prompt and timely intelligence about the situation.

Reforms in Education System to Evolve Secular Education

Jai Prakash Narain recommends Mass Education as a part of the tonic to remedy the communal virus. " Apart from what the Government, should do–it is the duty of those whether they belong to political parties or not who have the interest of their country at heart and who understand the danger of communalism to undertake an intensive campaign of mass education. Just as the communalists are working all the time, they should also be working all the time to counter the propaganda that goes on". The real remedy is political educatiion, national from the primary to the post-graduate stage should be reoriented :

1. To serve the purpose of creating a sense of Indian-ness, unity and solidarity;
2. To inculcate faith in the postulates of Indian democracy; and
3. To help the nation to create a modern society out of the present traditional one.

The role of teachers in combating communalism is particularly important since anything they do will soon percolate to the minds of their students, thereby helping the idea to blossom into a national ethos. The teachers can ingrain the ideas of national unity—harmony and mutal understanding. Education can transplant in the minds of children the concept of composite culture and inter-cultural understandings. In school, where children from different religions are brought together, the feeling of oneness and brotherhood can be easily fostered. The books must inculcate secular values and religious tolerance in the minds of students. The government can encourage the students at the college and university levels to play a proactive role as enlightened citizens to spread the words of amity, refrain from indulging in communal propaganda and processions. It is generally the young blood which falls prey to incitement and instigation by the communal elements. If these young minds can be well educated about how essential it is for all to live in communal harmony, many communal riots can be prevented. Educationists and academicians should be decommunalise the psyche of people through the means of their writings and mass contact programmes.

Ghetto Psychology of Minorities encouraging Fundamentalism need to be replaced by a Nationalistic Psychology and Inculcation of Scientific Temper

A national effort is needed to promote secular values and scientific temper amongst minorities so that their Ghetto psychology may not encourage fundamentalism. Failed expectations and a cultivated fear of communal riot have led to a situation where the strategy of building a united front of minority community seems to be the course of action which appeals to the bulk of the political organisers amongst the Muslims.[37] Secessionism fed by religious obscurantism and fundamentalism is not an isolated phenomenon pertaining to Gujarat alone. The entire nation's help is needed in fighting this malady.[38] This task should have been undertaken forty-three year ago. The present day Government can make a useful contribution to the communal peace and secularism of the country if they can take on this job even now on priority basis.[39] There is an urgent need to bring a psychological orientation in the masses to accept "Unity in Diversity" and respect for all religions". What is needed is a serious and deeper understanding of our classical and positive concept of secularism in the sense of Sarva Dharma Sambhawa and its dynamic interpretations as to ensure creative, constructive and dignified co-existence of all religions in our democratic republic. A secular state has to wage a resolute struggle against all forms of intolerance, credulity, superstition, emotionalism and irrationalism.

Encouragement to Inter-Religious and Inter-Community Harmony and Understanding

The national integration council 1968, has called upon all political parties, voluntary organisations, other citizen groups, the press, the leader of the public opinion, to actively encourage inter-religions and inter-community harmony. It also recommended halt to communal tensions by the following means:

(a) by discouraging communal ill will and regional animosities and weaning the misguided elements of society from path of violence;

(b) by active and energetic propagation of the principles especially of tolerance and harmony for which this nation stands;

(c) by mobilizing constructive forces of society in the cause of national unity and solidarity and giving them leadership encouragement and articulation; and

(d) by devising suitable community activities and programmes for fostering fellow feeling, emphasizing the privileges of common citizenship and in general raising the quality of national life. There is an urgent need for social mobilization to combat communalism. Karl W. Deutsch formulated the concept of social mobilization which according to him is "the process in which major culsters of old socio-economic and psychological commitments are eroded or broken and people become available for new pattern of socialization and behaviour." Against, this backdrop of social mobilization one may find a cule to the problem of communalism in India. Raghubar Dayal Commission Report has observed "As mutual mistrust between the two communities is the root cause of communal disturbances, it will really help people of all Communities form a permanent non-official organisation for doing necessary propaganda to allay the mistrust.

Implementation of the National Integration Council Recommendations

The recommendations of the National Integration Council held in 1968 can be divided into three parts namely (1) preventive measures; (2) punitive measures and (3) General measures.

Some of the main recommendations pertaining to preventive measures were as under:

(a) the constituting at the State and Central levels, of a special, intelligence unit composed of persons specially trained and possessing aptitude and absolute impartiality needed for this type of works;

(b) the furnishing by intelligence agencies, fo their reports and assessments to the District Magistrate and Superintendents of Police regularly and without delay;

(c) the charging of District Magistrates and Superintendents of Police with personal responsibility for scrutinizing these reports and for taking preventive action promptly to forestall any communal disturbances, and

(e) The keeping of a close watch on rumours mongering.

The Committee also recommended that places of workship should not be hold meetings which tend to create communal disharmony or ill-will and that special measures to prevent and deal with such meetings should be taken.

The Committee on communal aspects recommended the following punitive measures –

1. Making District Magistrates and Superintendents of Police personally responsible for prompt action to prevent or stop communal disturbances;
2. Detailing special teams of investigators for investigation of offences, committed during communal disturbances;
3. Considering the failure to take prompt and effective action as a dereliction of duty and dealing with the officers concerned accordingly and the amendment of Service Rules, if necessary to provide for this;
4. The introduction of a system of suitable recognition of services rendered in preventing or dealing with communal disturbances; and
5. The prompt investigation of offences and prompt prosecution of offenders, the non-withdrawing of prosecutions once launched, and the constitution of special courts with summary power to deal with offences connected with communal incidents.

National integration council has made several recommendations about other measures to curb communalism.

Need for a Political will and Reawakening Amongst Masses for Nation Building

Inaction on the part of Government or taking shelter under the cover of secularism will be disastrous for the unity and integrity of the country and therefore a strong political will is needed to combat communalism. Indian people and Indian Government must build up a strong political will to combat communalism together in an effective manner. It is time for our entire nation to wake up and bring forth a political leadership that is worthy of this great Republic and service it in such a manner that its foundations are reinforced and its pillars are bathed in the shining glory that rightfully deserves.[41]

Launching of a Crusade Against Communalism Through TV, Press and Other Mass Media

In order to fight communalism effectively, use of mass media like Television, Radio, newspapers and magazines etc. can play an effective role in reorienting people. Justice Ranga Nath Misra Commission of Enquiry Report (1986) has held the view that mass media including books, newspapers, cinema, radio and television have important roles to play in combating communalism. Psychological operations against communalism have to be carried out through the means of TV, Radio, Cinema, and other printed media of mass communication. Psychological feelings of prejudice, bias discrimination and distrust between communities have to be eliminated and controlled by psychological operations. Schools and colleges, social institutions, religious institutions can also play their respective roles in building up communal harmony. Press has to play its important role in reporting events in such a manner that it does not create communal tension and built up of communal frenzy. An exhaustive case study of media communalism, based on about 250 press clippings and interviews with 152 people including newspaper editors, reporters, politicians and officials of state administration reveal that certain sections of the media have been vicious combatants in communal warfare and not mere witnesses and neutral reporters. Here are some press cuttings on.

"Gorakhnath Mandir captured, terror among Sadhus; opponents flag hoisted on the main gate" was the headline given to a double column on page one of Gorakhpur's Swatantra Chetana on November 1. The story was denied by the temple authorities themselves.

"Pakistani flag hoisted on the Jama Masjid in Badayun" in Raj report on Nov. 4th, in the midst of the communal frenzy sparked off by the Ayodhya issue. The story was untrue.

"On Nov. 2nd, the Varanasi edition of a single paper Raj, said 100 had died in Ayodya, the Kanpur edition said 200 had died in an incident that dwarfed Jalhawaala Bagh", the Ranchi edition said 400-500 had perished and the Bareilly edition announced that Ayodhya had been bathed in blood on the day of Kartik Purnima with atleast 500 dead. As against this, Prime Minister Chandra Shekhar declared in Parliament that not more 16 died in Ayodhya.

"The Ram Mandir has been demolished in Ayodhya said a story published in Raj's Ranchi edition on Oct. 26. What had actually happened was that a canopy over the shilanyas pit at Ayodhya was removed. The story said that a Ram idol was also removed from the site by the administration, a fact contradicted by the VHP chief.

"115 killed in firing, said a banner headline in Swatantra Chetna on November 2. The body of the report did not say so. It was later found that in the main heading the editor had later inserted a 's' before the '15'.[42]

The press council's recently released report on press coverage of the Babri Masjid-Ram Janambhumi controversy are a revealing case study of communalism in India and point out the need for a code of conduct for the press for combating communalism. The strictures of Press Council has passed against four Hindi dailies— Raj, *Dainik Jagran*, *Swatantra Chetna* and *Swatantra Dhaiat*–for their gross irresponsibility in reporting the Ayodhya of late October and early November last year (1990). The press council has listed 12 guidelines for the press and governments on checking communalism in the press.[43] The need is that press understands its responsibility and plays an honest role instead of encouraging communal animosity on highlighting communal zealots. They must uphold the national spirit above the communal and sectarian ideas.

The mass media can leave a deep impact on the minds of literate and illiterate people. The first and foremost means of decommunalisation are government controlled TV and Radio which should not give coverage religious processions and ceremonies, or provocative speeches of religious leaders. They must have such programmes which teach the need and benefits of mutual cooperation and understanding among the members from different communities such "composite culture" enriches the lives of people by giving greater variety and virtue to lift it. The cinema is one of the most potent means to secularise the minds of men. People must not fall prey to the incitement by some selfish elements who only see personal benefits at the cost of public disorder, chaos, violence and death. This must encourage theories of amity and national solidarity instead of orthodox, reactionary, conservative ideas. "Strict legislation must be initiated" according to Amita Malik, "immediately to prosecute the makers and the distributors of audio and video cassettes inflaming communal passions". "Doordarshan is too strait-laced to attempt anything like countering the communal version on its own level with its captive audience, it can certainly go much beyond Saeed Naqvi's admirable vignettes of inter-religious tolerance and elite academic paril, discussion in Hindi and English to counter some of the communal version.

Leading Role of the State in Building up Active and Positive Secularism

The State including both Central and State Governments as the Chief Agents of the benevolent interventionism in social, political, economic and cultural activity is a given in the kind of order, we have sought to build since independence. State must vigorously propagate the ideology of scientific rationalism.[44] Through school and college text books, educational syllabi, the media it controls, the laws it passes, the example of non-identification with religious practice that it sets, the encouragement of scientific endeavour not merely in theoretical or abstract areas but in those that impinge directly on daily life and raise doubts about ordinary myths and superstition, in all these ways, the state must play an active and positive role in strengthening modern secularism and combating all forms of communalism. There are any number of ways by which state can combat communalism and build up a truly secular society. Deep commitment to secularism is needed among the leadership. Maintenance of communal harmony is as much the responsibility of minorities as it is of the majority community conflicts can always resolved and mutually adjusted if both communities have tolerance towards each other. Following measures can go a long way in combating communalism—

1. Communalism in India resolves around the compulsions of electoral politics and therefore the citizens particularly voters have to be educated and made aware of the pitfalls of communalism and its dire consequences. The political leaders, bureaucrats, educationists and police personnel should adhere to the secular values enshrined in the Indian culture and the constitution.
2. The national political parties should snap their ties and all contracts with the communal parties the organisations. Political parties should place the national interest above than the pitty electoral games and stop pleasing "the vote banks".
3. Government should caution people not to fall prey in the hands of the foreign powers who want to destablise India by creating communal violence and communal virus.
4. Dr. Gopal Singh has rightly said "If the minorities start thinking and acting in communal terms; the majority of necessity will begin to think and act likewise". Too much emphasis on minority psyche would be counter-productive." It would be in the interest of the minorities to appreciate that if they want India to retain its secular traditions and religious and cultural tolerance, they may not push the Hindu psyche too hard for that would be fatal not only for India's secular approach but also to their own survival."[44]
5. Prof. J.D. Sethi has observed "Pluralism of parties, is the essence of democracy but that essence can be destroyed by its own excesses. In India, pluralism has degenerated into anarchy because of the unlimited permissiveness of pluralism itself."[45] According to J.D. Sethi contradictions of the Indian polity have been now exposed and the mask of secularism was ripped off. Secularism was a fraudulent slogan used by the Congress party to beat the others". Communalism can be fought only when political modernization, party structuring institutionalization and economic development take deep roots in Indian polity.
6. To fight with Muslim fundamentalists and Hindu

fundamentalists, the first priority should be to resolve the two issues—Ram Janam Bhoomi Vs Babri Masjid case and the problem of uniform civil code bill. The ideal solution to the first issue has been suggested by Asghar Ali Engineer. He has suggested that "The Muslims should show magnanimity and a noble gesture of gifting away the mosque to their Hindu brothers and constructing another mosque elsewhere nearby"[46] Such Muslim gesture will strengthen the hands of the secular sections of the Hindus. Regarding the uniform civil code, the only viable solution is its immediate enactment so that Muslims may become part of the national mainstream. A. Engineer has rightly held that changing the Muslim Personel Law is not a question of accepting change under pressure from Hindu Communalists. The demand for change is basically a question of justice to the weaker sections particularly women"[47]

Censure or Ban on Communal Writings and Speeches

D.P. Madan Commisson report on communal disturbances at Bhiwandi, Jalgaon and Mahad (Maharashtra) in 1970 has recommended pre-censorship of news relating to Communal disturbances before it is published in the newspapers. District authorities should themselves issue news bulletins for publication. P. Jagan Mohan Reddy Commission has recommended pre-censorship of news and preventing the entry and distribution of any communal publications within an area. Severe action should be taken against any party or person propagating hatred against any community by speeches. Ananthasyanam Ayyangar proposed "no communal organisations which by its constitution or by the exercise of its discretionary powers is vested on grounds of religion, race or caste on any of them, should be permitted to engage in any activities other than those essential for bonafide and cultural needs of the community.

Correct Police Response to Communal Riots Need for Systems Approach

A systems approach provides the police with an integrated perspective of the internal operations and environmental relationships of police activities to communal disturbances. Police response to communal riots can be broadly divided into six phases–namely, preliminary preparations phase, deployment and planning phase, intervention and confrontation phase, withdrawal phase, post confrontation phase and post-riot normalcy phase.

(A) Preliminary Preparations Phase

Much before actual communal disturbances, police has to carry out preparations to deal with communal riots. Police organisation has to identify petty communal differences and tensions which can sow the seeds of discord for communal riots. Minor communal matters are prone to exploitation by communal organisations and political parties. The importance of meaningful intelligence based on well-defined data both in qualitative and quantitative terms must be realized by district level police officers. Preventive measures like control on ban of arms/ammunitions and explosives and rounding up of anti-social elements are necessary at the very beginning to contain communal riots. A realistic riot scheme prepared with imagination has to incorporate the following features—

(a) Complete background information of the district,

(b) A list of bad characters and anti-social elements,

(c) List of sensitive areas where the communal trouble could erupt, or has occurred in the past.

(d) The details of localities where minorities reside in sizeable numbers or have their business establishments.

(e) Statistical information regarding hospital, fire brigade, police stations, schools and other important installations.

(f) Details of previous deployment during communal disturbances and suggested future deployment.

(g) Areas where curfew needs to be enforced and where there is previous history of arson, looting and murders.

Emergency communal riot drill has to be prepared for every sensitive town. In U.P. in Moradabad districts such schemes were prepared for towns of Moradabad, Sambal, Amroha and Chandausi in 1974 and this helped police in crystallizing ideas about field work to be done during actual outbreak of communal riots.

Preliminary preparations also include availability of a control room at least in all those places which have been identified as prone to communal trouble. Control rooms have to be an ongoing facility available to the public for the purpose of communicating with the police authorities and should be under the charge of an adequate team of well-briefed police officers who can deal with communal riots with confidence and courage.

(B) Development and Planning Phase

During deployment phase mass briefing to the police personnel deployed for communal riots is most important. Spot briefing at deployed positions also help the policemen to understand their respective duties and responsibilities. Requisitioning of magistrates, mobilization of Home

Guards, alerting of Central police organisations, alerting of fire brigade, provision of P.A. equipment, transport for police officers, and preparation for all possible eventualities are some of the other important tasks for the police during deployment phase. Adequate resources have to be kept at various strategic points to deal with developing situations. Effective co-ordination between civil police, armed police and Central police organisations is required. Armed police should move only in proper formation alongwith full complement of their officiers and should be given specific tasks. All available resources both in terms of manpower and equipment should be deployed with imagination and after taking into account the vulnerable areas. The Force should not be dispersed in penny-pockets and sufficient striking resources should be kept. Detailed contingency plan for action to control communal riots has to be worked out to the minutest details. Sensitive places, such as mosque, temples, Idgah, and sensitive populated localities having mixed population have to be covered by police pickets. Vulnerable installation have to be given added protection. Deployment of armed police and CRPF has to be worked out with their specified duties.

(C) Intervention and Confrontation Phase

This is the most crucial phase of police task when the psychology of the communal mobs is to be assessed for adequate response. Police leaders have to determine the timing of intervention and set specific objectives for the police personnel, arrest of offenders, dispersal of mobs and control of unruly mob require effective police leadership. Registration of offences has to be done promptly and investigation of offences is to be done by specialized officers. Madan Commission Report (1974), has recommended that "the most effective way of bringing down the disturbance which has taken a serious turn or is about to take a serious turn is to use fire arms. Police firing should never take place in the air and should not be long delayed. During communal riots police leadership is always on the test because generally there is a tendency amongst the officers to avoid taking responsibility for dealing with the situation. A developing situation can be defused effectively by enlisting public cooperation and contradicting rumours set afloat by interested parties. Care of the dead and injured, identification of the dead and their subsequent inquest, guarding against looting of property and effective implementation of curfew are some of the other important tasks of the police force during this phase. Curfew should be restricted to these areas where curtailment of the movement of the people is absolutely necessary, for the control of communal disturbances. Once a curfew is imposed, adequate police should be moved into the area bound by the curfew. Anybody found violating the curfew should be arrested and prosecuted. Arrangements should be made for preparing photograph with moving cameras to keep record of various incidents and to monitor processions. If video camera can be made available, it will be very useful. Mobilisation of other emergency services such as ambulance service, fire fighting services, has to be realiatically assesssed and activated during this period. Emergency communal riot drill has to be a carried out to meet the situations as they develop.

(D) Withdrawal Phase

Once the communal riot is controlled and affectively dealt, regrouping of deployed personnel is needed. Injured policemen are to be sent to hospital, static guards are to be withdrawn gradually from peaceful areas and debriefing of the police personnel is to be done. Integration committees should be created both at the sub-division and at the Thana level to get popular mass support for restoration of normalcy. Through Radio broadcast and television, false and exaggerated rumours should be contradicted promptly. There should be more mobile patrols. No meeting should be permitted to be held and procession or demonstration march against communal disturbances should not be allowed in any case. Police should organise citizen committee at district and thana levels to promote and maintain communal harmony. During withdrawal phase, police officers should not develop any complacency and should keep a vigilant eye on the communal situation. Special investigation squads have to be set up to investigate crimes committed in the course of communal riots. Places of worship like Mosque, Gurdwaras, Temples, etc. should be searched by the police close to the time of communal disturbances to ensure that weapons and ammunitions and other lethal weapons are not collected.

(E) Post–Confrontation Phase

During this phase detailed reports are required to be sent to higher authorities and the Government. Police have to constantly brief mass media to prevent distortions and for rumour control. Relief and reduction of police personnel deployed on various duties has to be ensured during this phase. All documents and records are to be brought uptodate. All cases registered during communal riots are to be investigated by the special teams of experienced officers. Arms, ammunition and other police equipment is to be checked and fire arms used during riots are to be sent to fire arms experts for preparing required documentary evidence. Damages to Government property and police vehicles are to be properly assessed. All arrested persons are to be sent to jails and proper liaison with Jail authorities has to be maintained. Police should organise voluntary social service associations consisting of leading citizens of all communities to render assistance and relief to the victims and destitutes of communal riots. Psychological control of crowd, control of rumours, use of close circuit T.V., tape-recorders and cine cameras by the police are some of the routine responsibilities of the police. A joint report by the District Magistrate and Superintendent of Police should be generally prepared carefully giving details of all incidents in a chronological order.

(F) Post-Riot Normalcy Phase

During this phase all prohibitory orders and restrictive orders are finally withdrawn. Progressive withdrawal of policemen from vulnerable points is to be done and normal business life is to be restored to the community. Certain persons who can help in restoring normalcy can be released from the custody on their personal assurance of good conduct. Peace committees of respectable citizens are to be activated to bring and maintain communal harmony in communally sensitive areas. A close review of police arrangements to deal with communal disturbances should also be done once normalcy is restored. Research by police research cells should be carried out to draw lessons for future. Police should play a very active and positive role in the rehabilitation of the people affected in the communal riots. Training material and police guide books containing consolidated compilations of official instructions for dealing with communal disturbances should be prepared with greater care and should be made available to all officers upto and above the rank of Havildar and Sub-Inspectors. Communal organisations indulging in communal violence must be labeled as such and their activities should be kept under close scrutiny and watch in future. After the occurrence of communal disturbance, it is necessary to restore peace and calm as quickly as possible. Mobilisation of public opinion is a constant process and should be utilized for building communal harmony.

Effective Role of Peace Committees and Citizens Vigilance Committees

The National Integration Council in its conference in Srinagar in 1968 recommended among other suggestions:

"The constitution of citizen's committees as consulative bodies at the state and district levels to promote and maintain communal harmony, their functions being the holding of advance consultations with leaders of religious groups to ensure peaceful celebrations of festivals and to eneavour to promote joint participation by all communities in the festivals," and, "the constitution at the national level of a sub-committee of the National Integration Council to review from time to time the communal situation, the progress of implementation of recommendations of the National Integration Council in regard to communalism and to advise the government." Justice Ranganath Misra Commission of Inquiry observed that during riots in Delhi the local residents had formed combines and they succeeded in resisting rioter groups and the commission feels that such combines should be encouraged. These combines should be totally free from politics and maintain harmony and friendly relations with similar local organisations around.

Qualitative and Quantitative Reforms in Police and other Law-Enforcement Agencies

For combating communalism the police organisation will have to be revamped both in terms of quantity and quality and modernisation of police has to be carried out as a national priority. The National Police Commission has no doubt spelt out the administrative and organisational steps which can be implemented in dealing with communal violence. But we still need a clear cut policy, uninhibited by political considerations. Collective violence on account of this particular facet of our social life can be controlled to a remarkable extent if the administration is not only geared for such eventualities, but allowed to act with determination, independence and purpose. About the November 1984 riots in Delhi Justice Ranganath Misra Commission of Inquiry felt that the Delhi police requires both qualitative and quantitative expansion. The police personnel should be provided better training facilities, adequate reserves not only of armed police but also of Paramilitary forces should be built up. Riot squads with modern training should be available in riot prone areas. The need of higher levels of recruitment, training of the regulatory agencies are essential inputs to an efficient and effective functioning. Intelligence should be efficiently collected, uptodate and adequate enough to give a proper assessment of the situation. Strength of the police available locally should be sufficient. Communication and transport facilities available should serve well to reach reinforcements in time, at the required spot. The quality of the middle rank officers should be good to provide leadership when needed and take initiative. Action should be swift to prevent increase in tension. There should be desirable leadership to take action and build up a fairly good atmosphere of law enforcement. The orientation of the police force and training should prepare them, to adopt an impartial attitude to deal with communal riots firmly.

General Recommendations for Combating Communalism

1. India should effective use all available measures to fight and nullify the planned and mischievous propaganda against India and Pakistan. Cordial and good bilateral relations with Pakistan on the spirit of Simla agreement can also check propaganda by Pakistan.
2. Field officers who are present on the spot should be allowed to use their initiative in combating communalism. Raghubar Dayal Enquiry Commission Report has rightly observed : "Direction or interference from the highest level in government should not only restricts the local officers from taking independent decisions on the problem confronting them but also deprives their superiors of right to criticize the actions of the local officers if the results are not what they expected.
3. Better arrangements for water supply as well as an increase in the number and efficiency of fire fighting units are required to fight arson during communal rights.
4. Possession of arms such as daggers, knives, spears to communal trouble should be banned under Arms Act. Police should carry out effective searches and raids to detect unlicenced fire arms and ammunition.
5. The answer to the communal problems lies in maintaining constant vigilance by the local authorities and in taking prompt and effective preventive measures in time to nip the trouble in the bud. Ample use should be made to preventive sections of law to curb tendencies of people to commit breach of peace.
6. Punitive tax should be imposed on the people of the localities where communal disturbances take place.
7. To control communal riots if needed, effective police firing should be resorted to. Justice D.P. Misra Madan Commission (1970) has observed " what was wrong with the police firing in Jalgaon was that fire was not opened promptly but opened too late and that too in air and not on the mob. Had effective fire been opened on the rioting mobs at the first comment, when the situation required and justified it, so much loss of life and property would not have taken place in the Jalgaon.
8. A video movie camera with a proper technician to record the minute to minute events of the communal incidents can be very useful. District authorities should therefore engage a

proper photographer who has a movie video cemera to take photos and record events faithfully.

9. P. Jagan Mohan Reddy Commission Report (1970) has recommended that Control Rooms of police stations and districts should be reorganised to make their functioning effective and meaningful during communal disturbances. Police resources should not be wasted during riots on miscellaneous duties such as clearing debris, removing corpses, escorting persons, standing guards to protect personal properties and services of Home Guards or N.C.C. should be availed of for such duties.

10. Fraternisation between communities and participation in the festivals of other communities should be encouraged. Such occasions should be utilised for building up harmonious relations between communities.

11. Neil Smelser has suggested that social control measures involving institutionalizing of respect for law and other and orderly means for expressing grievances, the alleviating of condition of strain which generate dissatisfaction; the softening of prejudices and discrimination which deepen social damages; minimizing of divisiveness among the ruling groups in the society, should be utilised in an effective manner to cope with the problem. Government and all other social control agencies should: (a) prevent communication in general so that beliefs cannot be disseminated; (b) prevent inter-action between leaders and the followers so that mobilisation of beliefs is difficult; (c) refrain from taking a conditional attitude towards violence by bluffing or vacillating in the use of ultimate weapons of force; (d) refrain from entering into issues and controversies that move around and (e) remain impartial, unyielding and fixed on the principle of maintaining law and order.

12. In communal riots guilty must be punished. Lord Brijce rightly said: "It is not the severity of punishment but the certainty of it that deters the violators of the law. District authorities, courts and the prosecution should all ensure that guilty persons are surely punished. From time to time Central Government has made all possible efforts to deal with communal problems. The Union Government have decided to set up a special peace keeping force (Riot police) to assist the States in dealing with communal problems. Recently a decision has been taken to raise a highly mobile and will-equipped riot police mainly consisting of members

of the minority communities, Scheduled Castes and Scheduled Tribes from different parts of the country. The Prime Minister has also asked the country's top police and administrative officials to take proper action to remove any trace of communal bias in the police and administrative machinery with responsibility for communal disturbances. Due to inexperienced district level officials, the administration of districts in sensitive areas have been weakened and it must be strengthened by posting of experienced district officials if the drift into anarchy is to be stopped.

13. It is also necessary to restructure the composition of the armed constabulary of States to ensure proper representation of all sections of the society so as to deal more effectively with communal violence. (*Hindustan Times*, December 1, 1982). It is also necessary to take a fresh look at the training programmes of police so that the police developed the right attitude in dealing with the communal problem. However, secularism should not be stretched to the absurd extent of evolving a recruitment policy on communal lines. It is noticed that at times for political and communal considerations police is criticized for insensitivity, ruthlessness, excessive action and for punitively punishing the minorities not much represented in the police force. National Police Commission (1981-85) has recommended an elaborate action plan to deal with communal problem and it is high time that its recommendations are given concrete and practical shape by bringing required police reforms.

Establishment of a Secular Democratic Polity : An Operative Ideal

Secularism is an operarative ideal which must be achieved in India if communalism is to be rooted out from the society. Secularism or *sarv dharm sambhav* has been defined by Vinobaji as follows: "There are four essential ingredients of Sarv Dharm Sambhav —the feeling of equality of all religions. One of them is the faith in one's own religion, the second is the respect for all religions, the third is the reformation of one's religion and the fourth one is opposition to irreligiousness". Establishment of a truly secular and democratic polity is indeed a stupendous task and it adds to the magnitude of the problem if the society is multi-religious and multi-ethnic as our Indian society is—To establish a truly secular state, one must understand in all earnestness the psyche of Indian people and their religious cultural traditions. It is the duty of the secular intelligentsia to generate adequate pressure for politicians to give priority to peoples issues rather than non-issues like Ramjanam Bhoomi, Babri Masjid issue. There should be no pressures or pulls for assimilation of minorities in the name of national mainstream. There is lot of vitality and life in our secularism and there is no need to despair although secularism has been weakend to a large extent during the last decade. All out national efforts of all citizens must be made to further strengthen secularism and inject new blood into our secular polity. Prevention of enactment on communal laws, proper education with a secular bias, reorientation of the thinking of people by psychological operations through mass media, creation of a climate of peace and communal harmony and a change of hearts are some of the remedies to fight communalism and establish a secular polity. The greatest task that faces the nation today is to create a feeling, mood and atmosphere which did not allow communalism to grow. The fight against communalism cannot be fought by the police and law and order machinery alone. Certain amount of effective political action is necessary to restrict the menace. A new national initiative alongwith economic, political, human and socio-cultural development is necessary to combat communalism and to restore faith in the basic concepts of secularism. Building up of a secular ethos is easier said than done because of the conflict of interests, tendency of party politics to impinge on social problems and complexity of the emerging social forces. For combating communalism, guilty persons should be immediately identified, arrested and punished. It is necessary that minorities should be represented in all law-enforcement agencies, the intelligence network should be tightened to prevent the outbreak of violence and those who suffer loss of life or property should be fully compensated. For building up secular ethos we must guard against "minority communalism" for its breeds virulent reaction in the majority community. Secularism touches upon the condition of consciousness of the masses while communalism does the opposite the unconsciousness of the masses. How best the former could be promoted should be the concern of us all. Separation of the State and the functionaries of the state from religion is a necessary conditions for the development of a secular society in India. The state and the political leaders have a special responsibility to distance themselves from religious expression of the various communities by exhibiting secular ethos" only the emergence of a secular society and a civil culture can eradicate the fear of the minorities about majority intolerance. This is a sensitive balancing act which needs political acumen and vision.[48] Political leaders, human rights and civil liberties activists, social action groups, Gandhians, intellectuals, professionals, writers, artists, humanists, and the common man— all have to make all possible efforts to combat communalism for establishing a truly secular society. The anointment of Aneesa Mirza (Congress) as the first women Muslim Mayor of Ahmedabad on April 16, 2003, is a symbolic spark of hope of plural India secularism.

Why Communalism Could not be Controlled and Eradicated So Far

Ineffective police response, lack of timely intelligence, lack of political will and delays and distortions in the criminal Justice System are partly responsible for failure in combating communalism. Delhi witnessed widespread violence in the first week of November 1984 following the assassination of the Prime Minister Mrs. Indira Gandhi. Apart from large scale of looting and arson, about 2600 people were killed. One of the factors for the deterioration in law and order, especially in relation to communal riots, is the poor technical knowledge of I.A.S. and I.P.S. officers compared to their own predecessors in the fifties and even more to their predecessor services, I.C.S. and I.P.S. in pre-independent India. Generally communal riots could not be effectively controlled because there is lack of sincerity on the part of the political masters and each occasion is calculated in terms of election politics. Every communal riot has been followed by a high level declaration that not a single culprit will escape but even administration fails to punish even two per cent of the guilty persons. "The public is sought to be pacified by the following types of declarations : (1) there was a high level cabinet meeting to review the law and order situation; (2) the Chief Minister or Union Home Minister has rushed to the scene of disturbance; (3) a high level peace committee has been formed; (4) a high level judicial enquiry is being ordered. These make good press headlines but are of little or no use of curbing communal violence.[49]" For reasons of history. Indian political system is today overwhelmingly dominated by parties which operate with. The community as their analytical category, through following different strategies and thus communalism continues to shape its politics. What has surfaced now is a new epoch with endemic communal riots, mass mobilization by both Hindus and Muslims over the Babri Masjid-Ram Janam Bhoomi temple issue and the overwhelming Muslim response to the Shariat controversy which finally led to the enactment of 1986 Muslim Women Act.[50] We can understand and endure a gap between what is desirable and what is possible. But it is difficult to accept the gap between capability and commitment, which is essentially a measure of the corrosion caused by the vested interest and political and official opportunists enjoying their positions at the pluralism of power and acting in collusion or even independent of each other. The following founding fathers of the Constitution committed costly mistakes and failed to fight communalism. "There is a school of thought which believes that the constituent assembly and framers of the Indian Constitution failed to combat communalism. They were afraid to take such measures which could completely root out communalism from Indian society. "When the opportunity came to the Indians to wipe out communalism, root and branch from the body politics the framers prevaicated, vassillated and even evaded the stark naked truth of life. They compromised on every issue, on principles, with everybody and with secularism as well as a matter of fact they bought time by conceding the demands of the smaller groups and interests"[51] In the words of M.R.A. Baig, India can only have the humanism if it deserves. Those who preach humanism but do not practice it, who condemn communalism but do not combat it, who are anxious to reform but afraid to be radiant, and who treat the symptoms but not the disease might tell their rosary every morning. It could runs like this — Jabalpur, Jamshedpur, Ranchi, Hazaribagh, Meerut, Bhiwandi, Delhi, Aligarh, Ahmedabad, Poona and on and on and on.[52] Every enlightened citizen perhaps shares the agony and anguish expressed by M.R.A. Baig. It should be therefore the endeavour of every citizen to ensure that forces of unity, stability, integration and secularism ultimately triumph over the forces of communalism. Time has come for bold actions and radical reforms. In a multi–religious society it is highly necessary for secular rulers to maintain a delicate balance between different religious communities — Majority community or minority, certain religious sensibilities have to be respected.[53] The security and prosperity of the minorities as much as of the majority his, according to Arun Shourie, not in building fortresses around our parochial groups but in all of us joining together to ensure that the institutions of parliamentary democracy work.[53a]

Concluding Remarks

Communalism is a dirty word which none is anxious to use but it is a dirty act which everyone who wants to stay in the power game is anxious to do.[54] For effectively combating communalism the battle for genuine secularism merges with the struggle for faster economic growth, social justice and the defence of the multi-ethnic, multi-lingual and multi-religious character of the Indian society. If communalism is to be eradicated from the Indian society the political will to govern must be exhibited by the governments of the day. "Governance ultimately requires the will to govern. Such will can be generated only if the ruler is prepared go give up power but his principles. In other words, the party in power must first decide its policy and thereafter avoid any knee jerk reaction to situations as they develop. Populism must be avoided if communalism is to be effectively fought.[55] The country has to be save from communal virus and communal politics." In the totality of our policies the struggle for national unity is still to get priority over consideration of electoral politics. I hope this will happen without delay."[56] A plural society wedded to – the ideals of secularism can become a functioning and self fulfilling reality only when the majority conducts itself even under the most provocative conditions in a manner that it does not alienate or antagonize the minorities. Secularism has to grow silently in the minds and hearts of men by a process of correct education. Television, cinema and other mass media will have to play a positive and constructive role in bringing secularism and combating communalism. Every citizen has to play his role in combating communalism by developing secular values and right attitude to the other members of the community. It is appropriate to refer to Gurudev Rabindra Nath.

Tagore's vision of the India of tomorrow, which in inspiring language, symobises the philosophy of communal harmony in following poetic terms:

"Day and night thy voice goes out from land to land,

Calling Hindus, Buddhists, Sikhs and Jains round, thy throne

and Parsee, Musalmans and Christians, offering are brought to thy shrine by the East and the west to be woven in a garland of love, thou bringest the hearts of all people into the harmony of one life.

Thou dispenser of India's destiny,

Victory, victory, victory to thee"

References

1. Randhir Singh "Theorising communalism – A fragmentary note in the Marxist Mode", *Economic and Political Weakly* July 23, 1988.
2. P.K.B. Nagar "A Sociological Analysis of Communalism with Reference to Kerala", in *Secularism and Indian Policy* edited by Bidyut Chakrabarty 1990, p. 211.
3. Rajni Kothari " On communalism".
4. S.K. Ghosh Communal riots in India. Meet the challenge unitedly, p. 57.
5. Quoted by Bipin Chandra from A.V. Vidyalankar, National *Integration and Teaching of History*, New Delhi p. 3.
6. A. Ali Engineer – An appeal to Muslims after Meerut riots in communal problem. A symposium. Dr. Ramji Lal.
7. Kuldip Nayar – Home coming to strange land – *Tribune* 5/2/199. Chandigarh edition, p. 6.
8. Dr. Krishna Mohan Mathur – *Internal Security Challenges and Police in a Developing Society* —RBSA Publishers, Jaipur, 1989, p. 186.
9. Jai Prakash Narain, *Nation Building in India*, edited by Brahmananda, Indraprastha Press (KET), New Delhi, pp. 21-22.
10. Gopal Krishna–National integration–Not a lost cause – IV- 26th December, 1988.

11. Jai Narain – Secularism – The way out to communalism in communal problem in India –A symposium – Dr. Ramji Lal.
12. Kuldip Nayar – Home coming in a strange land – *Tribune* 5 / 2/1991, Chandigarh edition, p. 6.
13. Nikhil Chakravarthy. *Mainstream,* December 13, 1990.
14. Coomi Kapoor – The Saffron upsurge – *The Illustrated Weekly of India,* Dec. 22-23, 1990, pp.10-11.
15. V.M.Tarkunde – Hindu Communalism – Is it the beginning of Fascism – *Times of India*.
16. Asgar Ali Engineer – Meerut Shame of Nation - *Delhi Meerut Riots* – p. 16.
17. Asgar Ali Engineer – Meerut Shame of the Nation in the book *Delhi Meerut Riots* – p. 17.
18. Inder Jit – Double Talk on Communalism – May 9, 1989.
18 (a) See Asgar Ali Engineer – " Process of Nation Building in South Asia. Some Ethnic and Communal Aspects" in *Nation Building in South Asia*. Edited by Ramakant and Upriti – 1991, p. 60.
19. Ramji Lal – Communal Scenario in India in Communal Problem in India. A symposium, p. 30.
20. Syed Shahabuddin – Rejoinder Darkness gathers in the horizon. *Illustrated Weekly India,* 10th Aug. 1986.
21. Nikhil Chakravarthy – The communal winds blow – *Political Diary*.
22. Kuldip Nayar – Homecoming to a strange land". *Tribune* 5-2-1991, Chandigarh Edition, p. 6.
23. Randhir Singh – Theorising Communalism – An explanatory note in the Marxist Mode, *Economic and Political Weekly*. July 23, 1988, p.154.
24. Asghar Ali Engineer – Process of Nation building in South Asia – Some ethnic and communal aspects – in *Nation Building in South Asia* – Vol. I Edited by Ramakant and Upriti. 191, p. 64.
24 (a) Khusro J – Rustamji – Babri Masjid must be acquired – *Tribune,* 20/9/1990.
25. K.Z. Amani – Communalism Geography – History and Politics – Dec. 4, 1989.
26. S.S. Gill – Rich Government poor people – *Indian Express* – 5th April, 1988.
27. Ashis Nandi – New Ideology of Religious Tolerance, *Times India, Delhi* January, 21st 1981.
28. Kuldip Nayar – Homecoming to a strange land *Tribune* 5-2-1991, Chandigarh Edition, p. 6.
29. Ashis Nandy – Hindustan – I – Secularism disowned double. *Indian Express,* 13-1-1991.
30. N.S. Saksena – Riots in U.P. The Questions – II – *Indian Express,* 2 January 1991.
31. N.S. Saksena – Brutalised India – Who is to blame, *Times of India* – 16/1/1991.
32. S.K. Ghosh – Communal Riots in India. Meet the Challenge Unitedly, p. 96.

33. A.R. Saiyed – Secularism in Retreat – The Communal Secular Paradox in India – *Secularism and Indian Polity* – Edited by Bidyut Chakrabarty – 1990, p. 148.
34. (a) S.K. Ghosh – Social Order in India – 1990, p. 38.
35. Harish Khare - Sparring with communalism – Why Sadhus are setting National agents – *Times of India*, Oct 20, 1989.
36. S.C. Misra – *Communal Riots in India,* p. 195.
37. Shri Prakash Society – The Muslims Ghetto Psychology encourages fundamentalism – *Times of India*, 8-10-1989.
38. Satya Pal Dang – Fail out of Ayodhya Dispute on Punjab – *Times of India* – Sept 15, 1989.
39. P.R. Raj Gopal – Communal Problem – Approach is wrong – *Times of India,* January 10, 1990.
40. Kushwant Singh – *Indian Express,* 25th January 1987.
41. Nikhil Chakravarty – *Mainstream* – January 26,1991.
42. The author gratefully acknowledges the Newswatch Comments of Anjali Puri – "When the Press ran Riot" in Indian Express -10th Feb. 1991.
43. Times of India – Editorial on Justified Structures. 16 Feb 1991.
43(a) Arun Shourie – *Religion in politics* Roli Book Private Ltd. New Delhi, 1989, p. 297.
44. A.S. Abraham – Care for Active Secularism – Leading Role of the State, *Times of India* – October 15, 1990.
44(a) Devendra Chintan – Hindu Psyche Today , *Panchand Research Journals* – Inaugural issue, Vol. 1, No. 1987, pp. 43-53.
45. The State against the Nation – *Mainstream,* June 27, 1987, p. 22.
46. Asghar Ali Engineer – An Appeal to the Muslims – after the Meerut Riots – *Mainstream,* Sept 12, 1987, p. 23.
47. Asghar Ali Engineer – Personal Law and Communal Reaction Special Action—July-Sept 1987, p. 301.
48. Author gratefully acknowledge to above given ideas George Mathew – a social scientist and director of the Institute of Sciences, New Delhi given in his articles "Secular Ethos and Minorities" Published in Perestroika in India – V.P. Singh's Prime Ministership – Edited by G.S. Bhargav, pp. 69-79.
49. N.S. Saksena – Riots in U.P. – The Question – I, *Indian Express,* 2 January 1991.
50. Kuldip Nayar – *The Telegraph* – Calcutta, 5/1/1988.
51. Anirban Kashyap – Communalism and Constitution – 1988, p. 242.
52. M.R.A. Baig – *The Muslim Dilemma in India* (1974), p. 98.
53. Asghar Ali Engineer – Ram Janam Bhoomi – Karseva and Communal violence– Institute of Islamic Studies – Occasional paper – No.1. Vol. 7 January 1990, p. 4.
53(a) Arun Shourie - *Religion in Politics,* Roli Book Private Ltd New Delhi 1989, p. 297.
54. K. Raghuvendra Roa – *Secularism, Communalism and Democracy in*

India–Some theoretical issues in secularism and Indian Polity edited by B. Chakraborty, 1990, p. 44.

55. M.N. Buch. The Will to Governor. *Hindustan Times*, New Delhi, 10-8-1990.
56. S.G. Sardesai – Cry from the Heart to Save the Nation – *Times of India* – 24/10/1989.

3

Challenges to Police Professionalism

There are many definitions and different perceptions about profession. According to *Carr Saunders* and *Wilson*, "a profession is defined as the possession of an intellectual technique acquired by special training which can be applied to some sphere of every day life"[1] Talcott Parsons considers a profession as performance of certain functions valued in society in general and earning a Living as full-time job by these activities[2]. According to *Greenwood*, distinguishing attributes of profession are systematic theory (body of knowledge), authority (building confidence in the clients), community sanction (approval and respect by the society), ethical codes and professional culture (focus on certain values and norms, dedication and interest in mankind and society)[3]. Although there are so far no universally accepted attributes of a profession, some of the main characteristics of a profession can be as under:-

1. Professional competence based on a relatively coherent, systematic and transmissible body of knowledge, skills, attitudes, values and practices, rooted in scientific theories which enable the practitioners of the profession to utilize concepts and principles and to apply them to specific situations.
2. Performance of certain functions of public service valued in society in general.
3. Pride in work and self-esteem.
4. Fixed standards for admission, training and fitness to work.
5. Continued updating of education and training for keeping in touch with changing realities.
6. Functional exclusiveness and specializations.
7. Autonomous control and code of ethics.
8. Individual responsibility and social accountability for actions and omissions.

9. Professional solidarity and esprit de corps.
10. Commitment and dedication to the profession and earning a living as full time job.
11. Community sanction (approval and respect by society).
12. Professional authority (building confidence in clients).

Professionalism has vague connotations perhaps even an undefined message. Professionalism is only an ideal and the degree of professionalism is directly proportional to the degree of training, autonomy in decision-making and extent of operational freedom which members of any profession enjoy in any society. Efficiency and accountability are two indices for measuring the degree of professionalism. All professions strive to move towards excellence on a continuing basis. However two of the grand old professions - law and medicine have in the recent past held to ransom their hapless clientele in Delhi and are guilty of using the professional prerogative against clients by resorting strike.

The concept of professionalism in Police according to *Norman J. Greenhill,* may be represented as follows:

Social value of the work

1. Essential public service (especially handling people's emergencies, crises, etc).
2. High public esteem and social status enjoyed by practitioners.
3. High degree of pride in belonging to the profession.

Technical skill

4. Expertise based on a systematic body of knowledge (applied science or study).
5. Higher standards of admission and fitness to practice.
6. Lengthy candidate training and continued commitment to learning.

Internal control of the work

7. Autonomous control of the profession (code of ethics or discipline, rather than or in addition to external or administrative controls).
8. Individual responsibility for inaction.
9. Moral or vocational commitment to the service aspect of the work.
10. Functional exclusiveness and specialisation[4].

If the society wants a professional police force, Executives and other organisations must be encouraged to treat their Police Officer as professional when and if they in fact achieve the qualification standards, and competencies associated with professionalism. To recruit and retain a person in police committed for continued professional growth, society has to devise a work world that is psychologically richer. Job-enlargement, participative management and an intrinsic reward system are major components of such a job environment. "Plainly put professional police employees should be provided the means through their job for meeting higher-order human needs (participation, self evaluation, dignity, variety, task identity and friendship opportunities)"[5]. Can we expect the professionalisation of Indian Police to continue without thought restructuring and modernization to accommodate space for newer roles and better organisational development. The professionalisation of the police officers role is an essential requirement because of the developments in science, technology and increasing use of computers in our daily life. Bachelors degree has to be a mandatory requirement for recruits and advanced degree should be mandatory for Subordinate Officers, and higher level Police Officers. "The profession of Law Enforcement, even though young in the history of the honoured professions, is rich in traditions because of its many heroic and meritorious services to the public whom it serves"[6].

Emerging Challenges to Police Professionalism in the Changing Scenario

The emerging challenges to police professionalism can be broadly categorized under the following heads:

1. Changing patterns of crime, both urban and rural.
2. The changing political scenario.
3. The changing social scenario.
4. The changing religious scenario.
5. The changing economic scenario.
6. The changing environmental scenario.
7. The demographic changes in society.
8. The changing value system and the generation gap.
9. The rapid expansion and multiplication of Central Police Organisations.
10. The International campaign for Human Rights and dignity of the individuals.
11. Information over-load syndrome and how to cope with it.
12. The increasing challenge of violence, terrorism and insurgency.

13. The growing nexus between politicians, bureaucrats, businessmen and the criminal gangs/mafia.
14. Judicial activism and the professional autonomy of the police.

The Time of India, New Delhi, 20 1997 says: "Naxalites running parallel administration in Bastar" by imposing taxes on traders, forest contractors, and private bus operators, thereby collecting lakhs of rupees. In many parts of the country particularly in Bihar, U.P. and Andhra Pradesh extremists, armed gangs and P.W.G. are almost running a parallel administration.

Are We Becoming a Police State?

Many persons ask a question whether India is becoming "a Police State". In April 1997 policemen in New Delhi killed two innocent businessmen, mistaking them for gangsters. In another incident, Martin Massey, returning home after a tiring day, was beaten black and blue by overzealous cops on duty keeping the Prime Minister's route clear of obstruction. A staggering Rs. 76 crore has been earmarked in 1997-1998 for the Special Protection Group which guards the Prime Minister, former PMs and their families. There have been rampant violations of human rights by the State Police Organisations including fake encounters, custodial deaths, custodial tortures and even custodial rapes. Justice J.S. Verma and Justice A.S. Anand declared the principle of Sovereign immunity would not apply in cases of violation of fundamental rights. Justice Anand said "No civilized system can permit an executive to play with the people of its country and claim that it is entitled to act in any manner as it is Sovereign.............. No legal or political system today can place the state above the law as it is unjust and unfair for citizen to be deprived of his property illegally by the negligent act of officers. Over zealous policing and obsolete laws are making India a dangerous place to live in[7]. However cases of official brutality are an exception rather than the norm and the term "obsolete" is subjective. Things need to be seen in a more broader perspective.

Judicial Activism and Need for Police Autonomy

The Central Bureau of Investigation is being criticised for being politically partisan, seeking publicity, leaking out information prematurely and selectively, not preparing its cases thoroughly and of committing improprieties which prejudice a fair trial[8]. What is needed vitally to-day is complete autonomy of the police, and all Intelligence Agencies as well as investigating agencies. There is need for a comprehensive legislation defining the role of Civil Police, C.B.I., Central Police Organisations CPOs and other law-enforcement agencies having complete autonomy, with their clearly defined role, functions, responsibilities and relationship with other agencies of the Criminal Justice System, Central Security Council and State Security Councils can over see and monitor the activities and functional accountability. In such an institutional arrangement there will be reduced need for judicial activism and it will provide professional autonomy and desired accountability. The debate on the Police autonomy and professionalism should be carried out at national level in the larger framework keeping in mind the long-term good governance and security of the citizens.

Police professionalism should be viewed holistically. It is no professionalism that so much of lament should be made about the poor career prospects of the IPS Officers vis-à-vis other services, when so little is heard about the career prospects of Constables, thousands of whom retire every year, without a single promotion in 35 years or more.[9] Problems of Constables, Head Constables, Sub Inspectors, Inspectors and Officers of Central Police Organisations also need to be properly highlighted when problems of police professionalism are discussed. Actually for a democratic society like India, professionalism at middle and lower echelons should be properly analysed. To-day there is need of police leaders and not police managers.

Police Professionalism Getting Organisational Stress Due to Information Over-Load Syndrome

New information technology like fax, mobile phone, E-mail, pager, voice mail have submerged police professionals in what psychologists call information overload syndrome. A survey commissioned by Reuters found that half of 1300 managers questioned were suffering from more stress, less job satisfaction and greater degree of psychological illness and physical symptoms ranged from headaches and chronic tiredness to bad temper and stomach pains. The psychological effects included an inability to analyse information, increased anxiety, poorer performance, greater self-doubt and a growing tendency to pass the buck. Cary Cooper, Britain's leading occupational psychologist says that you can cope with information overload but only if you take control. Impose a restriction on the number of enquiries, messages you can deal with, if you are under 45 and just five if you are older[10]. Information overload could easily turn professionals into workaholics, but if we neglect home, we pay a price. Dr. Mark Griffiths, a psychologist at Nottingham Trent University admits: "I still often feel bombarded by information but I have now at least developed the capacity to shut off sometimes". Police professionalism has to face this emerging challenge of information overload syndrome by learning ways to cope with it and stop the world[11].

Problem Areas for Police Professionalism

1. Crisis of leadership.
2. Careerism and increasing unionism in State Police.
3. Growing Police indiscipline and organisational deviance.
4. Increase in non-ethical police practices and violations of human rights.
5. Growing corruption at all levels and its impact on service.
6. Collusion with criminals, politicians and organised Mafia gangs.
7. Lack of democratization.

Organisational Deviance

One of the most serious challenges of police professionalisms is organisational deviance.

In 1979, M.David Ermann and Richard J. Lundman had developed the concept of organisations as deviant. Lawrence W. Sherman has also expanded the idea further in extent of police in his book *"Scandal and Reform - Controlling Police Corruption."*

The following five conditions must be met for a deviant action to be the product of organisational system rather than an individual person:-

1. For an action to be organisationally deviant, it must be contrary to norms and rules maintained by the society to which the police organisation belongs.
2. The deviant action must be supported by internal informal norms which conflict with the police organisation's formal goals and objectives.
3. The deviance is organisational when police socialisation involves an introduction to internal norms supportive of impropriety to the new entrants through training and practical field experience, reinforced by peer group support.
4. A Code of Secrecy requires police officers to remain silent about deviant behaviour of colleagues and peer group support for the misbehaviour of colleagues.
5. It must be supported by the dominant administrative coalitions of the police organisation.

Police misconduct is organisational deviance when actions are in conformity with internal operating norms and supported by socialisation, peers and the administrative coalition of the department even though such actions violate external expectations of what the police organisation should do. Immunity of persons involved in gambling, narcotics, prostitution and planned theft only occurs when entire police organisation is deviant. Acceptance of free or discount meals and services, protection of illegal activities, planned theft and robberies, acceptance of kickbacks for referrals for services and organised corruption are some of the well know organisational deviances in police organisations. Corruption makes policing available for a price and it makes police into criminals. Needless and excessive police violence is a form of anarchy. Use of abusive language and excessive use of force over suspects make police misconduct a part of organisational deviance. Sociological research reveals that extra-individualistic or social forces are operative in the context of police wrong-doing.

Social deviance in police organisation can be of five broad categories:

1. *Criminal Misconduct* : This refers to violation of the penal code of the state and includes violations of penal laws like bribery, theft, perjury, criminal assault, rape and drug violations.
2. *Indiscipline and serious violations of conduct rules* : These violations involve insubordination, drunkenness on the job, gross neglect of duty, and failure to confirm to departmental orders and norms.
3. *Individual deviances while off duties* : Off duty deviances could include public drunkenness, involvement in extra-marital affairs, failure to pay debts and the like.
4. *Organisational deviance* : Police officers also engage in occupational deviance by providing protection of illegal but widely demanded services such as narcotics, gambling and prostitution. Police abuse of discretion, unnecessary use of force and corruption can be best understood as instances of organisational rather than individual deviance. The Police sub-culture of secrecy, a distrust of outsiders, willingness to tolerate the discriminatory actions of colleagues are some of the internal operating norms of the police organisations which encourage organisational deviance.
5. *Marginal Crime in Police Organisations* : In most of the communities large number of citizens are willing to provide money, goods or services to the Police Officers in exchange for police favours. Police Officers, particularly at the middle and lower levels, take advantage of these illegitimate opportunities and commit marginal crime.

Some of the main marginal crime are enumerated below :

(a) *Mooching* - It is an act of receiving free tea, coffee, cigarettes, meals, liquor, groceries and other items for the possible future acts of favouritism.

(b) *Chiseling* - It is an activity involving free admission to entertainment in crime houses, circus and other public shows.

(c) *Favouritism* - It is the practice of using license tabs, window stickers, courtesy cards to gain immunity from traffic arrest and is sometimes extènded to the wives, families and friends of the police personnel.

(d) *Shopping* - It is the practice of picking up small items such as candy bars, gums, or cigarettes at a store without payment.

(e) *Extortion* - It includes demands made for advertisements in police magazines or purchase of tickets to police functions or the "street courts" where minor traffic tickets can be avoided by small payments to police personnel without asking for official receipts.

(f) *Gifts* - It is in the form of payment of costly "gifts" and presents on some trivial occasions for future assistance to avoid prosecution and to gain favour under the cover of personal friendship.

(g) *Shakedown* - It is the practice of appropriating or procuring expensive items for personal use and attributing it to criminal activity when investigating burglary, and unlocked door or dacoity cases.

(h) *Premeditated theft* - It is planned burglary and premeditated theft involving use of tools, keys etc. for unlawful acquisition of property.

(i) *Perjury and little lies* - It includes alteration in crime statistics, padding up of evidence and even creation of false evidence to seek conviction of the accused. It includes lies which police officers provide as an alibi for fellow officers apprehended in unlawful activity covered by the police "code" and informal organisational sub-culture of secrecy.

(j) *Abuse of Police discretion* - It includes aggressive misuse of police discretion regarding arrest and use of force for personnel gains.

(k) *Police brutality, assault and encounters* - Numerous instances can be quoted where police are exercising unnecessary and excessive police force during interrogation and in police criminal armed encounters.

The Doctrine of Sovereign Immunity Not Applicable in Police Organisations

The doctrine of sovereign immunity is not only anathematic to the Republican polity in India but is also incompatible with the principles of human rights jurisprudence. The doctrine of sovereign immunity completely negates this fundamental human right. The Supreme Court now-a-days does not take cognizance of the doctrine of sovereign immunity while deciding cases involving violation of any fundamental right, and it has awarded compensation in a number of cases to the aggrieved person whose fundamental right had been violated, as for example, in Rudul Sah v. State of Bihar, AIR 1983, SC 1086; in Sebbastian M. Hongray v. Union of India, AIR 1984 SC 1026; in Bhim Singh v. State of J&K, AIR 1986 SC 494; in Saheli and others v. Commissioner of Police, Delhi, AIR 1990 SC 513; and in Nilabati Behera V. State of Orissa, AIR 1993 SC 1960. In the case of Nilabati Vehera v. State of Orissa, the Supreme Court made this point clear when it observed; "It may be mentioned straightaway that award of compensation in a proceeding under Art. 32 by this court or by the High Court under Art. 226 of the Constitution is a remedy available in public law, based on strict liability for contravention of fundamental rights to which the principle of sovereign immunity does not apply, even though it may be available as a defence in private law in an action based on tort.

How to Build up Police Professionalism in India?

Police professionalism in India can be built up only when police organisations are totally overhauled and long due police reforms are carried out in a given time-frame. The present police culture of defensiveness, suspicion, secrecy, cynicism, organisational deviance and corruption, occupational solidarity and isolation syndrome, conservatism, rigid hierarchical structure, police brutalities and use of third degree need to be replaced by a new police culture of democratic ethos, high level of professional training and commitment and new professional values characterised by social justice, due recognition of human rights, service to the community with a deep humane orientation. Better personal management, adequate organisational reforms, effective and job-oriented training and community support to police have to be some of the first few measures needed to build up professionalism in police. Police leadership in Central Police Organisations need to be developed from within by building CPO cadres because the challenges of the future will require new skills in personnel management and a much higher level of specialization, professional knowledge, competence and leadership from the senior officers. Full and effective implementation of the recommendations of the National Police Commission are imperative to build up professionalism in place in India. Police leadership has to be fully aware of the organisational and operational shortcomings and recognize what must be done to improve their organisations. Police leaders have to play an important role in building professionalism. Self regulation, social accountability, public credibility, professional ethics, emerging challenges of social change and public cooperation are the most important challenges faced by police professionalism in India. Increasing crime, social violence and terrorism are throwing serious threat to police professionalism.

Police profession is the most hazardous, dangerous, challenging and demanding in terms of commitment. No professional sacrifices so many lives for upholding the professional commitment. 516 police personnel of various ranks were killed and 4450 were injured in India while performing their duties during 1989. The highest casualty was in Punjab which alone accounts for 23.3 per cent of the total deaths in line of their duty as professional. If we see the rank-wise breakup 340 Constables, 86 Head Constables, 28 Asstt. Sub-Inspectors, 42 Sub-Inspectors, 6 Inspectors and 12 Gazetted Officers sacrificed their valuable lives at the altar of their duty. Similarly 3109 Constables, 473 Head Constables, 164 Asstt. Sub Inspectors, 47 Sub-Inspectors, 149 Inspectors and 147 Gazetted Officers making a total of 4459 police personnel were injured during performance of their official duty during 1999 only. Actually during last six months of 1991 (May - October 1991) more than 160 members of the police families were killed by terrorists of Punjab as part of their wrath against police persons who were putting up a gallant fight against terrorists. During 1988, 394 police personnel of various ranks sacrificed their lives at the altar of duty and 3829 were injured while performing their duties in India. During 1988 Punjab had the highest casualty of 121 which alone counted for 30.7 per cent of the total deaths of police personnel. Which other profession in the world has such high casualty rate?

Following measures will go a long way in building up sound professionalism in police in Indians:

1. Long term perspective planning should be done for state police organisations and the Central Police Organisations so that

their training, recruitment, and other personnel policies are properly planned and executed.

2. Proliferation of police organisations need to be restricted and specialised areas of duties, responsibilities and obligations have to be clearly demarcated for each organisation in order to avoid overlapping of jurisdictions and duplicity of command structure.
3. Recommendations of the National Police Commission should be implemented in a given time frame and police leadership must not be diluted by having eve-increasing upgradation of senior level posts of the rank of Director General and Additional Directors General and below.
4. Police science as an academic discipline should be introduced at higher secondary, graduate and postgraduate levels in the humanities and social sciences group of subjects and free access to police literature be made for researchers and social scientists. We should start a graduate qualification for middle level police officers and a diploma in police science as a necessary qualification for officers of the rank of Sub-Inspectors. Similarly all Universities should help social scientists and researchers to build up police science as a fully developed academic discipline.
5. There is need for a strong political will and determination at the Centre and State levels to bring out drastic reforms in police organisation.
6. Police efficiency and effectiveness have to be built up by reducing the response-time and building up an organisational culture of responsiveness to the changing needs of the society.
7. International bibliography on all available police literature should be made and proper Classification and Documentation of police literature should be attempted on priority basis so that police science builds up its academic contents and research orientation.
8. Police researches in the fields of police equipment, arms, ammunition, operational technology, training and personnel management should be carried out by police organisations and universities on a continuous basis.
9. A well-researched, documented approach and objective

evaluation of police-thinkers and practitioners should be carried out on a continuous basis so that police pioneers and thinkers are given due place in the history of police science. Police professionalism can be built only when police organisations build up their "Knowledgc-base" on scientific lines. The art and science of policing need to be constantly upgraded and given practical life-orientation.

Action Plan for Building up Professionalism

There is a need for an Action plan for removing the following impediments which throw up series challenges to police professionalism:

(a) Political pressure at all levels (succumbing to the same again is lack of professionalism).

(b) Inadequate training not envisaging the changing social need.

(c) Lack of rapport with people in general due to attitude not conducive towards interaction with general masses.

(d) An atmosphere of toral security in service conditions, developing a casual attitude to the job.

(e) Absence of feedback from below making the top echelon developing a closed mind.

(f) Lack of adequate resources - they are made available during any emergency.

(g) Inadequacy of force - overstretching them allowing no time for in-service training. (This arises out of lack of professionalism and generate a further impediments to professionalism).

(h) Absence of any specific cell charged with the task of doing a perspective planning for the States and the Centre as a whole.

For removing these impediments the following Action Plan is recommended :

(a) Lobbying at the Central and State level to remove political pressure through seminars and interface with mass media.

(b) Improved training facilities keeping in view the changing social needs.

(c) Underlining the requirement at the stage of training and making it imperative to hold periodic police - public meeting at all levels.

(d) In-service examination at all stages of promotion to higher ranks with specific age-limits, competing which should be made imperative. Failure would lead to departure/relegation to some other job.

(e) Suitable organisational network for required interface between different ranks.

(f) Lobbying again to meet the projected needs.

(g) Because of a fall in professional efficiency the hiatus is sought to be filled by quantity rather than quality. This results in lack of required routine in-service training. Increase in force continued with re-introduction of inservice training (routine, like musketry, rudiments of law, abstract course, etc).

(h) BPR and D can take up the task of perspective planning at the Central level and ISGP Training at the state level with a small body at their disposal.

A study by Shri P.S.V.Prasad about professionalism in police has made useful study about professionalism. It has recommended a 13 point Action Plan for building up Police professionalism which is as under :

1. Recommedations of NPC should be implemented in toto.
2. Transfers be made not by Ministers but by a board headed by judges.
3. Corruption and malpractices by subordinate ranks must be taken severe note of by the superiors.
4. Entry at a younger age, frequent deputation to the Government of India, periodic exposure to changing environment, very strict system of rewards and punishments.
5. Service Association Office bearers should visit NPA/BPR and D for briefing on the requirements of a professional service and monitoring of work needs.
6. Raising of police education corps at All India level.
7. Positive police philosophy, a healthy police culture, occupational commitment, professional specialisation, decentralisation, accountability, autonomy, modernization and brotherhood.
8. Police science as an academic discipline should be inducted at appropriate levels of education and should be made compulsory for entry to police.
9. Research on police equipment, arms, operational technology, and HRD should be carried out by police organisation and universities on continuous basis.
10. Courses on public relations, crisis management,HRD, collection of intelligence, surveillance and interrogation.

11. Intervention by politicians should be discouraged at all costs in police functioning.
12. In-service refresher training should be made compulsory before promotions of police functionaries.
13. Improve police training at all levels and emphasize importance of police code of conduct in training so that officers come out of the training institutions with a strong moral base.

A Case Study - Dilemma for Professional Policemen - Case of Shri Ajit Singh Sandhu

The death of Ajit Singh Sandhu is an indictment of the manner in which this nation treats the people it is indebted to. It probably true that in the course of discharging his duties in Tarun Taran, Sandhu used means that would not find place in any police manual. But such contraventions are inevitable in areas prone to separatist violence, where police are expected to carry assault rifles and conduct joint operations with the military. In Tarun Taran, the police were not engaged in keeping the peace. They were engaged in irregular, low-intensity war, fighting the Indian Government's battles against a parallel Government set up by the militants. While Sandhu's methods ought indeed to come under scrutiny, he should also have been given due credit for wresting control of Tarun Taran, where India's resolve to fight militancy suffered the acid test. He should have been subjected to the process of the law, but he should not have been robbed of all dignity before he was even convicted. But the Government, by giving the human rights lobbies free rein, did all it could to ensure his humiliation, even going to the extent of jailing him with the very militants he had helped pût behind bars[12]. It is a matter of serious consideration for the police professionals whether they should sacrifice their life and limb to restore law and order in situations as was prevailing in Punjab during hey days of terrorism. Shri K.P.S. Gill holds the view that law should be amended to protect policemen for their role during militancy in Punjab. However, former DGP of Haryana Shri S.S. Bar feels that no blanket protection from law can be given to the Police officers in a civilized society. The police officers are answerable under the law for any wrong doings. However most of the police professionals hold the view that while actions performed in good faith deserve proper consideration, the abuse of power through illegal or corrupt action do not call for any protection. The question of how perspective change with the change of Government at the Centre and in the States need to be noted by the police professionals. Can they be victims of changing perspectives of frequently changing governments in the States and at the Centre.

Need for Research on Organisational Stress and Occupational Health in Police

One of the most serious challenges to the Indian Police emerging due to changing scenario is the increasing occurrences of stress and related mental health problems. Even though police force has changed its role and responsibilities since the dawn of independence, problems are aggravating at a rapid pace and the inadequate police force is already stretched to a maximum. This limited manpower and increasing social problems have only contributed for increasing stress on police personnel.[13] In a research study P. Mathur noted that job stress remains a neglected area of research and reported that the following job-related factors act as specific stressors for the police:-

(1) Working conditions.
(2) Work over-load.
(3) Lack of recognition.
(4) Fear of severe injury or being killed on duty.
(5) Short-term, high intensity stressful events.
(6) Inadequate equipment.
(7) Shooting someone in line of duty.
(8) Anti-terrorist operations.
(9) Complaints by public against police.
(10) Confrontation with public.
(11) Lack of job satisfaction.
(12) Police hierarchy.[14]

In another research study by Mathur (1995) it was reported that nearly 90 per cent of the police personnel had expressed the need for further research. Among the senior officers the major stressors were neglecting family, inspection tours, frequent transfers, trouble with boss and staying away from family. Among the Subordinate Officers neglect of family, non-grant of leave, doing VIP security duties, performing unofficial work and staying away from family were the major factors.[15] A research study by Dr. S.M. Channabasavanna, an epidemiological approach indicates depression, dysthymia, anxiety and psychological morbidity are gradually increasing in Police personnel.[16] There is, therefore, a constant need for research in the organisation stress and occupational health of the police personnel.

Concluding Remarks

Criminalisation of politics and politicalisation of criminals, economic liberalisation policy, increasing caste violence and caste consciousness in our plural society, the growing fundamentalism of Islam and other religious groups, the environment hazards created by increasing traffic in metropolitan cities, the erosion of value system, growing population, growing outcry for human rights violations by the police, judicial activism, increasing challenges of terrorism, insurgency and hitech extremist groups, information overload syndrome are some of the most serious challenges to the police professionalism today.

Police organisation should prepare itself for meeting the following dissertations of recent developments of Indian society, namely, (a) increasing turbulence, unrest and violence, (b) increasing awareness among tribal-rural poor of their democratic rights in the face of their continued suppression by the feudalistic forces, leading to (c) human-rights, civil-liberties movements and upsurge in the form of Naxalism and terrorism, (d) state terrorism as reflected by torture, encounter-deaths and police-violence resulting in, (e) people tending to take law into their own hand on the basis of their perception that state and its administrative apparatus are not only irresponsive, but partisan too. Police organisation in India need to develop its role as a democratic agent with a high professional ethos, accountability and transparency in its functions.

References

1. A.M. Carr Saunders and P.A. Wilson Profession - *Encyclopedia of Social Sciences,* New York, Vol. XII Mac Millan 1959, p. 976.
2. Talcott Parsons - *Essay in Sociological Theory* - Glence, Illinois The Fren Press 1958, p. 372.
3. Earnest Green Wood - "Attributes of a profession" *Social work* Vol. 2, July 1957, p. 54.
4. Norman J. Green Hill - *Professionalism in Police Service in Modern Policing* Edited by David Watts Pope and Norman and Weiner, 1981, p. 56.
5. Paul M. Whiteland - *Police Supervision - Theory and Practice* - Prentice Hall In. New Jersey, 1976, p. 435.
6. Albert N. Brown - Foreword to the book *Professional - Police Human Relations* By Arthur I. Siegel, Philip J. Federman and Donglas G. Schulz - Charles C. Thomas - Springfield, USA, 1963, p. (vii).

7. Rakesh Bhatnagar - Are we becoming a Police State. *The Sunday Times,* Ahmedabad, 18 May 1997.
8. K. Subrahmanyam - Case to enquire into CBI's Functioning - *The Times of India*, May 20, 1997.
9 P.D. Malaviya - Police Professionalism at the District Level - SVP NPA Magazine Vol. 43. No. 2 July-December 1991, p. 30.
10. Cary Cooper - How to cope with information overload - The *Sunday Times of India Review,* May 11, 1997.
11. See Susan Clark - Stop the world. *The Sunday Times of India*, May 11, 1997.
12. *Indian Express* Monday - May 26, 1997 - Editorial - Death of a policeman - cases like Sandhu's call for sensitivity.
13. National Institute of Mental Health and Neuro Sciences Bangalore - Occupational stress and mental health of police personnel in India - HPR & D, MHA, GOI, New Delhi, July 1996 - Preface.
14. Dr. Pragya Mathur Kumar-Stress in Police Personnel - A preliminary survey-*NPA Magazine* 45 (2), 193. Also Stress in Police in India—Gyan Publishing House, New Delhi 1990.
15. Dr. Pragya Mathur Kumar-Perceptions of police stress - an empirical study of stressers and coping response among police personnel in India - *Indian Journal of Criminology* 23 (1), 9-19-1995.
16. Prof. S.M. Channabasavanna - Report on the Project "Mental Health Problems among Police Personnel" - An Epidemiological Study - BPR D 1996, p. 25.

4

Central Reserve Police Force and Internal Security Challenges

National Security can be divided into internal security and external security. National security basically involves not only national survival but also the protection of internal values and national interests. "India's greatest weakness is not its economy but internal dissentions. Perhaps the most dangerous threat the nation faces is not so much from its enemies on the borders as from the internal political struggle causing growing violence between ethnic groups, castes and creeds; the political scramble for votes at any cost, and the struggle which makes sworn enemies of those in power and those who wish to wrest this power by all available means fair or foul".[1] Terrorism, insurgency, communal riots, ethnic clashes, subversion, espionage and all other internal security problems pose serious threats to Indian federal political system. Law and order duties are clearly the primary role of Civil Police. But Internal Security problems cannot be managed by the state police forces alone without the assistance of Central Police Organisations. In the federal political system of India, Central Police Organisations have a very unique and important role in maintenance of Internal Security and nation-building activities. Central Police Organisation have become indispensable because of the serious constraints and internal problems of State Police organisations. The States have been over the years increasingly finding their meagre resources inadequate for augmenting their own police force to cope with emergency law and order situations such as widespread linguistic agitations, communal disturbances, political movement and growing violence in the society. In certain situations, State police becomes ineffective as they develop regional loyalties and vested interests.[2] State Police in most states are inadequately trained, overworked and lack adequate motivation to perform their duties honestly and with a social commitment. Organisational shortcomings, personal deficiencies, procedural and behavioural inadequacies have seriously hindered the effectiveness of the Civil Police in tackling complex internal security problems.[3] Internal Security, law and order and police are the responsibilities of the state under the Constitution. No State police can combat the challenging tasks of controlling and containing terrorist activities, border patrolling, anti-insurgency operations and anti-smuggling operations, security of VIPs, security of public undertakings and other internal security tasks without the assistance of Central Police Organisations. Central Police Organisations are really no threat to the autonomy of the States in the federal set up of India but they supplement state police and provide necessary additional manpower for large scale police operations like conducting elections and dealing with serious law and order problems. Central Police Organisations have a very important role to play in curbing and controlling crimes having interstate complexity in the larger national interest.

After independence the police role has undergone a vast change. In more practical terms, policing means giving a sense of security to the law-abiding citizens and bringing transgressors to book; to uphold fundamental rights such as freedom of speech, association and allow groups to express their demands, grievances and propogate their ideologies; ensure free and fair balloting; management of conflicting interests and tensions with minimum force; impartiality in dealing with communal and caste conflicts; agrarian and industrial disputes; and above all accountability to the law. [4] There is certainly no doubt that State Police performance in India has fallen short of public expectations due to various constraints and handicaps faced by the Civil Police.[5] Central Police organisations play an important role when State Police gets involved in State politics and the larger national interest are largely be neglected by the State Police, Central Police Organisations like I.B., C.B.I, CRPF, BSF, CISF, ITBP for their specialised role in their respective fields. In its broad perspective today, Central Police Organisations (CPOs) have in their ambit Intelligence Bureau (IB), Research and Analysis Wing (RAW), Central Reserve Police (CRP), Border Security Force (BSF), Railway Protection Force (RPF), Central Industrial Security Force (CISF), Indo-Tibetan Border Police (ITBP), National Security Guards (NSG), Special Protection Group (SPG), Bureau of Police Research and Development (BPR&D), Central Bureau of Investigation (CBI), National Police Academy (NPA), Central Detective Trg Schools (CDTS), Central Forensic Science Laboratory (CFSL), Institute of Criminology and Forensic Science (ICFS), National Crimes Records Bureau (NCRB), Directorate of Coordination of Police Wireless (DCPW), Jammu and Kashmir Militia and Assam Rifles.

Constitutional Provisions and C.R.P.F.

Article 352, 355, 365 and 248 of the Indian Constitution empower the Centre to actively interfere in the affairs of the State pertaining to police in unusual circumstances. Central Police Organisations are those agencies through which the Centre seeks to assist the State Police forces in various ways and discharges its constitutional obligations regarding the ultimate guardianship of the people of India and bringing qualitative changes in Indian Policing. The maintenance of parallel agencies by the Central Government is a very unusual feature of the Indian federal system.[6] The Administrative Reforms Commission of India has observed: "The Central Reserve Police and the Border Security Force are armed forces raised by the Union to meet the needs of the security of the country, both external and internal. In the circumstances, the use of the armed police forces of the Union in aid of Civil power of a state is perfectly constitutional".[7] In the large interests of the paramount need for national unity, the Indian Constitution has provided for centralisation in police administration in the country. The CRPF, BSF, Assam Rifles and Intelligence Bureau are rushed to the States to deal with serious law and order situations from time to time and are at times regarded as the intervention of the Union Government.

The Union list under 7th Schedule of the Indian Constitution specifies certain spheres of police work in which the Central Government (Union) has a vital role to play. They are as under:-

Entry 2: Naval, military and airforces; any other armed forces of the Union.

Entry 2A: Deployment of any armed force of the Union or any contingent or Unit thereof in any State in aid of the Civil power; powers, jurisdiction, privileges and liabilities of the members of such forces while or such deployment.

Entry 8: Central Bureau of Intelligence and Investigation.

Entry 9: Preventive detention for reasons connected with defence, foreign affairs or the security of India, persons subjected to such detention.

Entry 18: Extradition.

Entry 19: Admission into and emigration and expulsion from India, Passports and Visas.

Entry 65: Union agencies and institution for:

(a) Professional, vocational or technical training of police officers; or

(b) the promotion of special studies or research; of

(c) scientific or technical assistance in the investigation of detection of crime.

Entry 70: Union Public Services, All India Services : U.P.S.C.

Entry 80: Extension of the powers and jurisdiction of members of a police force belonging to any state to any area outside that state, but not so as to enable the police of one state to exercise powers and jurisdiction in any areas outside that state without the consent of the Government of the state in which such area is situated; extension of the powers and jurisdiction of members of police force belonging to any state to railway areas outside that state.

Parliament has an important role to play in union policing through:-

1. Law making on subjects in the union and concurrent list.
2. Amendment in Basic Police Acts.
3. Special measures during emergencies.

The concurrent list includes matters such as criminal law, criminal procedure, evidence, adulteration of food stuffs or other goods, drugs and poisons, trade in essential goods and prime control, etc.

In its annual report, Ministry of Home Affairs, it has been observed; "Though the responsibility for the maintenance of law and order rests primarily with State governments, the Ministry of Home Affairs have also a vital rolé to perform in this sphere. They give guidance and advice in important matters and provide assistance by arranging for deputation of extra forces either from the Central Reserves or from other States. The Home Ministry also help in securing arms ammunition, wireless equipment and vehicles for the State police forces.[8] Policing for Internal Security and maintenance of law and order are the basic responsibilities of the local state/civil police.[9] The Ayodhya incident indicates how Central Government failed to get deployment of Central Police organisations against the wishes of the State Government .

The Ministry of Home Affairs, G.O.I has to deal with the following items which have direct dealing with police functioning:

1. Administration of All India Service.
2. Administration of Police forces of Union territories.
3. Personnel management of IPS cadre/CPO Cadre Officers
4. Co-ordination of police administration of various states by calling annual meetings and conferences of State Home Ministers and to lay down policing directives.
5. Supply and control of arms and equipment.
6. Operation of homeguards and Civil Defence.

Government of India is also responsible for policing Union territories and the following subject comes under this category:

1. Public Order.
2. Police including railway and village police.
3. Administration of justice.
4. Prisons, Reformatories, etc.
5. Delhi Fire Service.
6. Offences against laws regarding matters in list II of Seventh Schedule of the Constitution.
7. Extension of State Acts to Union Territories.
8. General questions of administration other than those dealt with in other department and ministries.

Internal Security - Whose Responsibility?

Internal Security is the joint responsibility of the State and Centre. Under Indian Constitution, the State's power in respect of "public order" and "police" do not include "the use of any naval, military or airforce or any other armed forces of the union or of any other force subject to the control of the Union "............." in aid of civil powers". Read together, the provisions mean that should it be necessary to invoke the services of any Central force in "aid of the Civil power", situation gets out of the exclusive control of the State. Deployment of any of the Central Police Organisations "in aid of the civil power" is exclusively a union subject, while 'public order' is the primary responsibility of the State. A direct consequence of the deployment of central force is that under Article 257 the Union can give directions to the State in order to facilitate "the exercise of the executive power of the Union in respect of its forces.[10] "Public Order" is the exclusively a state subject where the Centre's legislative or executive powers cannot transgress into this sphere of state authority, but when 'public order' is flouted on such a large scale in a state as to constitute "internal disturbance" the Centre's duty in Article 355 gets activated: "It shall be the duty of the Union to protect every state against external aggression and internal disturbance and to ensure that the government of every state is carried on in accordance with the provisions of this Constitution". Here perceptions of Union government and State governments may differ on whether a situation comes under "public order" or "internal disturbance". When security of any part of India is threatened Article 352 springs into action. Imminent danger, according to Justice V.K. Krishna Iyer, is enough to activate the power.[11] Article 246 of the Constitution defines the respective jurisdictions of the Union and State legislatures as regards subjects for legislation. Police, public order and administration of justice are in State list. The Union has a duty to protect a State against internal disturbance under Article 355. Under Article 352 President can declare an emergency when any part of India is threatened by internal disturbances. "Therefore greater mutuality is clearly needed.[12] The Sarkaria commission has observed:- "In a two-tier system of government, with a single judiciary, where the administration of Union Law is largely secured through the machinery of the States, differences are bound to arise between the Union and the States in regard to the manner of implementation of Union laws and the exercise of Union's executive powers, specially if they conflict with the exercise of the executive powers of the State. Articles like 256 and 257 are essential to ensure harmonious exercise of the executive power by the Union and by the States, in keeping with the principle, by giving appropriate directions, in the event of irreconcilable differences on vital issues". The expression internal disturbance is wider in its scope. The Sarkaria Commission has said: "Obviously, they (the framers of the Indian Constitution) have done so as they intended to cover not only domestic violence but something more. The scope of the term 'internal disturbance' is wider than 'domestic violence'. It conveys the sense of domestic chaos which takes the colour of a security threat from its associate, expression, 'external aggression'. Such a chaos could be due to various causes. Large-scale public disorder- which throws out of gear the even tempo of administration and endangers the security of the State, is, ordinarily, one such cause. Such an internal disturbance is normally manmade. But it can be nature-made also. Natural calamities of unprecedented magnitude, such as flood, cyclone, earthquake, epidemic, etc may paralyse the government of the State and put its security in Jeopardy".[14]

The Mission of CRPF Gujarat Violence is a Watershed in Indian History

The mission of the CRPF is "to enable the Government to maintain Rule of Law, Public Order, and Internal Security effectively and efficiently, to preserve National Integrity and promote social harmony and Development by upholding supremacy of the constitution. In performing these tasks with utmost regard for human dignity and freedom of the citizens of India, the force shall endeavour to achieve excellence in management of internal security and national calamities by placing "Service and Loyalty" above self."

Objectives and Strategies

The objectives of CRPF are neither isolated nor exclusive. CRPF has a complementary role, derived from the constitutional and statutory provisions, as clarified and built up by the judicial dicta, parliamentary debates and various statements of policy. The objectives are:

(i) Lend specialist services to the States in the maintenance of internal security, arising from factors within or outside the national boundaries.
(ii) Support the civil authority.
(iii) Protect life and property of the citizens.
(iv) Aid and assist the civil authority in the management of natural disasters and calamities.
(v) Document and share expertise, derived from the wide-range of rich experience with other forces and the states in the management of internal security.

Strategies

These objectives of the CRPF may be secured by shaping the dominant organisational ethos on the following lines:

(i) Acquire knowledge and skills on a continuing basis in keeping with the ongoing and futuristic demands of internal security.
(ii) Promote through training and leadership, dedication to the mission and operational excellence.
(iii) Operate as a specialised force with both combat and non-combat capabilities.
(iv) Maintain effectiveness through a preventive ethos and use of minimum force, rather than through remedial engagement.
(v) Maintain alert for rapid entry, effective assistance and quick withdrawal.
(vi) Maintain impartiality and secular outlook with due respect to human rights.
(vii) Maintain highest level of dedication and discipline through appropriate and effective organisational management.
(viii) Develop relevant database on internal security scenario, and disseminate appropriately.
(ix) Undertake annual performance audit in order to redefine and reinforce role, and effect midcourse corrections as a part of organisational development.
(x) Establish and maintain close rapport with States including Union Territories.[15]

Basic Characteristics of CRPF and its Role

Central Reserve Police Force was constituted under CRP Act 1949 and Section of the CRPF Act lays down the following duties of the members of the force. Section 7 "(1) It shall be the duty of every member of the Force promptly to obey and to execute all orders and warrants lawfully issued to him by any competent authority to detect and bring offenders to justice and to apprehend all persons whom he is legally authorised to apprehend and for whose apprehension sufficient grounds exist. (2) Every member of the Force shall be liable to serve without any beyond, as well as within the territory of India". Central Reserve Police Force has the following salient features and characteristics:

1. It is a Mobile Force.
2. It is a highly trained Force.
3. It is a Secular Force—Free from Communal virus.
4. It is a Mini-India having all India Character.
5. It is well experienced in Internal Security duties.
6. It is fully equipped to deal with insurgency and terrorism and other armed disturbances.
7. It is an Armed Force of the Union but performing police duties.
8. It is a Unique force with capability of dealing multifarious duties—peace time to war/proxy war.
9. It forms Rapid Action Force.
10. It contained Women Armed Police—Mahila Bns/Platoons.
11. It has got high operational effectiveness.
12. It is built in mechanism for effective command and control purpose and discipline.
13. It is also performing internal security duties on reaching a new location-
    (a) Immediate reporting to the local authorities for deployment.
    (b) Sending detailed report about its assessment of situation.
    (c) Conducting Court of Enquiry where needed after police-firing.
    (d) Conducting judicial trials etc. for/maintaining internal discipline.
14. It has got effective communication network all over India.

The basic job of "Peace Keepers of the Nation" continues to remain in disturbed areas. It is deployed all over the country. During 1994, in 23 incidents, 40 CRP personnel were killed and 20 fire arms lost. The theatre-wise breakup of the incidents is as follows:

OPS/ theatre States	*No. of incident*	*No. of CRP persons killed*	*No. of arms lost*
J&K	8	9	2
Manipur	9	25	16
North Eastern States	2	1	1
Tripura	4	5	1
Total	23	40	20

The various roles performed by the CRP can be briefly enumerated as under:

1. The primary role of CRPF is to assist the civil administration of the States and the Union Territories in the task of restoration of peace and maintenance of law and order.
2. Protection and security of vital installations.
3. Combating natural calamities such as floods, fire, droughts, etc.
4. Carrying out anti-insurgency operations in insurgency affected areas.
5. Carrying out anti-terrorists operation in terrorists infested areas.
6. Assisting army during war and hostiles and guarding prisoners of war.
7. Combating extremists, political disturbances and other forms of internal violence.
8. Conduct of elections for parliamentary seats and state legislatures.
9. To act as a rapid action force for combating communalism and communal riots.
10. To be deployed as peace keeping force when so decided by the Government of India as in Sri Lanka.
11. CRP Force has recently been sent on peace keeping mission under UNO also.
12. CRP Force is a versatile, mobile and highly disciplined force which has been extensively deployed in preserving unity and integrity of the country.

Central Reserve Police has 10 Sectors/Zones, 21 Administrative Ranges and 6 Operational Ranges, 33 Group Centres and 155 Duty Battalions. It had made tremendous development during the last four decades.[16] By the end of the year 2005, the CRP Force will be 201 battalions and 37 Group Centres. CRPF officers cadre review is also expected. During January 2003, 2 officers has been promoted as ADIG, 25 as commandants, 10 Dy commandants as 21 and 15 as Assistant Commandant. State Police generally have developed and attitude of complete dependence on CRP. The worst result of deputing CRP freely has been that it has impaired the development of State police forces and the idea of self-reliance has more or less been abandoned.[17] With efforts at rationalisation, the number of interstate moves of the force was reduced from 2338 in 1993 to 2008 in 1994. Due to various reasons, stagnation in promotions in CRP was quite noticeable. Levels of stagnation in promotion in CRP is given in the table.

Table 'A'

Level of Stagnation in Promotion in CRPF

S. No.	*Promotion From*	*To*	*Minimum prescribed bed service*	*Actual time taken in 1988*	*1989*	*1990*	*1991*	*1992*	*1993*	*1994*
1.	CT	L/NK	4yrs	16 yrs	14yrs	13yrs	12yrs	9yrs	10yrs	10yrs
2.	L/NK	NK	Nil	4 "	4 "	4 "	3 "	2 "	2 "	2 "
3.	NK	HC	1yr	2 "	2 "	2 "	3 "	2 "	2 "	2 "
4.	HC	SI	4yrs	6 "	6 "	8 "	7 "	5 "	5 "	5 "
5.	SI	Insp	5 yrs	7 "	7 "	6 "	7 "	6 "	8 "	7 "
6.	Insp	A/C	3 yrs	6 "	6 "	4 "	4 "	4 "	-	5 "
7.	A/C	D/C	6yrs	8 "	8 "	7 "	7 "	6 "	-	N/A
8.	D/C	2-I/C	12 "	-	-	17 "	16 "	12 "	-	N/A
9.	2-I/C	CO NSG	14 " (including 2 years as 2-I/C)	15"	16"	17 "	18"	19"	-	N/A
10.	CO (NSG)	CO-(SG)	16" (including 2Yrs as CO) (NSG)	-	20 "	18 "	19"	20 yrs		20
11.	CO (SG)	ADIG	18 " (including 2 yrs as CO (SG)	-	21 "	-	23 "	24 "	-	24 "
12.	ADIG	DIG	20" (including 2 yrs as ADIG)		21"	-	-	24 "	--	27
13.	DIG	IG	26 yrs (including 6 yrs as DIG)		27"	28"	-	28"	--	32

Recently stagnation has been reduced due to its expansion after 2002 onwards.

CRPF Operational Commitments and Conditions of Work

CRPF operational commitments and movements have led to some

organisation specific working conditions and conditions of work. Some of them are:-

(i) Loss of contact with families, very little opportunity to satisfy psycho-physiological needs.

(ii) Inadequate parental supervision in the education of children.

(iii) Impediments in participating and fulfilling social obligations and in providing medical care to the family members.

(iv) Problems in arranging marriages of children, in supporting pursuit of employment by children and in constructing a house.

(v) Insecurity due to physical distance between CRPF personnel and their immediate family members.

(vi) Inadequate opportunities for personal growth and professional advancement, long and intermediate working hours.

(vii) Living in regimental atmosphere, disorientation due to frequent movements, and living on suit-case for long spells.

Details of movement of CRPF during the last 10 years are given below :

Table 1
Total Movements of CRPF Coys

Year	*By Road*	*By train*	*By Air*	*By ship*	*Total*
1987	290	420	104	02	816
1988	184	230	66	09	489
1989	386	676	125	17	1204
1990	380	645	83	06	1114
1991	393	830	51	-	1274
1992	646	808	42	04	1492
1993	896	1881	51	10	2838
1994	636	1358	04	10	2008
1995	978	1784	29	23	1814
1996 upto 4/11/96	1012	1180	92	04	2288

Table 2
Month-Wise Movements of CRPF Coys During 1996

Month	*By road*	*By train*	*By air*	*By ship*	*Total*
January.	89	69	-	-	158
February	86	38	-	-	124
March	73	43	-	-	116
April	113	192	6	4	315
May	291	190	68	-	549
June	104	150	5	-	259
July	29	136	-	-	165
August	73	89	11	-	173
Sep/Oct	86	122	2	-	210
Nov upto 4/11/96	68	151	-	-	219
Total	1012	1180	92	4	2288

Table 3
Year-Wise Details of Movements of CRPF Coys and Ops-Misconduct Cases

Year	*Total No. of Coys*	*Average No. of Coy deploped*	*No. of Moves*	*No. of Ops mis-conduct cases*
1992	764	702	1492	47
1993	764	749	2838	44
1994	764	665	2008	41
1995	764	716	2814	19
1996	764	734	2272	40

CRPF's operations are characterised by hard working conditions and harsh conditions of work. Extensive movement throughout the length and breadth of the country, shifting from problem to problem, without adequate logistic support or notice, problems such as absence of bullet-proof vests, even in insurgent-terrorist areas, absence of transit camps, poor medical facilities to the men in the front, and the like represent poor working conditions of CRPF. They are required to be taken care of in order to improve the operational efficacy of the organisation. Near lack of living accommodation to the men fighting on several fronts all the time, severance of contact with family members even in times of distress, and many other similar problems have demoralised not only the men but more so their families—affecting the image of the organisation. It is noted that the pay and allowances of men could not be reached often to the families merely because the men were found operating in remote areas and moving from place to place. The negative factors such as unemployment or lack of alternatives should not be allowed to operate as the only motivating force that prompts people to join and stick on to the organisation. There is an urgent need to step up the satisfaction-level by constructing more family quarters to meet a minimum of 25 per cent as against the existing authorisation of 14 per cent and actual availability of a mere 6 per cent. The existing authorisation compares poorly with many of the Civil Police Organisations. Most of them have 30 to 60 per cent and are aiming to achieve 100 per cent, with the creation of Police Housing Corporations exclusively for the purpose, and headed by DG level officers. The organisational health of CRPF is indicated in terms of voluntary retirements, suicides, and homicides, mental ill-health and the draining of provident fund reserves of men. Periodic medical tests are important to keep the force fighting fit, by initiating preventive measures. The scope for improving the working conditions of men is immense.

Management Issues in Deployment of Central Reserve Police

Not many people, including some senior civil servants and political leaders, are aware of the terrible conditions in which the Security Forces (CPOs) have to operate in disturbed areas like Kashmir. Imagine the mental state of a policeman holed up in a bunker day after day and night after night in bitterly cold conditions, not knowing which direction the bullet will come from.[18] Those who are conversant with the living conditions of our constabulary will vouchsafe this. Those who are aware of the manner in which the police forces are deployed for long hours and days on and would agree that men and officers of the CPOs are under enormous psychological stress. The pressures on them are enormous. It is patriotism and commitment of the highest order which enthuses them to accept such challenges even in the face of grave adversities.[19] Driven by nerves, frustration, humiliation and lack of recreation, troops of the various security agencies (CPOs) in Kashmir are having more incidents of suicides.[20] In Punjab, CRP and BSF have done very good job in fighting and rooting out terrorism. BSF and CRP were deployed initially in Punjab to tackle terrorism and their deployment for six years has been as under:

Year	CRP Coys	BSF Coys
1984	110	48
1985	134	37
1986	190	50
1987	200	86
1988	193	75
1989	171	67

The Companies of ITBP were deployed in Punjab for Bank Security duties.

Optimum Utilisation and Better Coordination of CRP

"The need of the hour is coordination for optimum use of all the available resources of the army, the paramilitary and the armed police including CRPF. The coordination has to be done at a sufficiently senior professional level.[21] When Central Police Organisations reach at a new place, on reaching the destination they require basic amenities like accommodation, water, electricity, transport and briefing about the task they will be required to perform. Their utilisation can be optimum when they get full support and cooperation from local police. CRPF is moved out from place to place in short notice and their deployment during the last three years is given in the table.

Table Showing Statewise Deployment of CRPF for the Last Three Years

State/UT	Oct'93	Jan'94	April'94	April'95
1. Andaman & Nicobar Island	2	2	2	2
2. Arunachal Pradesh	19	16	15	19
3. Andhra Pradesh	8	8	10	3
4. Assam	22	27	60	40
5. Bihar	13	2	1	168
6. Chandigarh	22	22	22	6
7. Delhi	62	51	62	24
8. Daman & Diu	1	-	-	-
9. Gujarat	2	-	-	-
10. Himachal Pradesh	4	2	-	-
11. Jammu &Kashmir	83	96	95	120
12. Karnataka	-	-	-	1
13. Lakshadweep	2	2	2	2

(Contd...)

(Contd...)

14.	Meghalaya	6	6	5	5
15.	Manipur	54	54	55	55
16.	Mizoram	2	2	5	9
17.	Nagaland	28	27	30	30
18.	Pondicherry	1	-	-	-
19.	Punjab	250	157	115	19
20.	Rajasthan	9	9	13	9
21.	Sikkim	3	5	7	5
22.	Tamil Nadu	29	8	8	8
23.	Tripura	22	22	25	-
24.	Uttar Pradesh	43	43	43	37
25.	W.B.	6	6	2	2
26.	Maharashtra	-	10	-	-
27.	Orissa	-	1	1	1
		Coys under MHA Reserve			48
		Coy on Spl Escort duty			01
		Coy in UNO operation			01
		Coys under move			02
		Coys under Pre-induction training			07

Need to Stop Proliferation of CPOs

Proliferation of police and Central Police Organisation is justified upto a certain point on grounds of functional requirements and specialisation. Duplication and multiplicity of Central Police Organisations can lead to unhealthy rivalries and effect operational efficiency. Each organisation wants more funds, more officers, better weapons, more accommodation additional transport and more training institutions. The concept of "Family Planning" is applicable to police organisations in the sense that too much proliferation and growth of police organisations is detrimental to their steady growth and development.[22]

Problem of Management of Training in CRPF

Main problem of management of training in CRP are as under:-

1. Existing CRPF Training Institutions are not able to train the CRPF personnel as per the needs and requirements of the force due to various administrative handicaps.
2. Competent, motivated and willing trainers are not available in adequate numbers.
3. Most of the training institutions are located at places where local guest faculty is not available.
4. There is tremendous gap between field realities and training imparted.

5. Training institutions are not fully equipped with modern training aids and modern techniques have not been adopted.
6. There is no long term training policy and training is not getting adequate support from higher formations on many occasions.
7. Training needs of CRP have not been identified by the CRPF.
8. Training allowances and other incentives are not adequate to attract willing and qualified trainers.

Personnel Policies for the CRP

Upender Baxi has found the following features of personnel policies about the subordinate police:-

(i) Low salary;
(ii) Undefined and long hours of work;
(iii) Lack of housing and related facilities;
(iv) Relative insecurity of service;
(v) Low mobility to higher ranks of police Force;
(vi) Authoritarian nature of police hierarchy and management system;
(vii) Exposure to exploitation both within and outside the Police organisation;
(viii) Last but not least the constant risk of physical danger. In 1973 out of 184 police personnel killed, 181 were from subordinate police; out of 5248 police personnel injured, 74.8 per cent were Constable.[23] The living and working conditions of CRPF men and officers are most inadequate and unsatisfactory. CRP men deployed in various parts of the country have to depend for accommodation upon the State authorities who are indifferent, helpless and at times unwilling to provide suitable living accommodation to the force personnel.

The key to basic change is transition to a more democratic and humanised police with adequate grievance redressal machinery, adequate and timely promotions, more humane working environment in the organisation and adequate housing and welfare measures.

Problem of Morale and Motivation of CRP

Morale is basically a group phenomenon. It is a mental condition of groups and individuals with respect to courage, discipline, confidence and willingness to endure hardship. In operational areas like Northeastern states and Kashmir, proper rotation of personnel from hard to soft areas, rest and recuperation, adequate steps to solve their personal problems and obligations need to be taken care of. When death or casualties occur, great care need to be taken to motivate the personnel into greater dedication and relief should be promptly arranged for the family– Morale can be built and developed over the years as a result of sound management and personnel policies and procedures, good supervisory practices, effective leadership, better working and living conditions and use of correct motivational techniques. Motivation is very important for those who are performing hazardous duties in Kashmir, North-Eastern States and other disturbed areas. Exemplary good conduct of leaders, genuine concern for the subordinates, guts to take up deserving cases for promotions, fair play and justice in matters of promotions, transfer postings and other service conditions can go a long way in motivating subordinates and other ranks of the police forces.[25]

The Problem of Professionalism in CRP

The state of police professionalism in India stands at the cross-roads today. "Professionalism in India" is a lofty ideal a distant dream and an immature claim of expertise. Profession has yet to mature and build up its professional base by perfecting its methods of operation, by modernising the techniques, by demanding the more strict admission standards and by building a Code of Conduct. Police Science is a developing branch of knowledge which has not yet acquired academic recognition and universal acceptance. The maturation of police science can be brought about by bridging the separatipn of basic and applied research on police through synergetic relationship between police theory and police practices. All over the world police studies and analytical researches need to be carried out to understand the expanding frontiers of the science of policing, general theories of police science, and its relevance in the socio-economic realities of governance. Police Professionalism needs higher doses of academic input and professional knowledge. Policemen as a friend, guide and philosopher to the common man has to be one of the ideals of the police profession. Due to non-professional approach of police leaders and malfunctioning of the police system, most of the police organisations suffer in India from resistance to change, rigid adherence to rules, reluctance to delegate authority, sycophancy towards superiors, target mentality, indifference to standards of efficiency, ignorance of the purposes behind regulations, hostility towards new technology, insistence on status and prestige symbols, corruption, secrecy, abuse of power, perversity, inertia, enophobia and nepotism. Corruption, misallocation of resources, technical inefficiency, unsatisfactory management, lack of innovation, ineffectiveness, subservience to the powerful, lack of coordination, conflicting objectives, spoils system, displacement of mandated objectives, favouritism, foot dragging, arbitrariners and arrogance of power are some of the prevalent ills of CRP professionalism in India. Professionalism in CRP today faces challenges of distortions of democratic development declining credibility, rising crime rate, drug menace, increasing violence, terrorism, communalism and growing police indiscipline. Professionalism is at a discount today in all professions. Professionalism in CRP can be built up only when police organisations are totally overhauled and long due police reforms are carried out in a given time-frame. The present culture of defensiveness, suspicion, secrecy, cynicism, organisational deviance and corruption, occupational solidarity and isolation syndrome, conservatism, rigid hierarchical structure, police brutalities and use of third degree needs to be replaced by a new CRP culture of democratic ethos, high level of professional training and commitment and new professional values characterised by social justice, due recognition of human rights, service to the community with a deep humane orientation. Better personal management, adequate housing facilities, better equipment and technology, organisational reforms, effective and job-oriented training and community support to police have to be some of the first few measures needed to build up professionalism in police. Leadership in Central Police Organisations need to be developed from within by building CPO Cadres because the challenges of the future will require new skills in personal management and a much higher levels of specialisation, professional knowledge, competence and, leadership from the senior officers. Full and effective implementation of the recommendations of the National Police Commission are imperative to build up professionalism in India. CRP leadership has to be fully aware of the organisational and operational shortcomings and recognise what must be done to improve their organisations. Police leaders have to play an important role in building professionalism. Self regulation, social accountability, public credibility, professional ethics, emerging challenges of social change and public co-operation are the most important challenges faced by police professionalism in India. Increasing crime, social violence and terrorism are throwing serious threat to police professionalism. CRP profession is the most hazardous, dangerous, challenging and demanding in terms of commitment. No profession sacrifices so many lives for upholding the professional commitment.

Following measures will go a long way in building up sound professionalism in CRP:-

1. Long term perspective planning should be done for state police organisations and the Central Police Organisations so that their training, recruitment, and other personnel policies are properly planned and executed.
2. Proliferation of police organisations need to be restricted and specialised areas of duties, responsibilities and obligations have to be clearly demarcated for each organisation in order to avoid overlapping of jurisdictions and duplicity of command structure.
3. Recommendations of the National Police Commission should be implemented in a given time frame and police leadership must not be diluted by having ever increasing upgradation of senior level posts of the rank of Directors General and Additional Directors General and below.
4. Police science as an academic discipline should be introduced at higher secondary, graduate and postgraduate levels in the humanities and social sciences group of subjects and free access to police literature be made for researchers and social scientists. We should start a graduate qualification in police science as a necessary qualification for middle level police officers and a diploma in police science as a necessary qualification for officers of the rank of Sub-Inspectors. Similarly all Universities should develop "schools of police studies" to enable social scientists and researchers to build up police science as a fully developed academic discipline.
5. There is need for a strong political will and determination at the Centre and State levels to bring out drastic reforms in police organisations.
6. Police efficiency and effectiveness have to be built up by reducing the reponse-time and building up an organisational culture of responsiveness to the changing needs of the society.
7. International bibliography on all available police literature should be made and proper classification and documentation of police literature should be attempted on priority basis so that police science builds up its academic contents and research orientation.
8. Police Researches in the fields of police equipment, arms, ammunition, operational technology, training, and personnel management should be carried out by police organisations and universities on a continuous basis.
9. A well-researched, documented and objective evaluation of police-thinkers and practitioners should be carried out on a

continuous basis so that police pioneers and thinkers are given due place in the history of police science. Police professionalism, can be built up only when police organisations build up their "knowledge-base"on scientific lines. The art and science of policing need to be constantly upgraded and given practical life-orientation.

10. Positive police philosophy, a healthy police culture, a deep occupational commitment, professional specialisation, decentralisation, accountability, autonomy, modernisation and genuine professional brotherhood can be some of the main factors which can nurture and bloom professionalism in police and help it to achieve the goals of excellence.

Central Forces—No Threat to State Police

Galloping increase in the strength of Central Police Forces has raised fears in certain quarters about the demoralising effect it may have in the long run on the State Police Forces to the detriment of the federal structure of our Indian nation[26]. There has been a near five-fold increase in the numerical strength of the Central Police Forces during the last thirty-five years. Five major Central Police Organisations (CPOs) are the Central Reserve Force (155 Battalions and 33 Group Centres), Border Security Force (150 Battalions), Assam Rifles (31 Battalions), Indo-Tibetan Border Police (25 Battalions) and Central Industrial Security Force (84000 personnel). One Former Home Secretary held that "There is need for raising such force as an assertion of authority, Central Forces alone can match the sophisticated weaponry of terrorists and check increasing sectarian and communal tension, economic blockade and take care of VVIP Security". Central Police Organisations are no threat to the State Police Organisations because "Law and Order" is a state subject and State police alone is responsible at present for requisitioning and deployment of Central Police Organisation. The basic need is to improve the performance and effectiveness of the state police. The aim should be to improve each man of Civil Police by better training, better facilities for living, better transport, better powers and an improved image in every way.[27] CRPF has authorised strength of 2 Lakhs 6 thousand seven hundred and forty two personnel.

Future Challenges for the CPOs

Relations between the Centre and States come under strain when parties in power happen to be different in the States as happened during Kalyan Singh's Government in Uttar Pradesh. Central Police

Kashmir Valley in the face of armed threat of terrorists and secessionists. Central Police Organisations, due to their high level of training, alone can match the sophisticated weaponry of militants. Central Police Organisations should not be considered as "Unwanted intruders upon State autonomy" but as "useful additions" to supplement the State police force. At times states are relying more on Central Police Forces as they find it convenient to shift the blame if situations goes out of hand and claim credit for the good performance of the Central Forces since these forces operate under State Police. Shri S.C. Misra, retired Director, National Police Academy Mount Abu has observed "The (Civil) Police have been moving for quite sometime on crutches provided by the paramilitary forces and now their limbs have become so weak that the armed forces have to prop them". Civil Police today is a severely damaged instrument and cannot work without the help of paramilitary forces.[28]

Protection of Human Rights

Sopore and Bigbehara incidents have focussed our attention to the challenges of Human Rights. It is therefore high time that we chalk out a plan of action aimed at adherence to the basic requirements of human rights and humanitarian laws, maintaining the delicate balance between the dictates of security and integrity of the country on the one hand and the need to honour human rights not merely in thought but also in action on the other.[29]

Politicised State Police and Deployment of CRP

When State Police operates under the dictates of State political masters to the detriment of the national interests, Central Police Organisations deployed under State police force face dilemma. One of the primary aims of a newly elected regime, soon after coming into power in any state, is to position and "deposition" police personnel at all echelons and keep on shifting and shuffling them to suit their political requirements.[30] According to N.S. Saksena two-thirds of the SHOs in the country—the pivotal police functionary were political appointees. As a fall out of this, the rule of law is the main casualty and an environment of total inaccountability prevails. Why should deployment of Central Police Organisations be made by State police, police which has been highly politicised? Can deployment of CPOs be controlled by some IGP/DIGP of CPO who can act as nodal authority in each State?

Recommedations for Better and Effective Management

1. Need for a Central Police Commission and Police Board. On the pattern of the Planning Commission of India, there should be one Central Police Advisory Board to serve as think-tank for the government of India. This body can take up strategic police planning for national security at the national level as well as carry out planned changes by resource planning, mobilisation of man and material.[31]

2. Amendment in Police Acts and CRPF Act. The Police Act of 1861 and other corresponding State Police Acts should be thoroughly amended to identify the role of Central Police Organisations and to cater for the federal, democratic decentralisation demands for autonomy and compatibility of Police with Panchayat Raj.[32] As Panchayat Raj marches ahead and its legitimisation of power politics becomes an accepted fact of rural life, the police administration can ill-afford to stay as a passive spectator of the whole Phenomenon[33] CRPF Act should also be amended

3. Other Miscellaneous Suggestions. The problems connected with internal security have much larger dimensions than are commonly understood. If the political ethos have infected the imprincipled search for power, if fundamentalism and parochialism are instigated for personal or party gains; if business and administration are permeated with the culture of corruption; if people are divided on caste and communal lines; if rich are callous in pursuit of consumerism and poor continue to groan under the burden of their poverty, it would be virtually impossible to ensure internal security at reasonable cost and on continuous basis.[34] Indian Police has to provide good quality policing and effective responses to the internal security challenges. For building an effective infrastructure of Central Police Organisations for meeting the challenges of the 21st century, they need

"(a) depoliticalisation and decommunalisation;
(b) democratisation and decentralisation;
(c) professionalism and decriminalisation;
(d) socialisation and humanisation;
(e) sensitisation and culturalisation;
(f) reorganisation and revolutionary reforms".[35]

Public co-operation, restructuring of Police organisations at various levels, structural reorganisation of the entire criminal justice system, revamping of internal security structures at the national and State levels and effective job-oriented training of police organisations are needed for internal security duties. A changing society demands qulalitative and quantitative changes in the outlook, value system, procedures and technique of police and CRPF.[36]

References

1. General V.N. Sharma—National Security—More Threats from Within—*Hindustan Times*, Delhi, December 18, 1994, p. 13.
2. Dr. Krishna Mohan Mathur, *Internal Security Challenges and Police in a Developing Society*, R.B.S.A Publishers, Jaipur, 1989, p. 261
3. Dr. Krishna Mohan Mathur - *Policing for Internal Security-Administrative Change*, Jaipur, Vol. XIX, No. 1-2, July 1991 June 1992, p. 91.
4. Padam Rosha-Law and Disorder-*Indian Express,* 23 April 1995.
5. Krishna Mohan Mathur-*Police Law and Internal Security*-Gyan Publishing House, New Delhi, 1994, p. 17.
6. C.P. Bhanbari-Public Order, Paramilitary Organisations and Indian Federalism-*The Indian Journal of Public Administration,* Vol. XXIV, January - March, 1978, No. 1, pp. 30-31.
7. Centre-State Relations, Govt. of India, Ministry of Home Affairs, Administrative Reforms Commission, New Delhi 1969, p. 36.
8. Ministry of Home Affairs, Government of India, New Delhi, *Annual Report,* 1966-67, p. 38.
9. Dr. Krishna Mohan Mathur-*Police, Law and Internal Security*-Gyan Publishing House, New Delhi, 1994, p. 42.
10. A.G. Noorain —The Centre and Law and Order-*Indian Express,* 26 December 1986.
11. Justice V.K. Krishna Iyer-A "Barbarity and an Otiosity-*Hindu* 10, December 1992.
12. President R.V. Venkataraman-Conference of State Governors on 29 October 1987-See *Hindu* dated 30 Oct. 1987.
13. Commission on Centre - State Relations, Vol. I, Chapter III, p.106.
14. Commission on Centre-State Relations, Vol. I, Chap VI, Para 6.3.04, p.168.
15. A Bench-Mark Study of working conditions of Personnel in CRPF-Administrative Staff College of India, Bellavista, Hyderabad Feb. 1996.
16. For history and development of Central Reserve Police Force. Consult Dr. K.M. Mathur *Police in Indian-Problems and Perspectives*. Gyan Publishing House, New Delhi, 1991, Chapter 7 pp. 118-167.
17. Dr. K.M. Mathur - *Police, Law and Internal Security*-Gyan Publishing House, New Delhi, 1994 p. 2.
18. Ved Marwah-Police and Internal Security-*The Time of India,* New Delhi-22 Oct. 1993.
19. T. Ananthachari-*The Times of India,* 22 October 1993.

20. For similar views-Girja Shanker Kaura-In the Valley of death, they die disheartened-*Hindustan Times*-Delhi 27 Aug. 1994.
21. Ved Marwah—Army has to be used to combat Terrorism. *Hindustan Times,* 2 March 1992.
22. Dr. K.M. Mathur—*Internal Security Challenges and Police in a Developing Society*- R.B.S.A. Publishers, Jaipur, 1989, p. 316.
23. Upendra Baxi- "The crisis of the Indian legal system" p. 88.
24. Dr. K.M. Mathur- *Police in India-Problems and Perspective*-Gyan Publishing House, New Delhi, 1991, p. 116.
25. Dr. K.M. Mathur—Management of Internal Security and Related Issues-Gyan Publishing House, New Delhi, 1995, p. 25.
26. L.F. Rustamji -Internal Security Tasks-Rebuilding from the bottom-*Indian Express* 1 November 1985.
27. Pushp Saraf-Are Central Forces a threat to State Police? *Indian Express,* 12 April 1993.
28. Dr. K.M. Mathur-*Role of Police in Changing Social Scenario-Police Research and Development*-July Sept 1994, p. 9.
29. T. Ananthachari-Human Rights and Law. *Hindustan Times,* 14 July 1994.
30. Satyinder Singh-Politicised Police-*Hindustan Times,* 26 May 1995.
31. For similar views see C.C. Singhvi-National Planning and Police-*Indian Journal of Public Administration,* October December 1971.
32. For similar views see Dr. (Mrs.) Anjali Nirmal—*Role and Functioning of Central Police Organisations*-Uppal Publishing House, New Delhi, 1992, p. 416.
33. P.D. Sharma—*Police, Internal Security and Development disorder in India*-Uppal Publishing House, New Delhi, 1988, p. 251.
34. Jag Mohan—Internal Threats to India's Security National Security Lecture organised by the United Services Institution, 1991.
35. Dr. Krishna Mohan Mathur—*Indian Police Role and Challenges,* Gyan Publishing House, New Delhi, 1994, p. 250.
36. Dr. K.M. Mathur—*The Problem of Police in a Democratic Society,* R.B.S.A Publishers, SMS Highway Jaipur, 1987, p. 243.

5

Low Intensity Conflicts in India

In the present day world, the connotation "Low-intensity conflicts" is a valuable term but one that embraces a host of quite different conflict forms and even different connotations to different people. It is also potentially dangerous to assume that lower levels of threat and conflict pose only minor challenges. The social, economic and political problems of the third world nations, create fertile ground for developing and promoting low-intensity conflicts. In all multi-ethnic societies, generally called plural societies, many types of conflicts emerge either explicitly or implicitly which have direct impact on internal security of the state system. The arena of conflicts that have arisen during the process of economic development and nation building in India, need to be analyzed in depth and their impact on internal security has to be surveyed. Conflict manifests itself in a variety of shapes, sizes, and even disguises through the entire gamut of human interactions. Conflict usually refers to a process of interaction between individuals and troups of parties involving a struggle over claims to resources, power and status, beliefs and other preferences and desires. Conflicts itself, is a form of association, is designated to resolve divergent dualisms; and in fact dissociating factors—hate, envy, need, desire—are the causes of conflict; it breaks out because of them. Conflict within a group may help to establish unity or to re-establish unity and cohesion where it has been threatened by hostile and antagonistic feelings among the members.[1] In all ages, in every type of social structure, there are innumerable occasions for conflict, since individuals and sub-groups are likely to make from time to time rival claims to scarce resources, prestige or power positions. Internal social conflicts which concern goals, values or interests that do not contradict the basic assumptions upon which the relationship is founded tend to be positively functional for the social structure.[2] Conflict is conceived as a socio-psychological phenomena of deviance which is to be contained for insuring structural stability of a plural society. Talcott Parson equates deviance and conflict when he says, "cultural patterns which either fail to define a minimum of order or which place impossible demands on people….. generate deviance and conflict".[3] Many classifications of conflict like the one attempted by Stuart Chase, Ross Stagner, Lassewell, Adorne, Boulding and Kardiner are either merely catalogue of contemporary conflicts or their analysis at the psychic level.[4] Karl Marx has given the most powerful and realistic approach to the problem in his books. *The Communist Manifest* (1989) and *A Critique of Political economy*. George Simmel, A.W.Small,Coser and Dharendorf have made valuable contributions with respect to the consequences of conflict rather than the process itself.[5] Karl Marx recognized that class conflict was bound to be political and "the struggle between class and class is a political struggle".[6] Karl Marx held that with the change of the economic foundation, the entire immense superstructure is more or less rapidly transformed. In considering such transformations distinction should always be made between the material transformation of the economic conditions of production which can be determined with the precision of natural science and the legal, political, religious, aesthetic or philosophic—in short ideological form in which men become conscious of this conflict and fight it out . . . No social order ever perishes before all the productive forces for which there is room in it have developed; and new higher relation of production never appear before the material conditions of existence have natured in the womb of the old society itself".[7] Briefly conflict theories are economic, sociological, psychological and political—depending upon the emphasis assigned to the particular fact by thinkers. Social conflict has been defined as "a struggle over values, or claims to status, power and scarce resources, in which the aims of the conflicting groups or parties are not only to gain the desired values, power or scarce resources but also to neutralise, injure or eliminate their rivals".[8] Social conflict may generally occur between individuals, between social groups, and between collectivities. Conflict is an important element of social interaction because inter-group as well as intra-group conflicts are perenial features of social life. Hegel, Karl Marx, Herbert Spencer, Gustan Ratzenhofer, Lud-wig guinplowiez, William Graham Suinner are some of the well known social thinkers who have paid attention to social conflict. The struggle for power and influence is one of the themes of Pareto's theories as well as those of Sorel, Michels, and Hoscal. Simmel has carried out a classical analysis of various form of conflicts and held that "conflict is a form of sociation" and that a certain amount of discord, inner divergence and outer controversy, is organically tied up with the very elements that ultimately held the group together. Robert Park (1924) Weber, Talcott Parsons, Gessic Bermard (1957) and Max Gluckman (1956) have analyzed various aspects of social conflict including a conflict model of society. Tolcott Parsons claimed that the Central Problem of Sociological theory was the "Problem of order". Conflicts are power struggles carried out by various ethnic groups for winning political and economic power as a generalize means to presue goals, ideals or interests.

Development of Low Intensity Conflict Environment in India

Low intensity conflicts are suited to the conditions of the modern age because they take advantage of social discontent, racial ferment and nationalist fervours. Possible factors for Low Intensity Conflict in India are as under :-

1. Changing attitudes and desires for self-determinations.
2. Media explosion - It enables people to influence thoughts and actions of the masses.
3. Limitations of higher forms of warfare.
4. Democratic society permitting protests and freedom of expression and association.
5. Religious differences and fanaticism.
6. Linguistic differences.
7. Ethno-centric sub-nationalism.
8. Migrations from other state creating problems for sons of the soil.
9. Regionalistic parochialism.
10. Economic disparity and economic imbalance.
11. Corruption in society at various levels in administration.
12. External support by Pakistan I.S.I. agency and other unfriendly countries to the insurgents and terrorists in terms of training, finance, ideological support, base and logistics.
13. Unresponsive and inept administrative set up.
14. Insensitive law and order machinery and lack of commitment on the part of the government officials, educationists and other revenue officials.
15. Other precipitating and psychological factors such as identity crisis and feelings of alienation by the certain groups.

For each low-intensity conflict, there are generally more than one factors responsible for discontent and alienation.

Plural Societies Create Low-Intensity Conflict

According to Rabushka and Shepsle a society is plural if it is culturally diverse and if its cultural sections are organised into cohesive political sections.[9] In a plural society competitive politics is characterised by ethnic politics and ethnic nepotism. All Indian sociologists agree on the point that India is a plural society with unity in diversity. Prof. Amartya Sen, renowned academician and economist delivering a lecture on "Indian Pluralism" in July 1993 at Delhi touched upon India's intrinsic cultural diversities, its inherent strengths and the need to practice and defend this pluralism against organised attack.[10] India's plurality was quite remarkable. "What is central to Indian pluralism is its religious diversity, added to it is the diversities in art and music." We are not unique in being diverse but there is something quite special in the tremendous extent of diversity in our traditions. Our religious diversity is a part of much wider experience, of which we can be legitimately proud.[11] The great thing about the basic "Hindu" heritage is not only that it is itself pluralistic but that it imparts this plurality to other 'Non-Hindu' communities too.[12] The vast majority of Indians may be Hindus, but we have more than a hundred million Muslims, we have more Sikhs than any other country, more Jains too and more Parsis as well. I don't believe there exist another country the religious diversity of which begins to match ours.[13] The main pluralities of Indian society can be explained by the following realities :-

1. As many as 1652 languages and dialect are spoken in India while the Constitution of India recognizes 18 major languages.
2. India has an estimated tribal population of 51.6 million in 1981. Major tribes of North Eastern states are Nagas, Angmi, Semia Aao, Tankkul in Nagaland, Lushais Chakma and Tripuries in Tripura, Lepchas in Sikkim, Kuki in Manipur, Khasis and Garos in Meghalaya, Jarwas in Little Andamans, Apatamis in Arunachal Pradesh, Abors, Mikirs, Khasis and plain tribal people in Assam.
3. India has people belonging to almost all major religions and sects.

Indian society is seen to be developing in the direction of a full fledged pluralist democracy. India is a plural society with a nearly unfathomable diversity of languages, sects, castes, ethnicity, religions, regions and cultures. In a plural society conflicts may develop around (a) conflicts over the inheritance of land, (b) quarrel over adoption of sons, (c) quarrel over house sides and irrigation rites, (d) quarried over sexual offences and (e) conflicts over castes. According to Dr. Yogendra Singh conflicts and feuds by various groups can be analyzed as under :

1. Inter-caste feuds over the issue of land reported in 44 per cent cases.
2. Serious fights and court cases reported is 15.5 per cent.

3. Feuds and conflicts on the violation of the connubial rules of castes or sub-castes reported in 30 per cent cases.
4. Conflicts over the inheritance of property reported in 10.2 per cent.[14]

In addition to a fairly high level of extremist and secessionist activity in Jammu and Kashmir and the north-east region during 1995, law enforcing agencies had to deal with increased incidence of left extremist violence, particularly in Bihar and Madhya Pradesh. Though there had been an overall decline in the number of caste-related incidents in 1995 as compared to the earlier year, caste tensions in states like Tamil Nadu, Maharashtra and Bihar had registered an upward trend. The annual report noted that in Uttar Pradesh, the caste-related incidents had decreased by 50 per cent while in Tamil Nadu, Bihar and Maharashtra there had been a 25 to 30 per cent increase in these incidents. The report said of the 723 caste-related incidents, the majority of clashes were between Scheduled Castes and Other Backward Classes (OBCs).

There was also a visible increase in the number of cases of abduction and other targeted random attacks on innocent civilians and soft targets such a political workers, government officials and media persons. The 117-page report said a major feature of violence was indiscriminate use of explosive devices like mines, improvised explosive devices (IEDs) and grenades, which were responsible for comparative increase in casualities of civilian and security personnel. There were 1,304 such incidents and 396 deaths in 1994 as compared to 1,153 incidents and 377 deaths during 1995. Both in 1995 and so far in the current year it was observed there was an immediate spurt in violence whenever there was any serious talk of elections in the state. There was a significant escalation in the number of incidents since May 1995 when there were signs of election being held in June-July last year. This period also saw a number of high profile terrorist acts such as burning of the Chrar-e-Sharif shrine, abduction of six foreign tourists and major bomb blasts in Jammu, Srinagar and Anantnag. The militants continued their efforts to spread violence in the Jammu region, particularly the Doda district with the intention of spreading fear among the people, creating communal tension so that an exodus of minority community member from the district takes place. According to Baljit Singh factional conflicts in rural society centre around the existing systems of individual land ownership.[15] Lewis Coser has distinguished between two types of conflicts—realistic and non-realistic. In realistic conflicts, the attainment of desired goals is more important than the destruction of the enemy. In non-realistic conflicts, conflicts generally are not aimed at the attainment of concrete results but at the expression of aggressive impulse by gone party and generally spills over in the form of violence of remonstrance and frustration on the third parties. Conflict is the conscious attempt to oppose, resist or coerce the will of another or others. Conflict is manifested in physical confrontations between groups expressing or resisting demand for change or is expressed in actual physical clashes (e.g., armed attacks, riots) or in a symbolic ones (e.g., general strike, civil disobedience, political protests). The political conflict theorists focus on the role of organised group conflict for political power to explain collective violence and revolutions.[16] Insurgency, guerrilla warfare, terrorism, revolutions coup-detat, and violent political movements are all forms of political conflicts having their impact on internal security. Conflicts can range from disturbing law and order or public order or internal security depending on the following factors :-

1. The probability of the occurrence of disturbance to law and order caused by conflicts.
2. The potentiality of damage in term of lives and property.
3. The intensity and effectivity of the conflict and
4. The recurring nature of the conflict phenomena and its magnitude and dimensions.

There is a ruling class in every society which constantly tries to monopolize political power at the expense of the lower class and this conflict produces on unending ferment of endosmosis and exosmosis between a class that rules and a class that is ruled. Powerful classes shape the legal/structure to serve its own narrow interests. According to Neil J.Smelser, as profounded in his book *"The Theory of Collective Behaviour"*, the manifestation of conflict, in collective behaviour occurs only in the following six conditions :-

1. Structural conduciveness.
2. Structural strains.
3. A generalized belief.
4. Precipitating factors.
5. Mobilisation for action.
6. Ineffective social control.

Structural conduciveness refers to the structural contradictions which are the primary cause for conflicts and collective behaviour manifestations in the form of direct action, strikes and even riots. Low intensity conflict get manifested in violent aggressive collective behaviour.

Conflict is the outcome of psychological feeling of relative deprivation. Relative deprivation can be understood as" actors" perceptions of discrepancy between their value expectation (the goods and conditions of the life to which they believe they are justifiable entitled) and their value capabilities (the amount of these goods and conditions that they think they are able to get and keep)". The psychological response to perceived relative deprivation is discontent or anger and that anger is motivating stage for which aggression is an inherently satisfying response. There are however four important societal variables namely "Coercive Potential," institutionalisation, social facilitation and legitimacy of the political regime which determine the magnitude of the manifestation of the aggression into a civil strife. The figure shows casual model of civil strife.

/Coercive, Potential /
Relative / Institutionalisation / Magnitude of
Deprivation / Social Facilitation /
/Civil strife, Legitimacy/

In the above model coercive power includes the quality and quantity of coercive forces, the loyalty of the forces and the attitude they take in a particular context. Institutionalisation refers to the social, political, economic and other societal structures which minimize the intensity of strife. Social and structural facilitation comprises aspects of organisational and environmental facilitations of strife such as transportation net. Legitimacy refers to the degree of popular support for the regime. Manifestation of low intensity conflicts become civil strife and can take shape of turmoil, domestic conflict, conspiracy or insurgency. The magnitude of domestic conflict or civil strife depends on the following three factors :-

(a) **Pervasiveness:** The extent of participation by the affected population.
(b) **Duration :** The total span of time in term of days and hours.
(c) **Intensity:** In term of loss of property and life total estimated casualities dead and injured and destruction of property in terms of quantity.

Machiavelli, Bodin, Hobbes and Mosca have analyzed conflicts in terms of power relationships. Conflicts arise in every state in the distribution of scarce goods and resources between different groups. The conflicts between the centre and states arise on various economic, political and linguistic matters as their interest clash. States want to get more and more autonomy while centre wants to remain strong and all powerful. Non-realistic conflicts arise when states demand more and more powers and autonomy in various fields while Centre wants more powers for the union. In democratic form of Government, according to Mosca, an organised minority imposes its will on the disorganised majority and this itself is a contradiction of political system because the ruling class tries to monopolise political powers at the expense of the power class of citizens. According to some thinkers, conflicts arise when the individual freedom is completely subjudicated to the so called "national- interest", which in essence means the interests of the powerful elite ruling the country at times. Political conflicts arise over values and claims to status, power and scarce resources when the aims of the conflicting parties are not only to gain the desired values but also neutralize, infuse or eliminate their political rivals. Such conflicts are structural, long lasting and deep rooted.

The Concept of Low-Intensity Conflicts

There is lot of conceptual misunderstanding and doctrinal confusion about low intensity conflicts not only in India but even abroad; "Perhaps the most fundamental issue is still conceptual: disagreements and confusion over the nature of and response to low intensity conflict"[17]. Civil disturbance, civil disobedience, guerrilla warfare, insurrection, insurgency, revolutionary warfare, internal security, limited wars, small wars, periphery wars and subversions, etc. are some of the common terms which are used by different authors to project the problems of low-intensity conflicts. One can easily find no agreement among the scholars about the précise definition of low-intensity conflicts. John F. Kennedy in June 1962 at West Point, underlined the theme of low intensity conflicts when he said; " This is another type of war, new in its intensity, ancient in its origin, war by guerrillas, subversives, insurgents, assassins, war by ambush instead of aggression, seeking victory by eroding and exhausting the enemy....... It preys on economic unrest, and ethnic conflicts and these are the kinds of challenges that will be before us in the next decade". Low-intensity conflicts left unchecked may prove extremely damaging, confronted and controlled, they may become high-intensity threats"[18]. Low-intensity conflict is a dynamic integrated action including various varieties of violence and conflict, directed against all institutional instruments of the state with a view to establish a new socio-political order. It also covers the response of the state and its coercive institutions. The college of combat at MHOW (M.P) has attempted to define the concept of Low Intensity Conflicts in the following words. " It is a politico military confrontation between the established authority (state) and organised groups of people with or without external assistance beyond the scope of legitimate routine peaceful contest/agitation. Being on the low end of conflict spectrum, it imposes an undefined restraint on the execution of military operations". It is a conflict waged by irregular and unconventional elements. According to U.S. department of defence, it is a limited politico military struggle to achieve political, social, economical or psychological objectives. It is often protracted and ranges from diplomatic, economic and psychological pressure through terrorism and insurgency. Low intensity conflict is generally confined to a geographical area and is often characterized by constraints on weaponry, tactics and the level of violence".[19] No war, whatever its form, is entirely free of psycho political elements and this is especially true for low-intensity conflicts.[20]

Low intensity conflict are basically political in nature, having the low-intensity level of combat, generally fought in clandestine manner as an illusive enemy with unconventional methods of warfare giving a predominant role to psychological warfare. Generally low-intensity conflicts demand political control of operations and limits on the use of force. It demands small unit operations with relatively low casualties which requires large number of infantry and police units to keep the violence from escalating beyond politically accepted limits. Low-intensity conflicts is a clandestine warfare generally carried out by irregular and civilian populations by unconventional methods of warfare including terrorism and insurgency. Low Intensity Conflict (LIC) gives predominant role to the psychological warfare. To combat Low Intensity Conflict (LIC) generally special forces are used by the state for special operations. In India Central Reserve Police Force has been the most dependable force for combating low intensity conflicts from 1947 onwards.

Government Response to Low-Intensity Conflicts

No government can allow low intensity conflicts and therefore have to carry out low-intensity operations to meet the challenge. Counter-measure include, political, social, economic and psychological action plans to eliminate root causes of conflict and also to keep the conflict under control through effective policies and special operations. Generally armed forces and Central Police organisation have to be particularly selected, trained, equipped and motivated for low intensity operations over a protracted period. The main tasks of such specially selected forces are as under :

(i) The collection of information on the location and movement of insurgent forces.

(ii) The ambush and liquidaton of insurgents.

(iii) Sabotage, assassination and demolition parties into insurgent held areas.

(iv) Political measures.

(v) Social measures.

(vi) Economic measures.

(vii) Administrative measures.

(viii) Legal and judicial measures like enactment of POTA.

(ix) Educational measures.

(x) Border surveillance.

(xi) Limited community relations and peoples support.

(xii) Liaison with and organisation training and control of friendly guerrilla forces, operating against the common enemy.[21]

This is generally believed that low intensity operations have to carry out slogan of winning the hearts and minds of the people of the area in which LIC are being carried out. Each category of low-intensity conflict needs a different type of response from the state authority. Terrorism, insurgency, subversion, guerrilla warfare require different responses. Any LIC takes time to develop and the degree of violence differs according to the injustice and discrimination perceived by the affected group of population. Quick and prompt identification process of the problem can be taken up if the intelligence network is effective and the government gets the proper pulse of the sentiments and grievances of the people. A national strategy and effectively timely response has to enlarge from within the existing policy framework with a view to prevent, pre-empt, contain, defuse and eradicate LIC. Management of LIC at the Central and state level has to be carried out promptly and effectively. Planning, organising staffing, directing, coordinating and training of human resources for proper responses have to be done at both levels in a coordinated manner. Mobilisation of public opinion against the dissidents demands need for appropriate psychological operations supported by socio-economic measures to root out the causes of grievances. An apex crisis management body with suitable authority to monitor implementation of policy in every field is needed. State security apparatus has to be suitably strengthened by mobilisation of specialized forces to deal with LIC. A state level civil Military liasion conference should be held every month to review and modify appropriate operational matters. A suitable coordination committee at district level also helps in dealing with LIC effectively and appropriately at district level. Indian political system has acquired the capacity for sustaining and eventually resolving these low-intensity conflicts without compromising its commitment to democratic norms. Political conflicts arise according to Trotsky when there are deep divisions among governing elites and leadership groups or when there is great erosion of confidence in the regime, its values and institutions, afflicting all levels of the populations including the government. According to Felkins Gross, conflicts arise in the political system due to the following reasons :

(a) Perceived political inequalition, infringement of rights, injustice or oppression;

(b) Lack of adequate channels for peaceful communication of protests, grievances and demands (e.g., denial of franchise and other right of participation, representation or access to media);

(c) The availability of a revolutionary leader equipped with a potentially attractive ideology.

Government of India has enacted POTA (Prevention of Terrorism Act) to safeguard national security and sovereignty. Funding and financing play a vital role in fostering terrorism and have to be dealt sternly to contain the menace.

T.A. Critchloy holds the view that whenever in a civilized political system, a substantive section of the community has reason to feel on racial, social or religious grounds that it is under privileged or otherwise deprived of elementary political rights, its political protest is likely to take the form of direct action (manifested conflict). Most of such conflicts have a major impact on internal security of the country. Dr.B.R. Ambedkar, in his prophetic observation at the time of making of Indian Constitution has said "In politics we will have inequality.........we must remove those contradiction at the earliest moment or else, those who suffer from inequality, will blow up the structure of political democracy". The introduction of adult suffrage, alongwith huge plans of mass education and economic development have over-stirred the political system in Indian to the extent its inbuilt contradiction seem like racking the entire society in the absence of a requisite infrastructure. The political system's growth, with its teething troubles is further accentuated by the over-increasing regional imbalance in the economic field. Recently political agitations and public disorders have gained new dimensions, strategies, tactics and manifestations. The rising expectations of the under-privileged citizens, the emergence of new type of political leaders, spread of political consciousness in the society, lack of social discipline and the emergence of a "Soft state" have further given rise to political conflicts of intense nature giving rise to public violence, communal, regional and linguistic agitations.[22] In every plural society conflicts over power and authority are bound to continue as they are structural in nature. Ideological conflict and power conflict can take manifestations in the form of political protests, direct action, terrorist activates to insurgency, revolt and even full-fledged revolution depending on the structure and nature of political system. In democratic system, conflict generally remains constitutional and open while in other form of systems it at times becomes convert and revolutionary Political conflicts have great implications for internal security and therefore require proper analysis and systematic study.

Low Intensity Conflicts in Tripura

Since 1980 ethnic violence has claimed the lives of three million people. In 1996, 236 people were killed by insurgents. 70 police and paramilitary personnel were killed in 1996 while politicians claim that more than 5000 militants have surrendered over the past three years. Tripura continues to be the only insurgency - wreacketed state in north-east where the disturbed area act has not been extended on All Tripura Tiger Force (ATTF), National Liberation Front of Tripura (NLFT), Tripura Resurrection Army (TRA) and about 11 other militants outfits have been declared illegal only on 16 February 1997, infix police stations Khowai, Kalyanpur, Teliamura, Jirania, Sidhai and Takarjola, the disturbed Area Act was promulgated after 21 persons were gunned down and 100 houses gutted in Khowai sub-division. Tripura is surrounded on three sides by Bangladesh with which it has a 839 km border. Tripura has only 30 companies of armed police and there are 59 CRPF and 49 BSF companies carrying out low intensity operations against insurgents. Mandai Massacre of 262 (262) non-tribals on June 1980 started a series of low intensity conflicts that left over 4000 dead in Tripura. In 1988 Congress came to power and TNV came overground. On January 31, 1997 insurgents raided a colony called Taidu Bazar 90 km south of Tripura and gunned down 7 people. Many sociologists have seen in the process of syncretize-action a latent form of class-conflict which results because of the peculiar structural constraints of the Indian Society. (Harold Gould) 1961 E.R.Leach 1960 etc)[23]. According to Pareto and Mosca, the dynamics in the structure of elites and the process of circulation among elite operates through conflict, intrigues and competition by which each section of elites tries to overthrow the power elites and occupy its position. In a system of social stratification of a plural society, it posits a permanent conflict between classes which have command over power and wealth and those who do not possess them.[24] In order to understand the dimension of conflict within the frame of social stratification it is essential to realize that conflict and tension can only be examined with the help of significant diacritical features of their own. Class conflict and caste mobility occur because there are full-fledged differences between castes. Conflicts arise on a far more general scale in caste societies because of the existence of multiple caste hierarchies which are all separate and equal and support their positions through their own caste ideologies.[25] The incidence of caste conflicts and violence in recent times have not been confined to rural areas only but have taken place in urban areas of Gujarat and Maharashtra as well. Mobility, social stratification, mutual reinforcement of economic and social inequalities and culture and ideology of repression in promoting and aggravating conflicts need special focus today.

Factors Responsible for Conflict in India

Primarily the roots of conflict lie in the exploitation or attempted exploitation. and following factors are partly responsible :

1. Caste system with its prejudices against lower caste has aggravated the tension and conflict.
2. Democratic system has given way to rising aspirations of the people and the feudal outlook of the people are responsible for conflicts.
3. Complete absence of the culture of communication and accumulating grievances of the people give rise to conflicts. Psychological factors give rise to conflicts.
4. Indian economic system is partly responsible for many conflicts.
5. Political system of India with a federal polity with a written constitution has given rise to conflicts.
6. Unresolved and unjust wage system, unscrupulous exploitation of the working classes and growing criminalisation has resulted in conflicts.
7. Conflicts are emerging due to the development process in a developing society.
8. Religion and communal bias and prejudices are causing conflicts.
9. Conflict can be due to generation gap and value system. The value conflict theorists like Walker, Fuller, Cuber and Harper hold that clashes in value system are of basic importance in the origin and development of social conflicts.
10. Fanaticism and schismatic beliefs can give rise to conflicts.

Ethnic Conflicts in India and their impact on Internal Security

In North-Eastern states of India like Nagaland, Assam, Tripura, Mizoram and Manipur following types of conflicts are noticed :

1. Diffused conflict at the ideational level.
2. Conflicts within the tribal communities.
3. Between different communities.
4. Between tribal communities and the state.

These are four types of conflicts are not wholly exclusive. From times immemorial, conflicts of economic interests have perhaps been the most obvious aspects in North Eastern states of India. Even today economic conflicts continue to dominate other type of conflicts either explicitly or implicitly. In order to deal with L.I.C., operational analysis and various models of counter insurgency operations have to be carried out with the help of operations research.[25a] There is a competition for and exploitation of, natural resources, encouraged by a political system which promotes concentrated extraction and profits for a few. Diffused conflict at the ideational level arises with the need of recognition of identity of each ethnic group. While non-recognition of at least some ethnic identities in India as indigenous population will accelerate the conflict, even formal recognition will not clinch the issue.[26] Ethnographic accounts are replete with intra-tribal conflicts related to the question of control and management of land in the tribal areas of north East India.[27] Intercommunity conflicts in tribal areas of North-eastern states are quite common. Self styled ethnic extremists have continued gruesome killings in Manipur. In August 1993 as many as fifty people including women and children were killed in ethnic conflicts and whole villages were put to the torch. In August 1993 ambushes killed Six Army and two CRP Jawans, over a hundred people have been killed in clashes between Tangkhul Nagas and Kukis during Sept. 1993. On 15th September 1993 suspected extremists belonging to a particular community massacred Ninety Kukis in Manipur's Senapati district. It is difficult to disentangle the tribal conflicts between Nagas belonging to National Socialist Council of Nagaland (Muviah group) and the Kukis organised by well-equipped Kuki National Army and both groups make their claims over control of territory in Manipur. Manipur State Government is a helpless spectator to this ethnic conflict. Weapons once owned by the Khmer Rouge cadres of Cambodia had now reached militants of Nagaland and Manipur, according Lt. Gen. S.C. Grewal, GOC, 3 Corps. In an interview he said that weapons from Afganisthan might have also reached militants of the north-east region. 'Since ISI of Pakistan is involved, this possibility cannot be ruled out'. Weapons from some South-East Asian nations reached the north-east via the sea route. These were first unloaded in small ports along the Bangladesh coast and then smuggled into Nagaland and Manipur via the land route. Assorted weapons, including rifles of the

AK series, rocket launchers, communication sets, ammunition conventional rifles were freely available in the arms markets of Bangkok. Though some rebel camps were closed down by the Bangladesh government, several other such camps were still operating in Sylhet and the Chittagong Hill Tract (CHT) areas. The difficult terrain could be one reason why the government could not close down these camps. Indian troops were getting help from the Myanmar army in busting militant camps located in the Indo-Myanmarese border areas. Regular border meetings were being held at the level of company commanders as well as at higher levels between the two armies. In May 1997, at least 70 militants of the National Socialist Council of Nagaland (I-M) entered Manipur and southern Assam from Bangladesh, but some others were left behind to run the camps. One reason for the relatively new phenomenon of clashes between Kukis and Paites was the attempt to collect taxes from the Paite community by Kuki militants. Paities, who were more prosperous than the Kukis and were ethnically closer to Mizos, had refused to pay these taxes. Another reason for the clashes was the dispute over land, which was scarce in the N.E. region because of the hilly terrain, The Nagas, who were the early inhabitants of Nagaland and the hill areas of Manipur considered the Kukis as outsiders as they had come to these areas much later, mainly with British expeditionary forces. In clashes between Nagas and Kukis in Manipur 113 persons have been killed. 75 injured and 1067 houses gutted or damaged between January and August 11, 1993.[28] To enforce effective counter-insurgency operations, Army was inducted in Manipur in May 1993 with the support of the State Police and Central Paramilitary Forces. Conflicts in tribal areas involving tribal communities and the State are found in almost all north-eastern states which have non-ethnic conflicts with insurgent activities racking the state frequently. The July 7, 1997 agreement between the warring Kukis and the Paities in Manipur has done precious little to restore ethnic peace to the troubled state, the renewed suspect of violence could be a machination of vested interest to scuttle Prime Minister. I.K.Gujral's peace overtures to the Naga underground's. In the latest incident of violence on July 21 four persons were killed and over a hundred houses destroyed in a major flare up in the Veng Paite village surrounding the Churachandpur district town, eventually spreading to 13 adjoining villages. Curfew was clamped on the town and the adjoining areas. The same day Kuki militants raided a Manipur rifles post at Lamjang area under Singhat Police Station in the district. The jawan were killed in the ambush. Violence continued even as the peace efforts were being made and four days after the agreement was signed. Kuki militants gunned down, 12 people, including some women, and burnt down more then 50 hutments in the district's Mata village. Intelligence reports said another nine were killed by the Kukis in the Saikul Paite village on June 24 and over 250 huts were razed. The trouble-torn Chaurachandpur district bordering Myanmar and Mizoram is inhabited by both the communities with Kukis predominantly populating the interior and the Paities the Churachandpur town. The ethnic Kuki-Naga clashes which started in mid 1992 following demand of a 'Kukiland' and 'South Nagaland' had so far claimed over 700 lives and over 1000 houses had been set ablaze or destroyed. Intelligence sources suggest that the trouble appeared to have been caused by calculatedly wrong signals sent by some vested interest groups for creating confusion, particularly in view of Centre's peace drive with Naga underground leaders. A peace agreement was thus signed between Kuki National Front and ZRO on July 7, 1997. (*The Hindustan Times* 25/7/97). Due to lack of vision and political expediency, conflicts are not being resolved and managed in time. Most of the problems are glossed over till they emerge in their violent and extremist form causing serious threat to the internal security of the country. Many ethnic conflicts are due to unbalanced economic growth and question of ethnic identity. In the North-East India, the question of identity perpetuated isolation and lack of economic development, required a well-planned graduated and wholesome approach to modernisation. "Ethnic conflicts are common in all ethnically plural societies and it has been extremely difficult to create harmonious relations between clearly different ethnic groups". [29] Absence of declared policy results in disjointed responses, by the politicians, the bureaucrats and the managers of internal security. It is therefore essential that it is within the knowledge of all responsible for, implementation.[30] Sophisticated arms of eastern European origin are finding their way to the north-east region via the arms bazaars in South East Asia. The RPG, an anti-tank grenade which United Liberation Front of Assam ultras has used to ambush an army convoy on February 1 near Digboi was of Russian origin. It is a powerful weapon and had it hit the vehicle six inches above where it actually had, the casualty figure would have been much higher. The AK-47 rifles which the ultras in the north-east use frequently also have a Russian origin. In some of the fund-starved eastern European states weapons are even sold off by army units to garner resources, insurgent gropes in the north-east purchase the weapons in arm markets in South-East Asia and bring them by sea routes to small ports in Bangladesh. In 1995, the army had apprehended one such consignment on the Mizoram border, last year, the Bangladesh authorities had impounded a ship carrying arms near Cox's Bazaar. The ULFA was trying to purchase more arms, but it was faced with funds shortage. Substantial amount of money is believed to be locked up in banks in Bangladesh. This had prompted the underground outfit to step up its collection drive. The pressure by the security forces would therefore, have to be kept up, they said. After the formation of the unified headquarters about 165 ULFA and Bodo militants had been arrested. Eight of the twelve militants suspected to be connected with the blasting of the Brahmaputra Mail have been nabbed. They belong to the Bodoland Tiger Force. Seven Ultras were killed in encounters with security forces during the same period.

Naxalite Movement: A Manifestations of Conflict

Naxalite movement which was started in 1967 in West Bengal, gradually spread to Andhra Pradesh, Orissa, Bihar and Kerala with sporadic activities in the states of Punjab, Uttar Pradesh, Assam, Tripura, Maharashtra and Tamil Nadu. Agrarian unrest, and conversion of CPI (M) into a revolutionary party believing in annihilation of class enemies were the twin causes of Naxalite movement gaining mass appeal. Due to failure of leadership and unrealistic analysis of socio-economic-political reality of India, movement has gradually died out except in Andhra Pradesh. The Naxalite movement in Andhra Pradesh has taken a very violent conflict form and has seriously jeopardized the internal security of state.

Low Intensity Conflicts in Nagaland -A Case Study

The State of Nagaland lies between 2506' and 2704' latitude north of equator and between the longitudinal lines 93020' E and 95015'E having an area of 16,579 sq. Km. The state is bounded by Assam in the North and West, by Myanmar (Burma) and Arunachal Pradesh in the East and Manipur in the South and runs more or less parallel to the left bank of Brahmaputra. The topograph is very severe, full of hills ranges which break into a wide chaos of spurs and ridges. The altitude varies between 194 metres (636 ft) and 3,048 metres (10,000 ft). Most of the thousand and odd villages stand at 1 to 2 thousand metres high as it is very typical of the Nagas to build their houses on the hilltops and at higher dominating elevations. The highest peak in the state. Saramati in Tuensang district is 3,840 (12,598 ft) high. The population belongs to Mongolian family and their influence derivative of the Tibeto-Burman Group. But the Lingua-Franca is English. The insurgency in Nagaland in one form or the other is more than one and a half century old. Originally the Nagas resisted the British into their territory from 1830 to 1879. Following the battle of Khonoma (near Kohima) in 1879 the Nagas permitted the British to set up 3 Hill station at Kohima, Wokha and Mokokchug, in regions belonging to Angami, Lotha and AO tribes respectively along the Western border areas adjoining neighbouring Ahome (Assam). The Tuensang Hill area was included in thirties. Nagaland remained a district of Assam till 1.12.63 when a separate state was carved out with its capital at Kohima. At present Nagaland has seven districts viz, Kohima, Phek, Wokha, Zunheboto, Tuensang, Mokokchung and Mon and nine Police districts with one extra each in Kohima (namely Dimapur) and Tuensang (namely Kipre). All districts are connected by state Highways and one NH-39 runs from Numaligarh (Assam) to dimapur to Kohima to Imphal/Moreh. Except Kohima-Wokha road which is being maintained by state PWD, all other roads are maintained by GREF. The average rainfall in the state is 1958 mm and the duration of rainy season is for about 6 months from April to September. During rainy season road block occurs occasionally due to landslides but it is generally cleared in a day or two by GREF. There are about 16 major tribes, viz, AO, Sema, Koniak, Chaksang, Angami, Sagtam, Phem, Chang, Yimchungre, Zoliang, Khiemnunjiu, Rangam, Tikhir, Chirr, Makware, etc. in the order of their population. The literacy rate is quite high (about 66.09 per cent male and 55.72 per cent female). In Nagaland, the order of village Council regulates the special life. The regulation of 1945 gives power to the Tribal Council to try criminal as well as Civil cases and impose fines so far as both parties belong to the same tract. All civil suits are tried by the Tribal Council. The punishment inflicted by the Council is according to their customary law but within the limit to avoid heavy punishment. Under the tribal custom the land belongs to local inhabitants and government can purchase land from the owners if they are willing. The communication system though satisfactory within the state but much to be desired when it relates to outside. Only one Railway station (Dimapur) exists in the state and this serves both Nagaland and Manipur. The air-service has been gradually deteriorating, and from daily service to Delhi it has come to nought. There are only two flights per week from Dimapur to Guwahati to Calcutta and many times it gets suspended or altered. With the commissioning of new electronic exchanges in Kohima and other districts of Nagaland, telephone service (specially STD) has improved considerably and this is the only silver lining. Objectively speaking Nagaland and other states of NES have ample justification for establishing a few channels from satellite Communication system. After signing of Shillong Accord between representative of underground faction of Nagaland on 5/12/75, insurgency was almost controlled. However a few important leaders of the then Eastern Naga Revolution Council viz, Issac suw, Th, Muivah, Khaplang, etc did not endorse Shillong Accord and continued to work against it and formed Naga Socialist Council of Nagaland (NSCN).The NSCN members also went to China through Kachin area and brought arms/ama. They also established a liberated zone in the 'SOMRA' track of Burma. After about a decade sometimes in 1988 the NSCN suffered a major split on the basis of tribal loyalties which ensured fratricidal killing. Thus, NSCN (K) was formed and led by Khaplang and NSCN (I) was led by Issak and Muivah. The latter moved of its cadre to Manipur and bordering Nagaland. Since then there has been no going back and both the groups have strengthened their cadre to above 4,000 each. As against the strengthening of both the groups of NSCN, the presence of army and para-military forces was reduced to almost nil. The biggest 8 MTN Div of the Army was shifted to eastern theatre and the CRPF Battalion was reduced to merely one. In this vacuum the NSCN group flourished without any resistance and established deep roots and contacts all over especially in towns. After noticing several avert activities of UGs, more CRPF Bn started arriving 1992 onwards and they were dispersed to all the seven districts primarily to check the UGs activities in the town in the wake of neutralisation and ineffectiveness of civil police; Army, CRP, Assam Rifles along with civil police are fighting low intensity conflicts during the last five decades. Author has carried out a detailed case study of incidents of 1994 and 1995 to highlight the problems caused by LIC. Sometimes in 1993, about 5 underground outfits had formed a United group called Indo-Burma Revolutionary Front (IBRF) which included NSCN (K) and UNLF (Meghen). This organisation has not posed any serious threat to the state so far. To encounter the IBRF, some of the prominent underground outfits viz NSCN (IM) and UNIF; oken) having enmity with NSCN (K) and UNLF (Meghen) have formed a new underground front called 'Self-Defence United Front of the South-East Himalayan Region.' Twenty-three representatives from seven outfits signed the formal declaration on November 30, 1994. Following are the member organisations.

KKYL :- Kanglei Yawal Kanna Lup from Manipur comprising UNLF (Oken Faction), KCP (Ibopishak) PREPAK (Khomba).

NSCN (IM)—National Socialist Council of Nagaland (Issue-Muivah group).

HALC - Hyuniewtrep Achik Liberation Council of Meghalaya.

NLFT - National Liberation Front of Tripura.

KNV - Korbi National Volunteers of Assam.

HPC - Hmar People's Convention of Mizoram.

NDFB - National Democratic Front of Bodoland.

The new front has chosen general secretary of NSCN (IM). The Muivah the convenor. Member organisation of this front will have equal power and status for combating Indian Forces. They have also expressed support to the movements in Kashmir, Punjab, Uttarkhand and Gorkhaland. The member organisation will depend on NSCN (IM) for arms, Bodos, Nagas and Meiteis in the new front are capable of launching major strikes and have enough power. Of late, large number of Nepali youths are enlisting in NSCN (IM) group in Nagaland and Manipur. In Indo-Nepal Agreement 1950, Nepalis were given all facilties except political rights. The Restricted Area Permit (RAP) was not applicable to them but in 1976, through an amendment, this provision was curtailed. The community has been feeling alienated owing to harassment/biased treatment. This might have prompted a section of the youths to take up arms to assert their presence. In this venture ISI of Pakistan and NSCN (IM) Embassy in Kathmandu is playing a vital role in providing Naga UGs with false passport bearing Nepali names. This nexus might prove a dangerous proposition.

Manifestations of Violent Social Conflicts and their Impact on Internal Security

Caste riots are not uncommon in India and especially during the last three decades there have been a number of such riots in rural areas of various parts of the country. Caste riots are primarily rooted in disputes over land and wages and sometimes in deep-rooted caste prejudices among the upper castes on one hand and social mobility of SC-ST on the other. Some studies indicate that caste conflicts were mainly over the scarce resources and employment opportunities. In Gujarat State intensity of caste conflicts was found in Ahmedabad, Mehsana, Kaisa and Baroda districts. Caste conflicts and caste violence in Gujarat can be judged by the figures below :

Intensity of Caste Conflicts in different Districts of Gujarat [31]

S.No.	*Districts*	*Killed in firing*	*injured in firing*	*Days of continued disturbance*
1.	Ahmedabad	18	29	10
2.	Mahesana	8	11	12
3.	Kaira	5	12	7
4.	Baroda	2	7	11
5.	Surat	-	-	7
6.	Sabar Kantha	1	-	1

(Contd.)

(Contd.)

7.	Jain Nagar	-	-	3
8.	Rajkot	-	-	3
9.	Bhavnagar	-	-	3

Caste conflicts and atrocities on lower castes SC/ST have been estimated to be 40,000 during 1966-76 and during 1976-78 this figure exceeded 17000. Caste conflicts in urban areas are generally related to the mobility of the Scheduled Castes and Scheduled Tribes. Indian society is having various types of social conflicts in almost all the states. Articles on violent social conflicts published in 'India Today from 1980 to 1988' can be classified as under :

Table 1

The Frequency distribution of articles on violent social conflicts published in India Today—1980-89 by the type of conflicting groups[32]

Type of conflict	*1980*	*81*	*82*	*83*	*84*	*85*	*86*	*87*	*88*	*Total*
1. Hindu Muslim	2	4	3	6	1	2	8	5	5	36
2. Hindu Harijan	3	5	4	2	-	1	1	1	2	19
3. Tribal Non-tribal	16	6	8	5	11	8	7	11	13	85
4. Hindu Sikh and Sikh Terrorism	-	3	4	10	19	9	15	9	17	86
5. Other violent ethnic conflicts	3	4	4	7	3	10	2	2	2	42
6. Non-ethnic violent conflict including Naxalites	2	8	2	2	1	1	5	2	2	25
Total	31	30	25	32	35	31	38	30	41	293

Geographically Hindu Muslim violent conflict have mainly affected U.P., Assam, West Bengal, Bihar, Gujarat M.P. and Maharashtra, Karnataka, Kerala and Andhra Pradesh. Political violence and conflicts have been increasing in India and political murders have been reported in all states during the last ten years. In 1988 in West Bengal alone there were 182 murders. Caste conflicts and violence in Bihar and U.P. are generally over the issues of wages, sharecroppers, social oppression, land disputes and retaliation. The 6th December 1992 Ayodhya incident has sparked of serious communal conflicts resulting in violence taking a very heavy toll in major cities as can be seen in the table below.[33]

	Major cities	Killed	Injured
1.	Bombay	500	1000
2.	Surat	184	60
3.	Bhopal	139	450
4.	Calcutta	25	50
5.	Kanpur	62	118
6.	Ahmedabad	150	700
7.	Hyderabad	13	50
8.	Mysore	9	260
9.	Bangalore	28	150
10.	Total in Major cities	1100	3378
11.	Total Post-demolition violence victims in India	1700	5500

The state-wise break up of communal conflicts resulting in deaths and injuries caused after 6th December 1992 at Ayodhya as shown below indicate the intensity of the communal violence in India.[34]

Sl.No.	State	Total Toll	Property damaged	
1.	Maharashtra	259	3.9	crores
2.	Uttar Pradesh	170	5.5	"
3.	Gujarat	208	7.25	"
4.	Rajasthan	49	7.37	"
5.	Karnataka	78	5.97	"
6.	Madhya Pradesh	133	1.05	"
7.	Andhra Pradesh	20	6.00	lakh
8.	West Bengal	27	N.A.	
9.	Bihar	40	N.A.	
10.	Kerala	21	1.5	crores
11.	Assam	115	49.0	lakh
12.	Orissa	02	6.00	lakh
13.	Tamil Nadu	02	70.00	lakh
14.	Haryana	01	N.A.	
15.	Chandigarh	15	N.A.	
16.	Delhi	17	N.A.	
17.	Jammu & Kashmir	7	N.A.	

It is noticed by all enlightened persons that social conflicts, violence destruction of property are gradually increasing in our plural society. Conflict in Indian society has apparently been intensified by the Ayodhya outrage in a substantial manner. While are some whispered references to the possibility of the exacerbation of extremism among both major religious groups in India, there does not appear to be any serious concern about handling such an eventuality through pre-emptive political action.[35] In

Kashmir the low intensity conflicts have caused serious internal security repercussions and the situation can be visualized from the following figure of 1991 :-

1.	No. of civilians killed	- 1028
2.	No. of security forces killed	- 318
3.	Militants killed	- 1378
4.	Militants arrested	- 4323
5.	Militants surrendered	- 583
6.	Militants released	- 17

Due to low intensity conflicts between 1988 to 1992 in Jammu & Kashmir, there were 14542 incidents of 6565 number of attacks on security forces and 1387 attacks on others during the period. A total 4147 incidents of explosion and arson were reported in Jammu & Kashmir. During LIC 2256 civilians 1671 militants and 508 security personnel were killed during

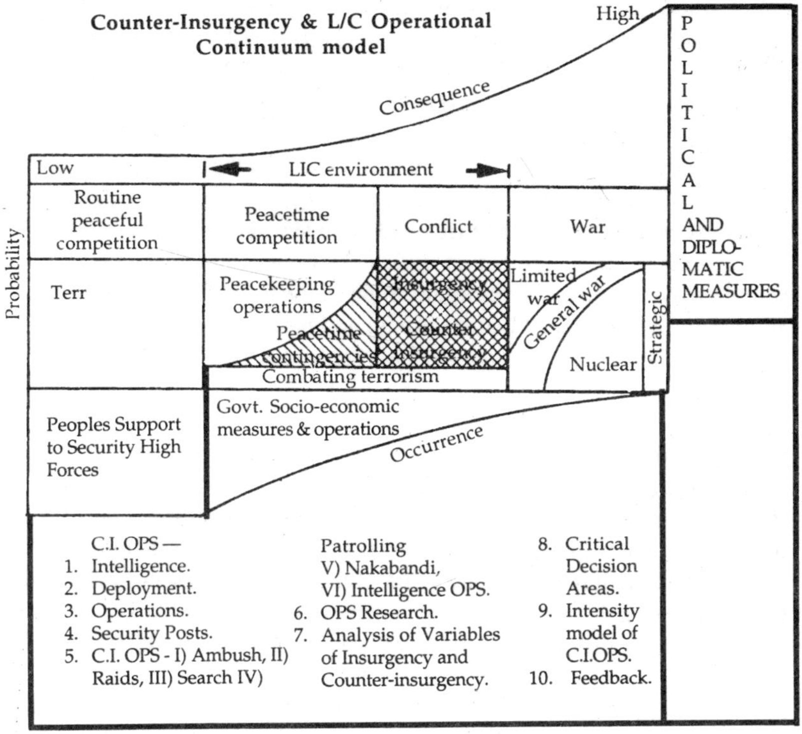

Figure

the period 1988 to 1992 in J & K. On July 20, 1997 at least 30 persons, including 22 militants and five security personnel, were killed in escalated violence is Kashmir Valley even as security forces destroyed a militant camp in inaccessible upper reaches of Pir Panjal ranges. Counter-Insurgency OPS and operations against LIC can be tackled through operational continuum model developed by the author in the form of the given matrix.

The author has developed counter-insurgency and L.I.C. operational continuum model which has been given on page 145. Counter-Insurgency operations can only be a part of the general political and administrative measures to control, contain and eliminate Low Intensity Conflicts. Every riot and every communal conflict between communities is an open invitation for criminals and anti-social elements to join in and share the booty. The Bombay riots between December 1992 and January 1993 were results of combined anti-social activities of criminals. Communalists and the partisan police who were in forefront of all the looting, killing and destruction.[35a] An estimated 784 people lost their lives in Bombay riots. In their long term recommendations the Bombay riot report has urged that the police force be removed and reoriented and special courts be set up to try riot-related offences. Two decade back between October 31 and November 4, 1984 2,773 Sikhs were killed in Delhi. Almost 10 years after the Delhi riots despite one commission and two committees, the subject is still not closed and even in several instances the FIR's had not been written. The committee has recommended severe action against 298 policemen and also urged complete overhauling and re-organisation of the Police force. Policemen all over the country need better training and better understanding of our problems. The Home Minister told Rajya Sabha that a total of 2132 persons were killed in 13 states in connection with 1149 cases of communal riots between June 1, 1991 and July 31, 1993. 14 persons were rendered handicapped, 22 homeless and 15838 arrested during the period[36] 142 persons were arrested in connection with the chain of bomb blasts in Bombay Conflicts. In a plural society like India have resulted in demands for separate states of Jharkhand in Bihar hill state of Uttarkhand in U.P. and Gorkhaland. It is a testimony to the resilience of plural society of India that it has been able to withstand the violent social conflicts like communal riots, terrorism, insurgency, caste wars etc. during the last 45 years and has been able to maintain its democratic, secular and plural characteristics. Police, administrators and the entire criminal justice system require restructuring and radical reforms to cater for the needs of the plural society which has the difficult task of managing various communal, religious, ethnic and social conflicts.

Low Intensity Conflicts and Insidious Subversion by Foreign Power

Low intensity conflicts involved irregular forces—guerrilla armies, national liberation movements, terrorist groups, private militia and narcotic traffickers arranged either individually or in various combinations, against state military and police forces in an unconventional warfare through mostly non-state actors abetted by foreign countries enemical to the state. India today finds itself embroiled in combating an effective low-intensity conflict predicament in Punjab and Kashmir, conflict fomented by Pakistan.[37] Following figure will indicate the violence caused by low intensity conflicts in J & K .

Year	*Total attack on Security force*	*Kidnapping*	*Incidents of in Killings*	*L.I.C,. incidents*
1988	390	6	NA	31
1989	2154	49	2	92
1990	3905	1098	57	1177
1991	3122	1999	100	1393
1992	4971	3413	124	1909
	14542	6565	283	4602

Since 1990, in J & K, will over 15000 Terrorists have been neutralised. In 2002, 1522 terrorists were killed in the state while the tally was 1432 in 2000 and 1522 in 2002 in J & K. Over 60 per cent of them have been foreign mercenaries.[37a]

Low-intensity conflicts can be seen as confrontation short of full scale war, generally waged in peace-time, in hostile neighbouring country with the aim of encouraging secession by creating disorder, subversion terrorism and religious struggles. Since independence, India has faced a number of low-intensity conflicts that have revolved around perceived concepts of secession in north-eastern states of Nagaland, Mizoram and Tripura and during the last decade in Kashmir and Punjab abetted and aided by Pakistan. Pakistan has played a master stroke by initiating an effective, well-coordinated and volatile LIC against India in Punjab and Kashmir.[38] Overhead Intelligence network, conduct of psychological operations, effective border management, coordination of media, effective civic action programmes are some of the suggested recommendations for combating LIC. Strong political will, effective use of army and border security force and effective large scale operations against LIC are needed.

Since low-intensity conflicts are complex in nature, the battlefield must be shared by soldiers, statesment economists, politicians, social reformers and the people of the area and a long range national policy has to be worked out. A recent analysis has revealed that Bangladesh has emerged as the new sanctuary for all the insurgents after the loss of Kachin camps to the Myanmar Army.[39] A considerable number of ULFA activists were still hiding in Bangladesh. Two aspects of proxy war waged by Pakistan through low-intensity operations in Kashmir need attention. "Firstly we donot seem to realize the implications of the fact that Pakistan is increasingly pushing in Afghans, Sudanese and nationals of the other countries. Secondly experience of the proxy war for three and a half years should make it quite clear that it would be far more cost-effective to squarely confront Pakistan at the border itself and to prevent its intervention rather than dealing with the infiltrators in the cities and towns in the interiors."[40] Low intensity conflicts have caused very serious violence in Punjab. A profile of low intensity conflicts can be estimated from the following figures of violence reported in Punjab.

Year	*No. of persons killed*	*No. of Policemen S.F. Killed*	*incidents*
1981	13	2	NA
1982	13	2	NA
1983	75	20	NA
1984	359	20	NA
1985	63	8	NA
1986	520	42	NA
1987	910	95	387
1988	1949	110	297
1989	1168	152	200
1990	2467	493	451
1991	2586	493	541
1992	1461	252	48
Total	11584	1689	19201

Due to effective anti-terrorist operations by CRPF, BSF and Punjab police, terrorism has been finally liquidated in Punjab and peace has been successfully restored. It symbolizes victory of peace over violence.

Conflicts in Indian Society and their impact on Internal Security

In Bihar, Maoist Communist Centre, (MCC), an underground organisation, inflicts crude brutal punishments to those it views as offenders. MCC is in full control of Gaya, Aurangabad, Chatra and Palamau and has strong influence in Jehenabad, Nawadash, Patna (rural), Hazaribagh and Giridh. The MCC activists have reportedly committed massacre of people in the past as can be seen in the table:

Table showing MCC Massacres in Bihar

Year and Month		*District*	*Massacred by MCC*
1986	(Sept)	- Aurangabad	- 11 Rajputs
1987	(May)-	- Aurangabad	- 42 Rajputs
1991	(Jan)	- Gaya	- 2 Policemen
1991	(March)	- Gaya	- 5 Muslims
1991	(May)	- Gaya	- 1 BJP MP
1991	(Dec)	- Gaya	- 3 Bhumihars
1992	(Feb)	- Gaya	- 37 Bhumihars
1992	(Sept)	- Chatra	- 1 Policemen
1992	(Sept)	- Gaya	- 5 MCC Rebels
1993	(Jan)	- Gaya	- 3 Yadavs

Source: India Today, August 31, 1993. p. 71 Farzand Ahmed—Bihar, Crime as Punishment.

MCC claims to fight oppression by the upper castes and has taken deep and dangerous roots in the impoverished stretch of Central Bihar. The MCC, according to a social researcher, has been responsible for massacres of caste exploiters including 37 Bhumihars killed in Bara village in 1992. 68,734 cases of atrocities were committed on Scheduled Castes in Uttar Pradesh and Madhya Pradesh and 14157 cases on S.T. in Madhya Pradesh during May 1993. 21 cases of atrocities were committed on SCs in the capital during June 1993.[41] 299 Rape cases were reported during 1992 against Tribal Women in the country with the highest of 21 being from Madhya Pradesh.[42] There seems to be no end of ethnic conflicts in Assam and North Eastern States upto Dec 1992. 3206 ULFA activists had surrendered with 141 assorted weapons and 2648 rounds of ammunition giving hope that peace will come to Assam but about 500 hard core activists are still at large and they are determined to carry on their struggle. The

National Socialist Council of Nagaland (NSCN) and Hmar Peoples Convention (MPC) militants have turned the inaccessible jungles of North Cachar hills district into their hideout. India as a plural society finds itself in a bind in the search for a solution to the prolonged social conflicts which constantly effect the internal security of the country.

In a plural society it is necessary to share power and make proportional representation with all parties offering seats in all decision making bodies, including the cabinet itself.[43] There are strong arguments for proportional representation and parliamentary system of democracy in plural societies. The four characteristics of consociational democracy are (1) government by a grand coalition of the political leaders of all significant segments of the plural society. (2) the mutual veto which serves as an additional protection of vital minority interests, (3) proportionality as principal standard of political-representation and (4) a high degree of autonomy for each segment to run its own internal affairs. Such a system can be suitable to consociational government and federalism. Lyphant message to the political leaders of plural societies is to encourage them to engage in a form of political engineering, if they wish to establish or strengthen democratic institutions in their countries, they must become consociational engineers[44] Juan J. Linz holds that plural societies should have parliamentary democracies because they provide a greater flexibility in the process of transition to a consolidation of democracy.[45] In a plural society many groups represent various interests and pluralism can be expressed by conflict or agreement of groups. Finally in a pluralistic society one group is quite, aware of what other groups are doing.[46] Conflicts arising out of the sufferings of the millions due to poverty, discriminations, hatred, vested interests and large scale industrialization need greater attention.

Low Intensity Conflicts Take High Toll

The official commissions of Enquiry in India, the Dayal report of the Ranchi Riots (1967), the Madan report of the Bhiwandi riots (1970) and the Reddy report of the Ahmedabad riots (1969) and press reports about police response to riots of December 1992 after destruction of Babri Masjid Ramjanam Bhumi disputed structure all over the country have indicated serious shortcomings in the police force of the country. In the lower and subordinate rungs of the police and probably the army, there is anti-minority prejudice. It is unfortunate that the citizen's approach to the police officer to give and not the obligation of the citizens to seek, is considered pestering.[48] In order to develop impartial attitude towards minorities, police training courses ought to evolve better techniques perhaps psychoanalystic in orientation, to make officers introspective about their attitudes to out groups such as the minorities and the scheduled Castes/Scheduled Tribes and sensitive to the implication of a pluralistic state system. Well structured police training courses should be able to recognize the realities of the low intensity conflicts of a plural society and particularly the psychological barriers to adequate role performance and devise orientation courses to break them down. Sensitivity to the implications of a pluralist state system can only come through the self conscious cultivations of attitudes which foster cordial relationships between communities.[49] Low intensity operations are wearing down army and security forces in India. More Indian's have been killed in terrorist violence in Punjab and Kashmir than army man killed in the three Indo-Pak wars. In the 1947-48 war between India and Pakistan the Indian Army reportedly lost about 2,500 soldiers, including about 1000 personnel declared missing-in-action. Another 3,261 soliders were killed, including 359 declared as missing-in-action, in the highly intensive 1965 war, while, 1,525 armymen died in the eastern front during the 1971 war. The total number of Indian soldiers killed in these three wars, excluding those killed on the western front during the 1971 war, stands about 7,286. In contrast, between 1981 and April 1993, as many as 21,476 citizens, including 81,26 militants, were killed in Punjab alone. In Kashmir, between 1988 and 1995, this figure works out to 11,656 deaths, including 5,405 militants. Thus, the total toll during the periods of insurgency in the two states alone stands at a staggering 33,132 — four times more the number of soldiers killed in the three Indo-Pak wars. The body count increases further if we include those killed in the March 1993. Bombay bomb blasts, or in periodic terrorist strikes in other parts of the country, especially in the North-West and Madhya Pradesh. In addition to human lives lost the nation has also suffered economically due to enormous resource diversion. This has resulted in considerable political instability. In the Kashmir valley alone, the army, has a complete mountain diversion and 25 battalion (25,000) soldiers of the Rastriya Rifles engaged in LIC operations. In addition, the two infantry divisions along the line of control are engaged in border security and LIC operation. In one of the largest counter-insurgency operation started on April 21-22, 2003, Security forces have killed 60 militants in J&K by using modified attack helicopters in the first phase of an offensive to cleanse entrenched Jihadi, in the upper reaches of Hill Kaka Area. (*Times of India* 17 May 2003). The scale of army involvement in counter-insurgency operation is less in the Jammu region but nevertheless appears to have become a major task of the Udhampur based Northern Command. Again, in Manipur and Nagaland alone an on entire corps comprising about 69 army and paramilitary force battalions are engaged in similar LIC operations. This does not include Assam and Arunachal Pradesh where yet another corps has engaged part of its troops for such operations. Thus, LIC operation in the North-East too remain a major task for the Calcutta-based Eastern Command. Although LIC operations in Kashmir alone have left about 400 soldiers dead and another 1,200 injured since 1990 the effect on the troops is not merely morale shattering. Sustained involvement in such an environment has left troops disoriented and both psychologically and physically worn out. The psychological impact of such operations on the troops deserves maximum attention especially so in a country where there is a lack of concern for national security and on defence matters.

Some Basic Issues

The basic issues which emerge from the analysis of low intensity conflict are as under :

(a) What kind of policies should the government implement to minimise the ill effects of low-intensity conflicts?

(b) How can plural society bring pluralistic adjustment and harmony and build up a strong united nation ?

(c) What lessons we can draw in this regard from the experiences of the past ?

It has been realized in India that an over-represented minority creates a commensurate anti-minority front. Similarly pampering or overdone protection can create anti-minority blacklash in a plural society as can be seen from the aftermath of Ayodhya December 1992 incidents. The time lag in the modernisation process of ethnic groups and the minorities is mainly due to their lack of representation in those sectors of the economy which are the vanguard of technical change and economic development. Sponsored development of one community vis-à-vis another runs into several different kinds of constraints and problems. One of the crucial problems is the limited spread-effect of the community based economic development measures because the masses of the community are unable to make the leap forward. A government wedded to the free market economy, inevitably confronts problems of irreconcilable class/community interest which further assumes sharper edges in the context of underdevelopment, delayed industrialization and uneven regional development.[51] Intra-community elite conflicts expose from time to time the nature and dimensions of the community based relative deprivations which inevitably nurse communal and ethnic unrest in plural societies. Plural societies have to carry out the difficult task of compromising and coalesce many different and conflicting group interests within its broad national-interest perspective. Integrative solution to conflicts are not merely compromises but should provide increasing benefits and fair play to all the parties concerned. The education system of plural societies must have sufficient grasp and appreciation of the plurality of cultures which constitute modern nations so that diverse ethnic, religious, racial and social groups may automatically participate in and develop their own culture and special interests, within the limits of the laws of a common civilization of a nation. In a plural society administrators and police personnel should be acutely conscious of their creative role in the healthy development of the pluralists state-system in modern time necessitates a more complex theoretical frame of reference for the understanding of the ethnocentric process than what is available in the social science today...... deeper understanding of the social reality of ethnocentrism should dictate policies" which are more relevant and in conformity with the pluralist state ideology.[52] Legacy of exploiting issues for short-term political gains must be put aside for a politics of consensus to re-establish a dialogue between different groups in a plural society. Management of conflicts need a very scientific and pragmatic approach by the State and the Central government.

Prof. Amartya Sen said it was the practice of this pluralism that had been deeply threatened by some recent political developments, particularly by sequence of violent events at Ayodhya in December 1992.[53] More than 150 places of workship were razed and 90 people killed in Assam violence following Ayodhya developments. Meanwhile Bangladesh immigrants added a new dimensions to the infiltration problem. The agitation for Bodoland has resulted in violence in Assam. According to figures given by the Rajya Sabha in April 1989, the Bodos had succeeded in killing 62 people in terrorist attacks with hundred of others dying in related violence. Since 1989 at least 600 people have died in Bodo-related violence.[54] The evolution of ULFA is rooted in the failure of the Government to address ethnic conflicts in Assam adequately and ultimately operation Bajrang and operation RHINO where carried out by the Army and Central Police Organisations. Results of operations are given below :[55]

Categories	*Operation Bajrang*	*Operation RHINO*
ULFA Activists Killed	15	-
ULFA Activists held	2867	4212
Weapons seized	1208	850
Cash recovered	Rs. 5 Crores	Rs. 64 Lakhs
Ammunition recovered	-	9946 rounds

The extremist violence in Tripura has been presenting a serious challenge and the All Tripura Tribal Force (ATTF) has been responsible for killing of 22 persons, looting market and banks and extorting money from transporters since April 1993.[56] The victims of the ATTF's killing squads altogether 137 in the last four years have been seriously threatening the internal security of the state. A proper solution to ethnic conflicts has to be found through political process and balanced economic growth of the country. The spreading rot in the Indian socio-political system is finding crass display in the increasing conflicts of our plural society. The functioning of the various organs of the state including the instruments of law and order as well as criminal justice system, is such that they have lost their credibility. The security situation within the country continues to deteriorate but no comprehensive strategic policies seem to emerge. The entrenched vested interests at different levels and points in the social order, economic structure, political alignments and administrative set are visibly weakening, indeed undermining, the plural democratic system of India, "The present government decided to set up a security council to deal with the increasing security problems but nothing of the sort has happened so far ".[57]

Experience the world over, demonstrates that for effective management of conflicts of plural societies, a clear policy can help. "If your policy changes from incidents to incident then you have already lost" In India unfortunately, the government is doing exactly that. It vacillates between softness and sternness having in the process the worst of both". Communal, ethnic and social conflicts have been with us for last four and half decades but inspite of these experiences, lessons have not been learnt and no comprehensive strategy evolved to prevent or combat conflicts. Except for empty rhetoric, nothing is being done to permanently cure the diseased base of our politico-social order. On the other hand politics is becoming more exploitative, criminalized and unaccountable to the people and economy more and more lop-sided, imbalanced and nihilistic forces is rendering the country incapable of solving, within reasonable time and at reasonable cost, any serious problems, of conflicts. It is time that we evolve a comprehensive strategy to eliminate the root causes of various conflicts from the plural society and meet the challenges thrown by various types of conflicts by adopting a well structured politics social strategy having short term and long term action plans as their essential components. The short term measures should includes putting strong and sustained pressure on the leaders of the various conflict groups and their collaborators, denying them extra supply of oxygen through psychological operations and removing subverting elements. From the government and semi-government organisation; prosecuting speedily through the designated courts and providing the honourable time of retreat to all these willing to side with the government launching an educational blitz through media and ultimately exhibiting a firm united national will be resolve the conflicts in a democratic spirit. The long term measures should include fundamental reforms of Indian polity and socio-economic system, having a culture of constructivity creativity and compassion.[59]

The Accommodation of Conflicts by Political, Economic and Social Reforms

W. Arthur Lewis has been one of the first thinkers to pay attention to the crucial role of political institutions in plural societies, In his book politics in West Africa (1965) he argued that in a plural society it is necessary to share power and it can be done by suitable political institutions. The plural society goes back to the primary meaning of democracy and through proportional representation all parties can be offered seats in all decision making bodies including the cabinet itself.[60] Arend Lyphart has referred to several plural societies in Europe which have achieved stable democracy by consociational methods. The four characteristics of consociational democracy are:-

1. Government by a grand condition of the political parties of all significant segments of the plural society;
2. The mutual veto which serves as an additional protection of vital interests of minorities and other group;
3. Proportionality as principal standard of political representation; and
4. A high degree of autonomy for each segment to run its own internal affairs.[61]

Indian security forces must learn lessons from various case studies of armies involved in low intensity operations such as U.S.A., Israel, France, Canada and British forces. CRP, BSF, Assam Rifles, Intelligence Bureau,

Research & Analysis Wing and the Army must arrange special orientation to the officers and man posted in areas where LIC are to be handled.

Ethnic conflicts must be preceded by an understand of the sources and pattern of that conflict. Democratic approaches entail measures to contain, limit, channel and manage ethnic conflict rather than to eradicate it and this needs careful political engineering followed by a good dosage of balanced economic development of the area concerned. The Anglo American plural electoral system is not well suited to plural societies because it produces discrimination against small groups. A well structured federal system with balanced economic growth and healthy spirit of consociational democracy can alone accommodate all conflicts of plural societies. Federalism can be used as a consociational method when plural societies want to live together by having political engineering to mitigate political, ethnic or economic conflicts. Some social scientists believe that the use of consociational methods can mitigate conflicts in plural societies.[62] Radical political, economic and social reforms with a spirit of the accommodation of conflict help the key in plural societies. The parliamentary system of government is better suited to plural societies because it makes possible to share the use of executive power among several groups. The success of failure of a plural society is principally related to the way in which all economic, intellectual and other power resources are distributed among competing groups in a fair and just manner. In India, the political institutions established by 1950 constitution have been sufficiently suitable to maintain a federal, democratic and plural society although not without serious conflicts but it seems that they have also caused malfunctioning over the years which could be corrected or mitigated by progressive institutional reforms in political, economic and social system. Democratic sharing of power on more or less equitable and just basis would strengthen the Indian socio-political system and mitigate various emerging ethnic, religious and social conflicts. The Centre-State relations and the nature of Indian federalism need fresh look in this context so that aspirations of all segments of the society are fulfilled.

Concluding Remarks

Where nations can flounder through internal or external conflicts, they can also grow in strength and stature when there is suitable resolution of conflicts. Half the battle is won if one were to foresee an approaching conflict situation and plan in advance to forestall it and be adequately prepared to resolve and sublimate the conflict situation.[63] Intelligence agencies and policy planners have an important role in combating conflicts. Unity in diversity and principle of co-existence along with open discussions for conflict resolutions are essential for a plural society which is wedded to the ideals of democracy, secularism, social justice and federalism. What is needed today is sound political leadership, combined with a strong vision of a secular, democratic and progressive nation, if India is to come in terms with the caste, ethnic, communal and religious conflicts which at times appear to tear the very fabric of our plural society apart by the frightening intensity of their outbreaks. The challenge in the years ahead will be to mould a frame of participative democracy that will accommodate the various interests of a multi-ethnic, multi-lingual and multi-religious plural society and allow federalism to develop in favour of devolution of power to the states and decentralisation of political authority to the Panchayat Raj institutions.[64] This should be a matter of concern to every Indian: how can we protect out plural society from endemic conflicts and ensure social justice to all citizens. At the grass root level, low intensity operations are generally to be carried out at company platoon or battalion level by highly trained and highly mobile special force equipped with modern sophisticated weapons and means of communication. The future generation of managers of LIC must understand that "as was between states exists through one side of history's revolving door, low intensity conflict among different organizations (and societies) will enter through the other.[65] For effectively dealing with low intensity conflicts, psychological operations and warfare by unconventional methods by specially trained, equipped and motivated security forces have to be carried out along with political economic, social measures. Many conflicts have been resolved in India in the past by political settlement and negotiations by mature political leadership and visionary leaders of the ethnic groups.

References

1. Lewis A. Coser, The Functions of Social Conflict, 1956, pp. 151-156.
2. Lewis A. Coser, "The functions of Social Conflict", 1956, p. 156.
3. Talcott Parson, *Social System*, Routledge & Kegan Paul Ltd. London 1956, pp. 227-28.
4. See for further details Stuart Chase-Roads to Agreement London: Ross Stragner(ed). The Dimensions of Human Conflict Distreit 1967; Harold Lasswell, Psychology and Politics, Chicago, 1930; T.W. Aderne, The Authoritarian Personality, New York, 1956; Kenneth Boulding, Conflict and Defense, New York, 1962; Abram Kardiner and Lienel Oversey, The Mark of Oppression, New York 1951.
5. For further details see George Sunimel Conflict Illusations 1955; Lewis A. Coser, Functions of conflict, London 1905; Lewis A. Coser,

Functions of Conflict, London 1956; Ralf : Dharendof, Class and class conflict in Industrial Society; London, 1959.

6. Karl Marx ; The Proverty of Philosophy in *Mar-Engels —Selected works,* Vol. 4, Moscow 1976.
7. Karl Marx, Preface to a contribution to the critique of Political Economy in *Mar-Engels-Selected Works,* Vol. I, Moscow 1951.
8. Lewis a Coser in Social Aspects of Conflict in International Encyclopedia of the Social Science, Vol. 3 & 4 Complete and Unabridged-Edited by Davis L. Sills, London 1972, p. 232.
9. Rabushka and Shepsle-*Politics in Plural Societies-A Theory of Democratic Instability,* 1972 pp. 20-21, 62.
10. *Hindustan Times,* 3 July 1993, p. 4. New Delhi.
11. Prof. Amartya Sen's lecture on "Indian Pluralism". *Hindustan Times,* 3 July 1993, New Delhi.
12. Rajni Kothari-Pluralism and Secularism; Lessons of Ayodhya. *Economic and Political Weekly,* Dec. 19-26, 1992. p. 2696
13. Prof. Amartya Sen's Lecture on "Indian Pluralism". *Hindustan Times,* 3 July 1993, New Delhi. p. 4.
14. Yogendra Singh-(1959) Group States of Faction in Rural Community. *Journal of Social Sciences,* Vol. I, p. 61.
15. Baljit Singh (1961) Next step in village India-A Study of Land Reforms and Group Dynamics, Bombay 1961, pp. 108-120.
16. Dr. B. Varma-*Insurgency and Counter Insurgency,* Uppal Publishing House, New Delhi-1988 p. 31
17. Sam C. Sarkesian; *The American Response to Low Intensity conflict. The Formative Period in Armies in Low Intensity Conflicts-* Edited by David Charters and Maurice Tugwell Brassey's Defence Publisher/ London 1989, p. 45.
18. David Charter and Maurice Tugwell- *Armies in Low Intensity Conflict.*
19. Gallagher, CSM James. T-Low Intensity Conflict also United States Army Field Manual 100-2 "and Air Force Pamphlet" Military Operations in Low Intensity Conflict.
20. Michael L. Martin - From Algiers to N'Djamena Francis Adaptation to Low Intensity Wars 1830-1987. In Armies in *low-intensity conflict.* Edited by David Charters and Maurice Tugwell Brassey's Defence Publishers, London 1989, p. 87.
21. David A. Charter, from Palestine to Northern Ireland British Adaptation to Low-intensity operations in Armies in low intensity conflict (Edt.) Charter and Tugwell. Also K.M. Mathur *Internal Security Challenges and Police in a Developing Society.* RBSA Publisher, Jaipur.

21a. Sorabjee—Pota better than Tada. *Times of India,* New Delhi 23 April 2003. p. 4.

22. Dr. Krishna Mohan Mathur-*Management of Internal Security,* Gyan Publishing House, New Delhi, 1995, p. 128.

23. Gould, Merold A. Dimension and structural change in an Indian Kuiship system-A problem of conceptual Refinement in Milton Singer and Bernard Cohn (ed) Structure and change in Indian Society.
24. Yogendra Singh-Social Stratification and change in India, 1980, p. 48.
25. Dipankar Gupta-*Hierarchy and difference - An Introduction in Social Stratification* edited by Dipankar Gupta, 1992, p. 18.
25a Col. A.K. Bhargav-Counter-Insurgency OPS-College of Defence Management Project-Report on Decision support System for LIC operations 1995-Also Banerjee, utpal, K, "Operational Analysis and Indian Defence-concepts publishing House New Delhi 1980.
26. B.K. Roy Burman - *Indigenous peoples and their Quest for Justice*. Social Action 39, Jan-March (1988).
27. B.K. Roy Burman- *Issues in Land Reforms in N.E. Tribal Areas-Mainstream,* Aug. 1 and 8 (1987).
28. Indian Express, 20/8/1993. Lok Sabha Questions.
29. Tatu Vanhamen- "Politics of Ethnic Nepotism- India as an Example."
30. For Similar views see Lt. General V.K. Nayar-Threat from Within-India's Internal Security Environment, Lancer, 1992, p. 250.
31. Source - *The Times of India* (Ahmedabad Edition), January 24 April 13, 1981. quoted by Pradip Kumar Bose- Social Mobility and caste violence - A Study of the Gujarat Riots - in *Caste, Caste Conflict and Reservation* 1985. Centre for Social Studies, Surat p. 144.
32. Tatu Vanhamen - *Politics of Ethnic Nepotism - India as an example*. Sterling Publishers Pvt. Ltd., New Delhi, 1991, p. 127.
33. Raj Chengappa and Ramesh Menon. The New Battle Fields. *India Today,* Jan 31, 1993.
34. See Dr Krishna Mohan Mathur, *Police, Law and Internal Security*, Gyan Publishing House 1993 and Also Rajya Sabha Questions.
35. Arvind N. Das-Maths of the Aftermath - Monday Dec. 21, 1992. *The Times of India*, New Delhi.
36. *The Hindu*, Delhi 19 August 1993.
37. V.K. Sood-*Low Intensity Conflict: The source of the Third World Instability Studies* in Conflict and Terrorism Vol.15. No. 4 Oct-Dec 1992 Crane Russak London, p. 233.
37a Rajat Pandit-Terror in J&K-*Time of India*. New Delhi-7th March 2003.
38. V.D. Chopra-*Genesis of Indo-Pakistan conflict in Kashmir*, New Delhi 1989 Chapter-2.
39. No Solution yet of ethnic unrest. *Hindustan Times* 31 December 1992.
40. Padam Rosha-Kashmir Policy-An Appraisal-*Hindustan Times*, 28 August 1993, p. 13.
41. Questions in Rajya Sabha-Mr. Sitaram Kesri told R.S. *Hindustan Times,* 22 August 1993.

42. *The Hindu*, Delhi 19 August 1993.
43. See W. Arthur Lewis. *Politics in West Africa,* 1965, pp. 55-74.
44. A rend Lyphart-Democracy in Plural Societies; a comparative exploration 1980-1977.
45. Linz, Jain J. (1984), Democracy Presidential or Parliamentary; Does it make a difference? Paper for the workshop on Political parties in Southern Cone, Washington.
46. Harold Koontz, Cyrial O. Donnel and Heinz, Weihrich-Management-M. C. Grain Hill Instructional Book Company Eight Edition 1984-86, p.75.
47. *The Hindu,* 21 January 1988, *Insurgency in North East.*
48. Justice Reddy Report into the Communal disturbances at Ahmedabad and other places 1969. Govt. of Gujarat 1970, p. 215-16.
49. Ratna Naidu- *The Communal Edge to plural societies-India and Malaysia*-Vikas Publishing House, Ghaziabad, 1980, p. 123.
50. For a detailed analysis-Dinesh Kumar-Low Intensity War Takes High Toll-*The Times of India,* 29 Dec. 1995.
51. Ratna Naidu-*The Communal Edge to Plural Society* 1980, p. 131.
52. Ratna Naidu-*The Communal Edge to Plural Societies-India and Malaysia*-1980, pp. 147-148.
53. Prof. Amartya Sen's Lecture on Indian Pluralism, *Hindustan Times,* 3 July 1993, New Delhi.
54. *India Today* April 30, 1989, p. 58.
55. *India Today,* January 15, 1992.
56. Indian Express-Violence in Tripura-Editorial, 30 July 1993.
57. A disturbing Security Scenario-Rajendra Nath. *The Tribune,* 26 August 1993 p. 8.
58. Jagmohan- Terrorism-Causes and Cure. *Hindustan Times,* 25 November 1992.
59. For similar views see Jagmohan Terrorism-Causes and Cure. *Hindustan Times,* 25 November 1992.
60. Lewis, W. Arthur (1965), *Politics in West Africa London* George Allen and Unwin, pp. 57-74.
61. Arend Lyphart-1980/1977-*Democracy in Plural societies. A Comparative Exploration*-London, pp-1-60.
62. For Similar views see Donald L. Horowitz-1985. *Ethnic groups in conflict* Berkely pp. 568-576. Nohlen Dieter 1988-Electoral system between science and fiction.
63. J.N. Nanda- *Conflict and Co-existence in India*. Concepts, New Delhi, 1991, p. 139.
64. For similar views see Alexandra George-*Social Ferment in India.* Orient Longman, 1986, p. 324.
65. Cleveld, Martin Van, "On Future War", p. 224.

6

Organisational Role Stress in Police Work

"Not all stress is bad. Stress is like a violin string. If there is no tension, there is no music. But if the string is too tight, it will break. You have to find the right level of tension for you-the level that lets you make harmony in your life" Dr. Allen Elkin.

H. Selye (1980) has written that stress suffers from the mixed blessing of being too well-known and too little understood.[1] During the last thirty-five years the popular interest in stress is growing and search is going on for a general model of stress response to the recognition of the importance of individual response patterns to specific stressers. A very important factor in the individual's response to stress involves the person's appraisal of the stresser and the manner in which the person "copes" with the situation. Stress is a highly individual, complex, multi-casual and interactive psychological and physiological phenomenon. Stress arises as a result of interaction of an individual with his/her environment. According to Prof. H.J. Eysenck, The concept of stress cannot be understood without reference to strain, the former being the stimulus, objectively measurable and identical for all individuals and the latter being the response of a given individual, frequently different from one individual to another.[2] The relationship between stress and strain can be in terms of a system of individual differences pertaining to neuroticism- stability and extraversion-introversion. Organisational stress can be compared to the electricity voltage. Given the right voltage, it can make the bulb illuminate but if the voltage is higher than the bulb can take, it can burn out the bulb. Similarly appropriate stress can bring effectiveness in a person but too much stress can cause burn out. Stress generally for a common man denotes unpleasant physical and mental reactions and in the field of organisational psychology, the stress concept obtained its own position under the label "Organisational Stress".[3] Organisational stress in police work in India is gradually increasing due to its complex role in a fast changing socio-political and economic environment in which police have to perform their duties. Stress is "essentially reflected by the rate of all the wear and tear caused by life".[4] Not many scientific studies have been carried out in India about police organisational stress, but researches carried out abroad indicate that police work is a high-stress occupation.[5] The following signs of stress, although not exhaustive gives a number of common stress indicators: (1) Pounding of the heart; (2) Dryness of throat and mouth; (3) Inability to concentrate; (4) Tendency to tire easily and to feel stale; (5) Feelings of dizziness or weakness; (6) Feelings of tension and being "keyed up"; (7) Feelings of generalized anxiety; (8) Trembling or shakiness; (9) Insomina; (10) Sweating; (11) Frequent need to urinate; (12) Stomach upset, indigestion diarrhea; (13) Migraine headaches; (14) Pain in the neck or lower back; (15) Increased smoking, drinking or use of drugs or medications; (16) Night mares; (17) Accident-proneness and (18) Depression.[6] These signs of stress can be easily perceived and noticed in Indian Police personnel who are generally working beyond normal duties hours almost everyday to carry out their various assigned duties. During the last three decades there have been a spate of writings on managerial and executive stress in India and abroad.[7] Burn out effect of stress can be noticed in police officers as a result of high stress level and not properly coped with, resulting in exhaustion, irritation, ineffectiveness and problems of health like hypertension, ulcers, etc. Rosenman R.H. and M. Friedman have found that people can be divided into two broad personality types and their behaviour patterns are characterized as under[8].

Type A Personality	*Type B Personality*
1. Ambitious wins	1. Seldom becomes impatient
2. Intense drive	2. Are not compulsive about use of time
3. Aggressiveness	3. Have more time for leisure
4. Competitiveness	4. Are less competitive
5. Pressure to get things done	5. Speak more quietly
6. Habitually pitting oneself against the clock	6. Are not concerned with constant and rapid achievement.
7. Obvious restlessness	7. Take enough time to make decisions carefully.

Dr Pragya Mathur Kumar in her book Stress in Police in India has carried out a detailed study of stress in police taking a sample of 252 serving personnel.[8a]

Many police officers in India, who has 'A' type personality, have been undergoing varying degrees of organisational stresses depending on their role and organisational environment. The hypothesis that some diseases are caused by stress and may be related to certain aspects of personality, has been widely accepted although the evidence for it is not always very cônvincing. It has been found that personality traits exert a mediating influence on the relation between stressors and strains.[8b]

Case Studies. On 23 May 2003 CISF Constable Raj Namdeo, posted at Mumbai Airport killed his senior officer AR Karandekar and detained six of his colleagues for six hours as hostages for not being sanctioned leave. On 24 May 2003 Assistant Inspector of Police Prashant Sawant, aged 39, shot dead his wife and son before shorting himself in his flat at chembur. Both cases show stress in police force.

Organisational Role/Stress

In police organisations, severity of stress differs from person to person and rank to rank. Severity of stress refers to the degree of disruption in the system that will occur if the individual fails to cope with the adjustive demands of the intensity, duration and magnitude of stress. The severity of stress, in turn, is determined primarily by three factors: the characteristics of the adjustive demand; the characteristics of the individual personality and the external resources and supports available to him.[10] The severity of cumulative stresses on an individual can be assessed by a variety of physiological and psychological measures including autonomic and cortical changes, level of muscle tension rating scales and self-assessment personality tests like K.S.P. The personality of an individual is an important factor in the development of stress. The Michigan group especially (e.g., French and Caplan 1972) Kalin in 1964 developed concepts such as role conflicts, role ambiguity and role over-load having direct bearing on stress. In police organisations, there is lot of stress on police personnel because of role conflicts, role overload and role ambiguity particularly in a democratic country wedded to the ideals of economic liberalism, social justice and democracy. Not all police officers will experience a given job situation as stressful, nor will a given policeman experience all job situations as equally stressful. Stress generally occurs when the abilities of a policeman are not congruent with the demands of the job environment or where clear obstacles exist in fulfilling strong needs or values. Stress is a dynamic psycho-physiological process, intervening between stimulous and response. Stress occurs when there is an imbalance between environmental demand and the response capability of the individual policeman. In Police organisations the level of stress differs in various ranks depending on the type of personality, his status, his responsibilities. Generally police officers of various ranks in India face following sources of stressful situations:

1. Stress within the person's system, which he brings with him such as his value system, family background and perceptual style when he joins the police organisation.
2. Stress arising from interpersonal relations within the police organisational environment and socio-political environment of the society.
3. Stress arising from hostile and unhospitable physical cultural and social environment in which policeman has to perform his duties.
4. Stress arising from tasks jobs and responsibilities assigned to the policeman.
5. Role based stress arising out his multi-dimensional roles as Police Officer.
6. Stress intrinsic to the behaviour setting of the police job such as the effects of over-crowding, noise pollution, air pollution and traffic hazards.

Organisational stress in police and Central police forces leads to suicides and depressions. On 18 May 2003, Shri Mohinder Singh Dy. Commandant 131 Bn. CRP, who was deployed at airport security duty at Dinapur Committed suicide by use of his service revolver due to serious stress and depression.

Generally there are there types of response to stress: emotional, behavioural and physiological. The most obvious is the emotional response like annoyance, rage or fear. The second type of stress response is change in performance or behaviour like increase in rate of error. The third type of response to stress is a physiological change; it can be psychologically induced illness. Stress can be a contributing factor in headache, back-aches, ulcers and even heart-diseases. The Police officers obviously have no control over various sources of stressful situations. Use of excessive force, resort to excessive sick leave, claims for faked injuries, excessive drinking in spare time, getting out of touch with family, causing spouse to call station to inquire or complain about him, continual behaviour requiring frequent internal investigation are some of the noticeable symptoms which often appear in the behaviour of police officers as a result of stress overload.[11] In police work most job tension results from suspense, excitement, anger, fear or anxiety when police men go out on patrolling activities. In police duties at the grass root level a perceived job threat is anxiety—a state of uneasiness or apprehension about future happenings whose course seems unpredictable. Prof. Udai Pareek in India has developed and standardized the organisational role stress scale to measure role stresses.[12] In all organisations there are inherent problems in the performance of various roles and therefore stress becomes inevitable. Organisational role stressors in police work can be broadly analysed as under:

1. ***(SRD) Self Role Distance:*** In police organisations, police officers very often find conflict of their values and self-concepts with the requirements of the organisational role. There are large number of honest, sincere and upright police officers who do not want to use third degree methods of interrogation, use of excessive force to disperse unlawful assembly burking or minimising of offences while recording of all first information reports but the organisational compulsions compel them to do so. Such officers suffer from stress created by self-role distance. Local politicians and corrupt senior police officers want police to connive against offences like prostitution, gambling, smuggling, black marketing, boarding child marriage, dowry deaths' etc on the assurance of protection social proferment and even pecuniary gains but honest and upright police officers find such political pressures as cause of stress since they do not want to succumb to such wrong practices.
2. ***(IRD) Inter-Role Distance:*** Police officers find inter-role distance when there are conflicts between the organisational role and other roles and when he is unable to properly divide time between work demands and family demands. Police Officers of Central Police Organisations like CRPF, BSF, CISF, ITBP have to generally leave family at their homes due to non-availability of adequate family accommodation. Even exigencies of services and long hours of work compel police officers to neglect their duties towards their families and this creates inter-role distance. A primary concern of police officer is that it is very difficult to maintain relations with non-police friends or communicate with non-police in general and as a

result frequently he loses his non-police friends and gets socially isolated. Frequent transfers, postings at far off places and non-availability of family accommodation or children education facility compels police officers to leave families home. This separated life creates its own stresses for both the policemen and their families. Most of the police officers and officers of Central Police Organisations are unable to plan social events, unable to attend to social obligations and don't see enough of children due to pressures of police work and absence from home.

3. ***(RI) Role Isolation:*** In Police organisations there are many occasions and situations when there is lack of linkages of one's role with other role in the organisation. Skolnick has suggested that danger and authority combine to isolate the police from the rest of society. Police Officers generally get alienated from the society because many citizens slur contacts with policemen whose work is often tainted with ugliness, evil and danger. In insurgency effected areas police and security forces have to keep their movements and plans secret and therefore generally they have camps away from the villages and towns. Such security forces camps create isolation in the men deployed for such duties. Officers and men of Central Police Organisations like CRPF, BSF and ITBP feel role isolation when they serve in north-eastern states of Assam, Nagaland, Mizoram, Manipur, Tripura and Arunachal Pradesh for many long years. Lack of adequate transport and railway facilities hostile and hazardous environment and camp life away from the people bring role isolation and causes deep psychological stress when they are unable to attend to their social obligations and even family commitments. Research studies indicate that in several ways, the individual police officers perceive that their own organisation fail to treat them as professionals and a strong role isolation feeling is experienced by the police officers.

4. ***(RA) Role Ambiguity:*** In Police organisations there is lack of clarity about expectations of others from the police and there is also lack of feedback on how police performance is regarded by others. There is role ambiguity as various thinkers, philosophers and people perceive different roles for the police.[13] The role of police has become increasingly diverse,

challenging and complex in a fast changing democratic society like ours and this role ambiguity creates stress in police officers. An average policeman is expected to have a multi-faceted personality. "Role ambiguities of the police have a bearing on the legal, administrative and public expectations from the police but these role ambiguities make it difficult to assimulate and accommodate their various roles to conflicting demands and public expectations, resulting in creating physiological and psychological stress upon the police. Different sections of the society have different concepts about the role of police and there is a good deal of confusion, both within and outside the police organisation, as to the precise role which police are expected to enact and the priorities of their varied roles.[14] Because of the wide range of discretionary authority wielded by the police in the field, he is peculiarly vulnerable to reprimand or censure for making mistakes and therefore role ambiguity causes lot of stress.

5. ***(REC) Role Expectations Conflict:*** Situations in which police officers are caught between conflicting orders role conflict and job related tensions are almost twice as prevalent and role conflict has been found to correlate more consistently with anxiety, irritation and depression. In police service, most of the officers find that conflicting demands are made by different persons in the organisation. Kalin (1964) has described role conflict as the simultaneous occurrences of two (or more) set of pressures, such that compliance with one would make more difficult compliance with the other".[15] Critical and dangerous situations in which police officers are caught between conflicting orders are too many in modern day life. Role expectation conflict has been explained by Ben Bhitaker when he said: "We expect a policeman to be human and yet inhuman, we imply him to administer the law and yet ask him to waive it. We resent him when he enforces a law in our own cases yet demand his dismissal when he does not enforce it elsewhere, we offer him to be a member of society and yet not to share its values".[16] There is a conflict between policeman's legal duty and his sense of compassion when he finds a semi-naked, sick and feeble starving man committing theft of a few loaves of bread to feed his famished children. Role conflict may arise when a police officer tries to please too many bosses or is

pressured to bend the law in favour of influential people. The police have to make a difficult choice in resolving the conflict between the dignity of the individual and the security of the society because of the job stress, police sub-culture organisational structure and power dynamics.[17]

6. ***(RI) Resource Inadequancy:*** In most of the police organisations, there is non-availability of adequate resources needed for effective role performance. Resources deficiencies at the grass root level relate to the totally inadequate financial resources in the shape of a duly authorised imprest amount in a police station to meet the expenditure on several legitimate needs such as stationary even to meet the minimum needs of scriptory work, expenditure on feeding prisoners in police custody, transport of dead bodies from distant places for post-mortem examination at the station headquarters, refreshment and transport charges for witnesses who attend Courts, etc. Indequacy of transport for movement of police sub-inspectors and Inspectors, lack of facilities of forensic science laboratories, inadequacy of communication and telephone facilities, lack of modern equipment, arms and ammunition are some of the inadequacies of resources which cause stress in police work. Mobility of police can not be enhanced in the absence of adequate transport facilities to the police. Non-availability of typewriters and tape recorders at the police station level causes loss of stress to the investigating officers. The police plead helplessness in the face of laws that openly distrust them; that make it, in several cases, impossible for them to discharge their duties.[18] Resource inadequacies are cause of various serious stress situations in police work.

7. ***(PI) Personal Inadequacy:*** With the fast changing socio-political changes the nature of crime is also changing. Police officers often find lack of knowledge skills or adquate preparation to be effective in their assigned roles-/"A number of IPS Officers find themselves as misfits in the jobs entrusted to them. They neither have the training nor the aptitude for these jobs. Imagine the lot of an officer leading his team in an encounter against the terrorists, who neither has the physical courage, nor the reflexes nor the confidence to handle fire arms and other equipments.[19] Such personal inadequacies are bound to create stress in police officers. All police officers

need reorientation courses, refresher courses to equip and train them in new skills, knowledge, attitudes and use of newly acquired equipments. Training in crowd control, terrorism and anti-terrorist operation, handling of communal riots and police community relations is required at the level of Inspectors, Sub Inspectors and other senior officers. Personal inadequacies in terms of knowledge of field craft and tactics for anti-insurgency and anti-terrorist police operations, lack of practical expertise in use of weapons, computers and sophisticated communication systems have been noticed in large number of police officers. Our entire police training has to be geared and there is a need to improve the training standards in the police.[20]

8. ***(RS) Role Stagnation:*** There are in police organisations very few opportunities for learning and growth and very often police officers find their role as stagnating and stressful. The vast majority of police officers start and end their careers as police Constables. Opportunities for promotion to higher ranks are very limited and promotions take long years and the promotional processes itself at time lack fairness and objectivity. As the police constables grow physically they expect career advancement with the passage of time and when they find no opportunities or very limited opportunities for promotions, they start suffering from stagnation. In Central Police Organisations like C.R.P.F., B.S.F., C.I.S.F., I.T.B.P. and others even at the senior supervisory rank, officers originally belonging to the Central Police Organisations, find role stagnation since they find very limited scope for promotions. Role stagnation includes stress related to career progression which is very clearly evident in police organisations from the grass root level to Inspectors' level in State Police Organisations and even at Gazetted rank in Central Police Organisations due to absence of IPS Cadre for CPOs. Most of the officers belonging to Central Police Organisations suffer from stress due to role stagnation.

9. ***(RE) Role Erosion:*** With the improportionate increase in higher posts in police hierarchy district level police officers feel role erosion. There is a general feeling in police officers particularly at the S.P. level that many important functions have been taken away from them and they feel that their powers

have been taken away by their superior officers. Role erosion is the subjective feeling of the police officer that some important role expectations he has in his role, do not match with the expectations other roles have for him. In Central Police Organisations earlier, recruitment and promotions upto certain ranks used to be carried out by Commandants but now these powers have been taken away by the superior supervisory officers even without changing the existing rules. Such role erosion creates organisation stress in Central Police Organisations. Role erosion causes stress in police officers when they perform the duties which they were performing in their lower ranks before promotions to higher ranks.

10. ***(RO) Role Overload:*** Role overload means "a condition in which the individual is faced with a set of obligations which, taken as a set, requires him to do more than he is able to in the time available."[21] Role overloads obviously have to do with lack of time and too many activities. When too many tasks are expected from some one we speak of quantitative overload and when an individual has to perform tasks which demand qualitatively more work, we speak of qualitative overload. A police station house officer is supposed to control a fire at 6 AM, provide assistance to injured scooter driver at 7AM, investigate murder case at 8 AM, collect intelligence about terrorist activities at 9 AM, supervise VIP Police Bandobast at 10 AM, provide dynamic leadership to deal with students at 11AM, handle a communal riot situation at 11.30 AM, attend to court work at 12.30 PM, and disposal of the grievances of the public from 2 PM and supervise to his office work at 4 PM. How do you expect a police station house officer to do so many roles and jobs in one day? The long and irregular hours of duties of the policemen, absence of time and facilities for regaining mental balance or healthy physical exercise result in psychological stresses upon the policemen. It has been established that organisational stressors have the strongest negative effects on police personnel, regardless of rank and age.

Role Stress studies In Police Needed

In modern life, pollution, noise,urbanisation, industrialisation and socio-economic complexity in human life are some of the reasons for rising stress. In an urban life when the telephone goes out of order, power is shut down, water supply is often disrupted, an expected promotion is denied, children perform poorly at schools, prices of essential commodities increase disproportionate to the income, etc, stress becomes inevitable.The term stress when applied to an organisational setting can be described as organisational stress. Udai Pareek has,in relation to organisational role, suggested ten stresses as worth considering.[22] In police organisations Role Ambiguity and Role Expectation Conflict (REC) are caused when the role boundaries and the expectations from various role senders lack clarity and precision. Organisational stress can be measured through psychological instruments which can have high reliability and validity and even detailed norms have been worked out for different types of organisations. Such studies and researches need to be carried out in Police Organisations with the help of Organisational Roles scale developed by Udai Pareek of Indian Institute of Health Management Research, Jaipur. National Institute for Mental Health Bangalore has also carried out a study of police stress and its impact on health of police personnel in India. Dr Pragya Mathur Kumar and Parviz Talili have also done research on police stress.[22a]

According to Parviz Talib ORS Scores for Police Personnel in his research were as under:[22a]

	Stressors	*Mean N-178*	*SD*	*Rank*
A	IRD	12.04	4.71	1
B	RS	9.51	5.03	5
C	REC	8.67	4.31	6
D	RE	10.76	4.24	3
E	RO	7.35	5.09	9
F	RI	10.03	4.22	4
G	PI	6.98	4.75	10
H	SRD	8.37	4.57	7
I	RA	7.70	4.47	8
J	RIN	11.06	4.05	2
Total		92.47	29.88	

Police personnel undergo intense stress, when they see their colleagues and co-wokers injured or killed during performance of duties.779 police personnel of various ranks were killed and 5,788 were injured in the country while preforming different types of duties during 1990. Of these, persons killed 356 were killed by 'other criminals'and 238 lost their lives in accidents which account for 45.7 and 30.6 per cent of the total deaths respectively. Rankwise 485 policemen of the rank of Constable lost their lives, which constitutes 62.3 per cent of the total number of policemen injured during the year 1990, 3888, i.e., 67.2 per cent were injured by "the riotous mobs''. Among the states the highest casualty reported in Punjab (271) which alone account for 34.8 per cent of the total deaths in the country.There were as many as 2039 occasions when police had to ressort to firing which resulted in deaths of 1182 civilians and 158 policemen. Police personnel undergo severe stress when they go out for controlling riotous mobs and anti-terrorist duties. Police personnel, who are the helpless witnesses of the ghastly scenes of tens of people killed in a terrorist shootout in a train or in some area can never forget the ghastly sight. A police guard standing alone in a platoon post in a distant land away from civilisation amidst Jungle area has to spend nights keeping vigil for others after nights away from their families. The unfriendly hostile locals, the unfamiliar and often hazardous terrain and extreme weather conditions which call for undaunted courage and fearless determination tend to take their toll on the mental and physical health of the policemen involved in fighting insurgents in North Eastern States of Nagaland, Mizoram, Tripura, Manipur and Assam. The Indian policemen are constantly facing rapid social changes such as breakup of joint family system, which gave security, increasing mental conflicts, and social disorders and these social changes have brought in their walk a number of stresses for them. Police in India, particularly, after independence, generally suffer from serious chronic stress due to job-ambiguity, conflicting values negative police image and job overload. Life threatening situations create serious stress over the police personnel particularly when they have a feeling of economic insecurity for their families and dependents. Officers and men of Central Police Organisations like CRPF and BSF remain under severe stress when they are deployed in violence ridden areas of north-eastern States, Punjab and Kashmir. In the recent past the magnitude and dimensions of stress have increased manifold and it is necessary that proper research is carried out in this important area. Unless the police themselves become concerned with job stresses and its short-term and long-term consequences on police personnel, social scientists will not take up any worthwhile research in the field.The most common prevailing myth is that stress is a part of the police job, if you can't take the heat, get out of the kitchen". It occurs to one that many of the police reactions which mar with police image in the society, were the direct results of police stress, the result of the unresolved fears and conflicts which are experienced by the policemen in their daily life. Indian police is generally criticised as "trigger happy", but some seemingly over reactions to threats to their personal life in the midst of violent environment over really defensive reappraisals (making their internal conflicts caused by stressful environment and external stressors).Indian policeman are unfortunately trapped between the outdated laws and instructions of the past and the fast changing socio-economic and political environment were increasing violence, economic offences, disregard for laws and open defiance to the social norms are the grim realities of the time.

Recognition of Stress in Police

How do we recognise the presence of stress in the policemen who are putting on uniform, do not know how to communicate with others due to their strict norms of discipline and general social isolation from the society? How can we measure the magnitude of stress and their dimensions when policemen are constantly moved from place to place to maintain law and order in the society? How can we diagnose the seriousness of the stress of CRPF and BSF personnel who remain deployed in terrorist infested areas and on the Indian borders and who carry out their duties faithfully year after year in a most dedicated manner. For a very sincere and keen observer following happenings can give clues that the individual police personnel are experiencing stress.[23]

1. Growing indiscipline in the police force, particularly in lower ranks who face the brunt mostly.
2. Increasing cases of discharges from police and paramilitary forces like CRPF.
3. Growing number of voluntary retirement cases in Central Police Organisations and the police.
4. Policemen becoming gradually smelling of alcohol even on the job.
5. Individual policemen generally overstaying leave in spite of liberal grant of leave.
6. Excessive use of several packages of antacid per day by the policemen.
7. Increasing number of accidents including vehicle accidents.
8. Policemen having serious suicidal tendencies and having frequent

temper tantrums with spouses and family members.

9. Policemen who believe that anything they do to enforce the laws and maintain internal security is perfectly justified.
10. Police officers who always handle situations with physical violence with impunity when they could handle them by talking.
11. Police officers who have utter disregard to the rule of law and believe in use of force and extra-legal methods to control the crimes.

Sources of Police Stress

Besides Role stressor, the author has closely observed the sources of stress to the CRPF and BSF personnel deployed in Punjab, Kashmir, North-Eastern States and other parts of the country and has identified the following main sources:-

1. Traumatic events like witnessing the dead bodies of their colleagues.
2. Dead bodies of innocent people killed by terrorists and insurgents.
3. Separation from their families and children.
4. Irregular grant of leave and refusal of leave.
5. Involvement in armed encounters and constant threat of physical injuries and life.
6. Authoritative style of leadership.
7. Lack of proper communication even with own family members due to long distances.
8. Inadequate training and lack of specialised preparation to face situations.
9. Lack of adequate emotional support from peer group and superiors.
10. Job ambiguity and subordination to local police.
11. Indequate resources and inequities in pay and job status.
12. Job overloads and almost twelve hours of duty under hostile environment.
13. Lack of clarity of orders and conflicting values of the organisation.
14. Unresponsive administrative set up.
15. Too frequent movements and uncertainty of tenure of stay.
16. Inadequate career planning and lack of job satisfaction.
17. Inability to plan and carry out personal and social obligations due to frequent changes of deployment.
18. Non-recognition of their hard and praiseworthy achievements

on many occasions.

19. Lack of adequate marital life due to inadequacy of family accommodation.
20. Unreasonable demands and expectations regarding duties from operational authorities.
21. Constant threat to life and subsequent tension.

Civil Police personnel constantly face stress due to the following factors: I) Satisfying too many people, II) Too much responsibility, III) Lack of time, IV) Conflictual orders, V) Inherent in capability VI) Neglected family life, VII) Most unpredictable role of Police organization.[23a]

Stress in police and Central Police Organisations need to be given due attention and stress-coping strategies need to be adopted on priority basis in India. Immediate and long-term consequences of stress in police can be easily noticed by any observer. Police stress is effecting their personality, health, job performance and even home life to a great extent. Increase in smoking rate, headaches, blood pressures beyond normal range, ulcers, heart problems are too well-known effects of stress. Chronic depression, alcoholism, high suicide rate and accident rates, social alienation and psycho-somatic problems are easily detectable problems of police personnel, which need attention. Stress related diseases are higher among police personnel as compared to the rest of the society and hence immediate long-term and remedial steps should be taken for reducing the stress among police personnel.

Coping with Stress

Police organisations and state police should adopt a proper stress management planning at both organisational and individual levels. Effective self-management of stress has to be done by police personnel themselves to cope with their increasing stress. Organisations also have to adopt suitable strategies to reduce the stress and actively support self-management practices taken by organisational members. Individual police officers can adopt the following measures to overcome stress:

1. Avoid isolation and take active part in organisational activities by keeping open channels of communication with colleagues, friends and the members of the family.
2. Stay alert and take note of their health problems.
3. Keep away from alcohol and drugs.
4. Carry out regular physical exercise or Yoga or games.
5. Devote sometime for spiritual relaxation exercises/prayers or

meditation.

6. Ensure good and balanced diet and keep physical fitness.
7 Increase self-awareness and identify early warning signals of stress and adopt suitable coping strategies.
8. Ensure regular medical check up.
9. Regularly avail leave and spend sometime with members of the family.
10. Utilize psychological counselling services if afflicted by stress.
11. Self-education about causes of stress, accurate appraisal of one's stress level and ability to learn successful coping methods and ability to behave flexibly to carry out comprehensive self-stress management.

There are many forms of self-help techniques which may be used to counter act stress and deal with problems when they are recognised and controllable.[24]

Concluding Remarks

In India, police officers are today undergoing serious organisational stresses and there is need for proper scientific research by police scientists, sociologists and psychologists with an inter-disciplinary approach. Members of Central Police Organisations like CRP, BSF and ITBP have a very high stress level due to various organisational and structural factors coupled with environmental factors. In a plural developing democratic society like India, the Organisational stress of police organisations require constant in depth study and subsequent organisational level coping strategies to reduce the stress amongst the organisational members. One of the major research findings on stress is that those police officers who had prior warning of a potentially stressful situation experienced considerably less stress than those who did not when the adverse conditions were actually encountered. This research finding has numerous implications for the training and supervising of police personnel in India. It is recommended that basic training and in-service training programmes for police officers of all ranks should be so designed to assist the officers in both anticipating and coping with conditions that can result in increased tension and stress for them. Coping with job related stress on police officers should be a paramount research subject for the next decade.

References

1. H. Selye (1980). The stress concept Today in I.L Kutash and L.B. Schle Singer *Hand Book on Stress and Anxiety*-San Francisco california Jossey Brass, pp. 127-143.

2. H.J. Eysenck- Stress, Disease and Personality. "The Inoculation Effect"- in Stress Research - Edited by Cary L. Cooper 1983, p.140.
3. Kalin, R.L. and D.M. Quinn, R.P (1964) *Organisational Stress-Studies in role conflict and ambiguity*-New York, Wiley.
4. Hans Selye- *The stress of life,* New York : McGraw Hill 1978, p. 271.
5. Martin Reiser-Some Organisational stresses on policemen Journal of Police Science and Administration, Vol. 2 No. 2, (June 1974); Also William Kroe's Bruce Margolis and Joseph Hurrill Job Stress in Policemen - *Journal of Police Science and Administration,* Vol. 2., No. 2 June 1974.
6. Hans Selye: The Stress of Life, pp. 174-177.
7. For further reference see Cooper and Marshall (1978) understanding Executive Stress Mac Millan Press London; Cooper and Payne (1978) Stress at Work - John Wiley-Chichester; Kalim, Wolfe, Quirm and other & (1964) Organisational Stress: Studies in role conflict and ambiguity, Wiley- New York; Marshall and Cooper, (1979), Executive under pressure-A Psychological study (1979) Mac Millan London: Udai Pareek (1981) Role Stress Scales, Indian Institute of Management, Ahmedabad.
8. Roseman R.H. and Friedman M. (1974) -Type A Behaviour and your Heart.
8a Dr. Pragya Mathur Kumar-Stress in Police in India-Recognition, Diagnosis, and coping strategies-Gyan Publishing House, New Delhi. (1999)- p. 178.
8b. Pragya Mathur-Police Research and Development April-June 1995, pp. 37-40.
9. H.J. Eysenck- Stress disease and personality -The "Inoculation Effect" -Stress Research Edited by Cary L. Cooper, 1983, p. 121
10. Jaines C. Coleman-Life Stress and Maladaptive behaviour. *The American Journal of Occupational Therapy,* Vol. No. 27. Issue No. 4 pp. 169-180.
11. Dennis L. Rowlison - Management considerations to combat Police Stress. *Michigan Police Journal,* Vol.53, No. 1. Jan 1978, p. 4.
12. Pareek., U., "Inter-Role exploration in J.W. Pfeiffer and J.E Zones (Ed). *The 1976 Annual Hand Book for Group Facilitators*, Lajolla, California, 1976, pp. 211-224.
13. Dr. Krishna Mohan Mathur-Police in India—Problems and Perspectives, Gyan Publishing House, New Delhi, 1991, p. 295.
14. Dr. K.M. Mathur. The Problems of Police in a Democratic Society RBSA Publishers, S.M.S. Highways, Jaipur, 1987, p. 236.
15. Kalin R.L, Wolfe D.M. Quinn R.P. (1964) Organisational Stress-Studies in role conflict and ambiguity, NewYork, Wiley, p. 19.
16. Ben Whitaker-*The Police,* p. 216.

17. Dr. K.M. Mathur - *The Problems of Police in a Democratic Society,* RBSA Publishers SMS Highway, Jaipur, 1987, p. 90.
18. Eighty and concluding Report of the National Police Commission, Government of India, May 1981, Para 62.35. p. 24.
19. Ved Marwah P. Marwah Training and Police Performance-*SVP NPA Magazine,* Vol. 45, No. 1, January-June 1993.
20. Dr. K.M. Mathur—Internal Security Challenges and Police in a Developing Society, 1989, pp. 50-55.
21. Sales S.M. (1969)—Organisational role as a risk factor in coronary heart disease, *Adminisitrative Science Quarterly* 14- pp. 325-336.
22. For details see Udai Pareek—Making Organisational Roles effective. Tata Mc Graw Hill Publishing Company Ltd., New Delhi, 1993, p. 48.
22a Pragya Mathur Kumar-Stress in Police in India-Gyan Publishing House New Delhi (1996) Also Parvaiz Talib-Role stress among Police Pessonel-Indian Police Journal 48 (4) Oct.-Dec. 2001.
23. Dr. K.M. Mathur—Indian Police Role and Challenges. Gyan Publishing House.
23a. Channabasavanna, S.M. Chandra P.S. Gururaj G., Chaturvedi S.K. and Subbakrishnan D.K. (1996) Mental Health Problems among Police Personnel - An Epidemiological Study-Report submitted to the Bureau of Police Research and Development, MHA. Govt. of India, New Delhi p. 21. Pragya Kumar has identified major stressors for police for gazetted offices and other ranks of police-refer-Stress in Police in India —(1996)—Gyan Publishing House, New Delhi pp. 84-85.
24. Alma Rosser—Talking About Stress—*The Police Journal,* Vol. LXI, Number 4, Oct-Dec 1988, p. 332. Also Talib, Parvaiz:- Stresses afflicting Police Personnel-India Police Journal 48 (4) October-Dec 2001. p. 77-84.

7

The Human Rights and Operations by Security Forces of India

Human Rights Violations and Terrorism will be always remembered in U.S.A. with what was done to World Trade Centre on Sept. 11.2001. Similarly India will never forget Dec. 13, 2001 when five well armed terrorists attacked the Parliament of India. Thanks to security forces of India, terrorists plan failed, but it was an assault on the whole nation and an attack on human rights.

The concept of "human rights" is a value loaded concept and human right discourses may be moral or axiomatic, or covenantal ; or logic-rational or universe experiential, or political.[1] Unfortunately, the civil society in India takes the major blame for numerous human rights violations and passes the buck to the police, Central Police Forces, prisons and the armed forces of the country without even appreciating the difficult role and responsibilities of these system in the context of Indian policy. Indian political masters never accept their own responsibilities for the mess but always make police, security forces or someone else scapegoats. Complete collapse of the criminal justice system at times and in certain circumstances, lack of adequate written directives for dealing with violent movements, growing cult of violence, armed insurgencies and terrorism, brutalisation of police forces, individual aberration of over—enthusiatic members of the security forces, the indifferent and apathetic attitude of citizen and super-cop Psyche and lack of professionalism are mostly accountable for human rights violations in India. There are many critical situations wherein human rights ideology is uncalled for particularly when a nation's survival, sovereignty and integrity are involved. Human rights are not for total anarchy or complete collapse of civil society.[2] Internal security operations are generally carried out by CRPF, BSF, NSG,Assam Rifles with the assistance of Civil Police to control, search, combat, raid and eliminate insurgents, terrorists and militant gangs. Human Rights in areas of Terrorism and Insurgency are often elusive, confusing and complex. The 1994 United Nations declaration of measures to eliminate international terrorism has affirmed in its paragraph 3, that "Criminal acts intended or calculated to provoke a state of terror in the general public, a group of persons, or particular persons for political purposes are in any circumstances unjustifiable whatever the considerations of a political, philosophical, ideological, social, ethnic, religious or any other nature that may be invoked to justify them and such acts in all its forms and manifestations are activities aimed at destruction of human rights." India has paid a very heavy price in terms of life, property and security of the citizens for fighting the menace of insurgency and terrorism in various operational theatres. Central Reserve Police Force, Border Security Force, Assam Rifles and other Central State armed police forces are continuously engaged in carrying out internal security operations in India. The containment, control and eradication of terrorism is no easy task and its relationship with human rights is complex, particularly since those engaged in acts of terror are quick to seek the protection of precisely those rights that they violate without compunction and hold in contempt.[3] Human rights in India face the challenges of credibility, challenges of scale and expectations, challenge of variety, challenge of good governance and challenge of protecting the human rights of the security force personnel engaged in combating terrorism and insurgency. Regrettablly, the invocation of human rights is now also an intrinsic part of the political and psychological under currents of "War-by proxy" and " low intensity conflicts" carried out in north-eastern states of India and Jammu & Kashmir. India has been suffering grievously from terrorism of different shades - insurgency in Nagaland, Manipur, Tripura, Assam, terrorism by the Sikh terrorists during ninetees in Punjab and terrorism/Proxy War in the Kashmir Valley. According to National Humam Rights Commission Report, of all the assaults on human rights that the people of India have had to endure since independence, Proxy war of Kahmir have been most cynical and skillfully organised for political and propaganda effect.[4] Status have an obligation to eliminate terrorism and are called upon to take all necessary and effective methods of prevent, combat and eliminate all acts of terrorism. There is a need for a full, open and continuing dialogue involving members of the Police and Security Forces, political masters and policy makers. The acts and practices of terrorism in all its forms and manifestations ... are activities aimed at the destruction of human rights.[4a]

About forty thousand lives have already been lost as a result of terrorists violence in different parts 8 of the country and security forces have suffered very heavy casualties fighting the menace. During my service tenure nearlyfor thirty-four years as a CRPF Officer, I had the opportunity to serve in almost all the troubled theatres of India—Assam, West Bengal, Manipur, Nagaland, Mizoram, Tripura, Punjab and Kashmir and witness violations of human rights at close quarters. In J&K, 762 civilian were killed as a result of the acts of militants in the course of the year 2000. Of them 563 were Muslims. Kashmiri Pandits, more than 3 Lakhs, had to leave the valley due to terrorism.[4a] Unfortunately the national security system of India has grave deficiencies and the Subrahmanyam Committee report is worth quoting: "The political, bureaucratic, military and intelligence establishments appear to have developed a vested interest in the status quo. National security management recedes in the background in time of peace and is considered too delicate to be tampered with in time of war and proxy war". The security forces of India are always vulnerable to the charges of violations of human rights when they engage themselves in combating insurgency and terrorism. Police, the security forces and armed forces do deserve our appreciations for their difficult role and responsibilities in combating insurgencies and terrorism in north-eastern states and state of Jammu and Kashmir. During the period 1 January 1988 to 30 April 1997 the army suffered 1375 killed and 2237 injured in the Jammu and Kashmir Sector. In north-eastern states, the Army and Security Forces lost 459 personnel with 250 injured during the period 1 January 1995 to 30 April 1997. "The rights and responsibilities of security personnel must be clearly defined and not be subjected to policy vacillations or sudden change".[5] In J & K as many as 1341 security personnel and 2671 civilians had been killed in terrorists acts since 1999.

The U.S. Department report "Patterns of Global Terrorism" recognises that India continues to be the worst victim of terrorism. India was subjected to 67 terrorist attacks in 2002, compared to nine in Israel, eight in Pakistan and seven on the west Bank.[5a] The September 11, 2001 attacks have proved to the world that no amount of high tech devices can guarantee fool-proof security. The world now knows that 19 or 20 terrorists hijacked four American planes and flew them right into three of the best known global landmarks, the two World Trade Centre towers and the Pentagon. We all knew how USA has retaliated this attack of terrorists. Where was the question of human rights then? We can not afford to have double standards. Washington's inability to bring Bin Laden to book can be considered a victory for terrorism and US has failed to win the support of the people in Islamic Countries. Security forces all over the world have to take effective measures to control and contain terrorism, violence and mass destruction of property. In Punjab, Police, CRPF and security forces have been successful in effectively containing and liquidating the terrorists violence. In the unfortunate fallout of petty political backlash, there have been serious charges of violations of human rights against the security forces specially Police Officers who had battled against terrorism at the cost of loss of several lives for their members. State Police, CRPF, and Border Security Forces have to carry out anti-terrorist and counter-insurgency operations to combat terrorists. Road protection duties, combing and search operations, surprise raids, attacks and intelligence operations are part of routine duties of security forces. Generally security forces and intelligence agencies are not able to coordinate their activities and there is always inadequacy of timely intelligence and security forces have to face heavy casualties in terms of lives of personnel and injuries to the security personnel. Sporadic fighting and fierce encounters with terrorists and insurgencies have increased in recent years due to availability of most modern and latest weaponry and explosive to the terriorists. Leadership of security forces and police plays an important role in promoting and enhancing the morale and motivation of the security personnel. Security forces operate under great stresses and strains in terrorist infested areas due to long hours of work in hazardous terrains, inadequate training, shortage of equipment and transport and lack of latest weaponry and explosives.

There were over 2500 writ petitions filed in the Supreme Court and the Punjab and Haryana High Courts. More than half have been since disposed off, but about 1200 petitions are still pending and about 120 Police Officers including 6 Superintendents of Police are still pending and facing prosecution. Sekhar Gupta in Indian Express of 20 Aug' 1996 had raised some pertinent questions and issues: "It is incredibly and shamefully low of us to ask our security/armed forces to put their lives on the line, do the dirty work of fighting terrorists and then when all is back to normal and the debris of war is cremated and buried to hark back to the "Law is supreme in a civil mode . . . we simply ask one question; did the police as in punjab or the security forces in Kashmir and Jaffna, act on their own into their own hands in defiance of civil authority or were they specifically asked by the Government of the day to do so . . . The Punjab crisis saw five Prime Ministers and as many Internal Security Ministers. Each one knew precisely what was going on . . . why are they hiding now? Why are they not being charged with genocide? If the way terrorism was fought in Punjab was such a crime against humanity, surely the buck should not stop at a mere Superintendent of Police". The unfortunate grim reality of life today is the fact that human right have today became more of a political weapon to attack an adversary and to demoralize Police and security forces of the country rather than the liberal concept to uphold the dignity of man. The basic issues at the international and national level which are yet to be satisfactorily addressed can be broadly as under:

(a) How does a democratic society deal with insurgents and terrorists who refuse to accept civilized norms of the society?

(b) How can peace, security and normalcy be maintained in a plural, secular and democratic republic when insurgents and terrorists are determined to destroy the democratic society, its normalcy through violent aggressive actions.

(c) Should the democratic state be a silent spectator to the destruction of its various socio-legal institutions, vandalizing of its property and killing of its innocent citizens including women and children.

(d) Should Police and security forces of the state be hamstrung in dealing with the perpetrators of violence by laws and rules which are generally applicable in normal tune?

(e) should extraordinary situations created by terrorists insurgents and perpetrators of criminal violence, destruction of property and insecurity of the state be dealt by extraordinary treatment and special laws empowering state to deal with situations effectively?

It is in such a context that Lord Denning asserted that "the freedom of the individual must take second place to the security of the state". Arun Shourie has deplored the "double standards" of the human right organisations and the courts and raised one pertinent question; " why should anyone (members of Police, security forces and armed forces) risk his life the next time the country is in peril when this (trials by Courts for actions to combat terrorists and insurgents) is what he is to got in return? It is unfortunate that about 1200 petitions are pending against Police and security forces in Punjab alone and they are facing prosecution. The Government of India and the state Governments need to evolve a comprehensive long-term strategic policy to tackle these human rights problems and must address the problems at its roots.[6] Since the outbreak of Pakistan sponsored terrorism in 1990 in J&K, 26421 people lost their lives and 2482 security personnel lost their lives,. According to reliable data Pakistan sponsored militancy claimed 2389 lives including that of 1520 militants in the year 2000 in Jammu & Kashmir. Only 51 militants were killed in retaliatory actions by the security forces in December 2000, whereas their toll in November was 163. During the year 2000, militants gunned down 762 civilians, 98 of them in December and injured 1258 despite the unilateral ceasefire as against 69 killed in November 2000. While the highest number of 397 security personnel including 86 J&K Policemen lost their lives in anti-terrorist operations and 864 were injured. In December-2000 alone 31 security personnel were killed while 180 civilians lost their lives in incidents of cross firing or terrorists attacks. During the year 2000 approx 768 terrorists were killed in Kashmir Valley and 752 in the Jammu region. 128 civilians were killed in explosives and grenade blast.

The Subrahmanyam Committee has rightly observed "National Security Management recedes into the background in time of peace and is considered too delicate to be tempered with in time of war and proxy war". The continuing proxy war and violation of human rights of citizens by the terrorists and insurgents justify a thorough review of the national security system in its entirety. The First Prime Minister of India, Jawahar Lal Nehru once said "The difficulties which the police (including security forces) face should be appreciated. They have often to face both external dangers and internal disorders and is doing so, they often suffer serious damage, injuries and even lose lives. When disorders worsen, their difficulties increase". Past September 11, 2001, the United States has came with a most tough law to deal with terrorists and Indian states must have stringent laws to deal with organised crime and terrorist organinsations every year for the past decade and more a thousand or so innocent civilians are killed by terrorists in India and a like number are maimed. At the same time 300-400 security forces personnel lay down their lives in combating them.[7] Each death brings in its train shattered families widows and orphans whose human rights are violated by terrorists. To deal with such terrorist activities Government of India has recently passed POTA in a joint sitting of Parliament. Mahrashtra, Karnataka, Andhra Pradesh, West Bengal and Tamil Nadu have passed special laws to deal with such cases. In the famous Bijbehara case of B.S.F. the Supreme Court has rightly uphold denial of information by MHA to the National Human Rights Commission on grounds of "national security" and wisely the NHRC has quietly withdrawn its petition in September 2000 and closed its own file relating to the incident.[8] The police, CRPF and BSF had been bearing the brunt of terrorism, insurgence and proxy war during the last forty years, performing most difficult assignments under very hazardous circumstances at times under great provocation and utter indifference of the local people. The stresses and strains of serving under such difficult conditions over prolonged periods at times likely to lead to the breaking posts crossing all limits of tolerance and patience. Despite all this the performance of these security forces can be rated as very impressive if not excellent. The high morale and motivation of the armed forces (including Central Police Organisations) remain an enigma despite the shortage of officers, paucity of hi-tech equipment or force multipliers and poor career prospects.[8a]

About 2000 people between the ages of 10 and 40 have disappeared from Kashmir valley since 1990. Civil liberties groups allege that these are results of covert arrest and extra-judicial killings by police/security forces. The Government insists that most of those missing have crossed over to Pakistan and are in terrorists training camps.[8b] The 13 year long Pakistan backed terrorism in Kashmir has not only taken the lives of over 30,000 persons but has in the process altered the social and cultural fabric of the state.[9] The 13 long-years have seen militancy turn from an emotional upsurge demanding Azadi in the valley, to a Pakistan Proxy War against India using a slew of Islamic fundamentalist organisation like Laskare-Toiba and The Jaish-e-Mohammad. Independent Market Research Agency "Mori" has found that 61 per cent of the respondents would like to remain Indian citizens and 81 per cent wanted the unique cultural identity of J&K to be preserved and feel that the return of Kashmir Pandits to their homes would help in restoring peace. An overwhelming 92 per cent opposed the religious and ethnic division of the State. There is an intrinsic link between the proper promotion of human rights and the pursuant of political, economic and social policies that are just and that open the doors of opportunity to all of the people of our country. The nation, its police, security forces and armed forces have a duty to fight and triumph over terrorism and insurgency with the active cooperation of the people and effective functioning of the criminal justice system.

There is need for appropriate training programmes for the members of the police, security forces and magistracy in human rights jurisprudence and sensitization to the human rights of the common citizens. Amnesty International and many other human rights organisations are clamoring all the time about the human rights of merchants of terror, succession and mayhem and remaining silent about the rights of the innocent victims of the killer gangs.[10] Certain bold and out spoken policemen say that the security forces are at times compelled to ignore legal bindings and use unconventional method because punishments to the terrorists and insurgents are not certain for years due to complete collapse of criminal justice system in India. Shri K.P.S. Gill said "We have registered 17391 cases under TADA since its reinforcement and only 111 of them were convicted with a percentage of conviction being just 0.05 and this is in a state where terrorism was at its peak". Even Justice V.K. Krishna Iyer agreed that special situations require special laws to deal with terrorism.[11] Those who are fighting terrorism and insurgency need effective laws and protection for their bonafide performance of duties carried out at the highest risk to life. The issue of human rights education to all citizens requires a long-term strategy and involvement of all possible players. If parliamentary democracy and human rights are to endure constitutional, legal, economic and political reforms have to be brought about in an integrated manner.[12] The Article 29(1) of the U.N. Declaration of Human Rights mentions that "every one has duties to the community". The ancient Indian tradition of emphasis on "duties" must be given its due place in education about human rights and fundamental duties now incorporated in the Indian Constitution. Under Article 51A, citizens of India have ten fundamental duties.[13] The doctrine of sovereign immunity is archaic principle which cannot be applicable generally against the redressal of human rights at any forum.[14] Police and security forces must realize their accountability and responsibilities to the Constitution of India and to the people of India. In a famous case Supreme Court has held that "Maintenance of Law and Order or repression of crime may be inalienable function, for proper exercise of power which the state may exact a law and may delegate its functions, the violation of which may not be seeable in torts, unless its trenches into and encroaches on the fundamental rights of life and liberty guaranteed by the Constitution.[15] Successive Indian Governments have persistently resisted all attempts to establish the right to monetary compensation for wrongful actions of their agents and officers. They have argued that the state is not liable for the acts of its officers when discharging sovereign functions.[16] The Supreme Court of India has brought about revolutionary break through in the human rights jurisprudence by evolving the principle that mandatory compensation has to be paid to the victims of police atrocities in appropriate cases for doing complete justice and enforcing the fundamental rights.[17] The Indian Police and security forces need to build up a new culture of respect for human rights and sensitization to the various human right issues.[18] Means are as important as ends and listening to the call of conscience and ethical mode of righteous living must be essential requirements of ethos of security forces. Prolonged stress due to long hours of work, social isolation, trauma due to frequent movements and continuous deployment in difficult hazardous areas have led to (a) Lack of self-esteem, (b) abnormal behavioural patterns, (c) deterioration in physical and mental health, (d) premature ageing, (e) growing cases of indiscipline and, (f) cases of absenteeism and high turnover of members of security forces.[19] There is an urgent need for transformational reforms in CRPF, BSF and other Central Police Organisation. There is a crying need to improve the training, weaponry, equipment and deployment pattern of our central police and para-military forces, particularly when they are deployed in counter-insurgency and anti-terrorists operations over a long stretch of more than two years. Prime Minister of India, paying tributes to the martyrs of 13 Dec 2001 attack upon Parliament said : "The war against terrorism had entered its last phase. It would be a fight to the finish."[19a]

Addressing the state Chief Secretaries and Directors General of Police, National Human Rights Commission Chairperson Justice J.S. Verma stressed that it is the states responsibility to protect human rights of everyone within its jurisdiction.[20] Justice Verma also took potshots at the "global frenzy which looks at nationalism being inconsistent with human dignity". It is unfortunate that on various occasions Indian Government seems to buckle under threat the recent case of swapping of three terrorists for the Indian Airlines Passenger hijacked from Kathmandu to Kandhar and the foreign minister Jaswant Singh escorted the three terrorists in his aircraft. India has become a known "Soft State". The three terrorists Masood Azhar, Mushtaq Ahmed Zarger and Ahmed Omar Sayeed Seikh (Umar) were dreaded terrorists who were in Indian jails. Why the criminal justice system of India jailed to punish them quickly—justice delayed was justice denied. Senior police officers often ask the question: why the India criminal justice system moves so slowly that men like Azhar Masood and Qmar Sheikh, in India fails for five years without facing trial and why should they be released by Indian Government? How can then police and security forces protect human rights? Such cases hurt the morale and motivation of security forces and make a mockery of our criminal justice system. In order to deal with terrorists, certain special laws are needed and enactment of POTA (Prevention of Terrorists Activities) is a useful legislation. The civil society must equip its security forces with realistic and effective laws to combat terrorism. Evidence collected by the Police through interception of telephonic, wireless or e-mail messages, during investigation into a terrorist act, will be admissible against an accused booked under Prevention of Terrorism Act which has been recently passed in a joint session of both houses of Indian Parliament. After September 11,

2001 incident, the high level of alert, the enhanced cooperation with organisations like Interpol and US Federal Bureau of Investigation (FBI), CBI has been designated agency to liaison with other international agencies and this will raise our level of intellignece on terrorist groups, their training camps and their activities.

Police Leadership has to adequately measure up to the various challenges and responsibilities in the context of protection of human rights and motivation of the security forces. Leadership must not only take care of the welfare, training, equipment, weaponry and morale of the security personnel but also use modern management techniques like information technology and use of operation reasearch modules. Various studies of successful counter insurgency operations in Arabia (1916-18), Ireland (1916-21), Cuba (1958-59), China (1929-49), Vietnam (1954-62) carried out by Utpal K. Banerjee, must be adequately studied and useful lessons should be drawn for our security forces.[21] Security forces of India should become "Learning Organisations" and must draw useful lessons from every important incident, failure and successes. Each member of the security forces should be motivated and inspired to learn new skills and should become truly a knowledge worker committed to the security and integrity of the country. Indian security forces, under able leadership, are capable of successfully winning anti-terrorists movements and securing human right of the people. In spite of all handicaps, problems and difficulties, the morale and motivation of security forces in India is high and it would be a good idea to reflect on the verse of Shakeel Badayuni :

"Mere Honsle Itney Buland Hein,
Kee Parai Sholon Ka Dar Naheen,
Mujhe Khauf Aatish-e-gul Se Hai
Yeh Chaman Kaheen Jala Na De"

(My soaring confidence has no fear of alien fires,
what I fear is the fire in the rose
which could burn my garden down)

No outside country or force can affect India. It has its own resilience but she can only be destroyed or harmed by the fire within fanned by burglary, violence, intolerance, decisiveness, hate and hatred. Human Rights have to protected and promoted by the security forces during anti-terrorist operations in letter and spirit of Human Rights Philosophy, although it is high time that criminal justice system should be revamped to quickly punish the merchants of violence and terror.

References

1. G. Har Gopal, "Good Governance Human Rights Perspective"- The Indian Journal of Public Administration Vol. XIIV No 3, July-September, 1998, pp. 297-306.
2. For similar views see (R Prasad Rao & Others-State, Civil Society and Human Rights Scenario in India-Indian Journal of Public Administration, Oct.-Dec. 2001, Vol. No. XI-VII, No. 4, p. 671.
3. National Human Rights Commission, Annual Report 1998-99, New Delhi-110001, p. 11.
4. National Human Rights Commission, Annual Report 1996-97, Sardar Patel Bhawan, Sansad Marg, New Delhi-110001, p. 8.

4a. National Human Rights Commission Annual Report 2000-2001-New Delhi, p.11.

5. National Human Rights Commission, Annual Report 1996-97, Sardar Patel Bhawan, Sansad Marg, New Delhi-110001, p. 14.

5a. Audit of Terror-*Times of India,* May 2, 2003, New Delhi-p. 14.

6. For similar views see Prakash Singh— "Kohima to Kashmir" on the Terrorist Trail-Rupa & Co. 2001, New Delhi, p.173.
7. Manoj Joshi— "Targeting Terrorism - To work POTO Must have Teeth – *The Time of India,* 13 Nov. 2001.
8. Akshaya Mukul — Times News Network - *The Times of India,* 5th July 2002.

8a. Armed Forces—*India Today,* August 19, 2002.

8b. *Times of India,* 16 May 2003—Time News Network.

9. Manoj Joshi — The Mori Message — Silver lining in Kashmir's Cloud-*The Times of India,* 10th June 2002.
10. Baraj Puri—Human Rights - Key to Kashmir Policy—The Times of India 11 February 1992.
11. V.K. Krihna Iyer — Human Rights and TADA—Seminar Held at Lucknow on 16 January 1994.
12. Krishna Mohan Mathur—Elections in the Indian Tradition and good government—in Governance and Human rights edited by Bharat Jhunjhunuwala—Kalpaz Publication, Delhi, 2002, p. 87.
13. Krishna Mohan Mathur—Management of Internal Security and Related Issues, Gyan Publishing House, New Delhi, 1995, p. 254.
14. Dr. K.M. Mathur—Crime, Human Rights and National Security, Gyan Publishing House, New Delhi, 1996, p. 237.
15. N. Nagendra Rao and Co Vs State of A.P. Air 1994 SC 2663
16. Amnesty International—India-Torture, Rape and Deaths in Custody—London, Amnesty International Publication, 1992, p. 86.
17. Dr. K.M. Mathur, Crime Human Rights and National Security, Gyan Publishing House, New Delhi, 1996, p. 230-240. See Nilabari Behera Vs State of Orissa 1993 —2 SCC 746. Arvinder Singh Bagga Vs State of UP - Air 1995 SC 117 Sec 565.

18. Dr. Krishna Mohan Mathur—Policing in the 21th Century - Challenges and Agenda for Reforms in Policing in Twenty First Century - Editor J. Guha Roy Indian Institute of Public Administration, New Delhi 1999, p. 42.
19. Bench Mark Study of the working conditions of personnel in CRPF carried out by the Administration Staff College of India, Hyderabad.
19a Attack on Parliament-Prabhu Chawla—India Today December 24, 2001. New Delhi p. 32.
20. J.S. Verma—State must guard citizens, *The Times of India,* 2nd May 2002.
21. For further details consult Banerjee Utpal K - "Operational Analysis and Indian Defence "— Concepts Publishing Company, New Delhi, 1980. Also 44th DisGP Seminar Background papers May 1997—Internal Security Academy—Mount Abu, p. 38-53.

8

Police Leadership and Protection of Human Rights

"Terrorism and Insurgency are specific violations of human rights." The notion of Human Rights is the most precious legacy of the classical and contemporary human thought to culture and civilisation.[1] Although Human Rights have been guaranteed as fundamental rights under the Indian Constitution and various other laws, in practice, Human Rights situation is precarious and prevalent state of affairs can be termed as "the Crises in Human Rights." In India, the institutions of a strong press and Judiciary with substantive powers have not succeeded in extending effective protections to hundreds of citizens who have died by torture and ill treatment at the hands of the police. Human Rights violations in counter insurgency areas, especially in the State of Punjab, J&K and North East, have raised sensitive questions relating to the performance of the Security Forces and role of their leaders. Human Rights violations have been attributed to the police, army and paramilitary forces although they form a very small fringe of the total spectrum. Police aberrations generally get greater media and public attention than other agencies which do much the same things. Supreme Court of India in 1980 has observed: "we are deeply disturbed by the diabolical recurrence of police torture resulting in a terrible scare in the minds of the common citizen that their lives and liberty are under a new peril when the guardians of the law gore Human Rights to death. The vulnerability of human rights assumes a traumatic torture and poignancy; the violent violation is perpetrated by the police arm of the State whose function is to protect the citizen and not to commit gruesome offences against them as has happened in this case. Police lockup, if reports in newspapers have a streak of credence, are becoming more and more awesome cells. This development is disastrous to our human rights and humanist constitutional order. (Raghbir Singh vs. State of Haryana (1980) 3SCC 70). Supreme Court in 1985 again observed "Police Officers who are custodians of law and order should have the greatest respect for the personal liberty of citizens and should not flout the laws by stooping to such bizarre acts of lawlessness. Custodians of law and order should not become depredators of civil liberties. Their duty is to protect and not to abduct." (Bhim Singh vs. State of Jammu and Kashmir, 1985 (4) SCC 677). It is in this background that we should examine the role of the leadership of police/security forces in safeguarding number of cases of violations of human rights by the police and security force, the blame cannot be put entirely upon the individuals but upon the entire criminal justice system.

A mature and well informed national dialogue is needed to define and identify the obligations of the police/security forces leadership in the protection of human rights in a plural, multi-religious democratic society which is in the thick of battle against terrorism, ethnic insurgency, religious fanaticism and low-intensity-operations by foreign powers. The frequent "encounters" the police (and security forces) have with terrorists, extremists and hard-core criminals make the public wonder about the role and the limits of the police as an important player in a democracy.[2] The problem of human rights in areas torn by intense strife and such manifestations as extremism, terrorism and secessionist activities, needs to be looked in a more holistic and realistic perspective. Are human rights more important than the preservation of the nation's integrity?[3] What should be the strategy of leaders of Police/Security forces to protect and enhance the respect for human rights? Can draconian measures help in curbing such situations without infringement of human rights? Under what compelling circumstances and pressures human rights are being violated by police/ security forces? What exact role can leaders of the police/security forces play in protecting human rights and in building a new culture and ethics of human rights protection? How can leadership of police/security forces inculcate in their subordinates more familiarity, greater awareness and respect for the human rights of all citizens, particularly the rights of the most vulnerable and weaker sections of the society? What should human rights imply and mean in practical real life situations? Are the maintenance of internal security and the protection of human rights antithetical or symbiotic? Do the perceptions of human rights differ from society to society and individual to individual? How can leaders of the police/security forces urge their subordinate to protect the human rights "through personal examples and orientation to a human rights police sub-culture?" All these issues need a national dialogue and serious indepth analysis. Democratic society alone can provide the fullest protection of human rights and eternal vigilance is the price which each citizen has to pay for nurturing the democratic institutions on healthy lines.[4] The present chapter is the effort of a vigilant humanist to find a few answers to some of the questions and issues raised above. There is an urgent need to generate serious thinking about the obligations of the leadership of the police/security forces in the protection of human rights so that present and future leadership of the police/security forces may rise above "the tunnel vision". The leadership of the police/security forces can bring about a significant improvement in the protection of Human Rights through a professional approach and can inculcate a human rights culture by reorientation, closer supervision and non-partisan approach.

Concept of Human Rights

In India human rights have been defined under "the protection of human rights 1993 (No.10 of 1994)" as under:

2 (I) (d) "human rights" means the rights relating to life, liberty, equality and dignity of the individual guaranteed by the Constitution or embodied in the International Covenants and enforceable by Courts in India.

If we analyse the Constitution of India, we find that Constitution of India has guaranteed the following fundamental rights:-

(a) Right to Equality

(i) Art.14 - Equality before law.
(ii) Art.15 - Prohibition of discrimination on grounds of religion, race, case, sex or place of birth.
(iii) Art.16 - Equality of opportunity to matters of public employment.
(iv) Art.17 - Abolition of Untouchability.
(v) Art.18 - Abolition of titles.

(b) Right of Liberty

(i) Art.19 - Protection of certain rights regarding freedom of speech, etc.
(ii) Art.20 - Protection in respect of conviction for offences.
(iii) Art.21 - Protection of life and personal liberty.
(iv) Art.22 - Protection against arrest and detention in certain cases.

(c) Right against Exploitation and Right to Dignity

(i) Art.23 - Prohibition of traffic in human beings and force labour.

(ii) Art.24 - Prohibition of employment of children in factories etc.

(d) Right to life

(i) Art. 21 of the Indian Constitution included within its scope:

1. The right to speedy trial (Hussainara Khatoon vs. Secretary, AIR 1979, SC 1360).
2. The right to free legal aid to the poor (Hussainara Khatoon vs. Home Secretary, AIR 1979, SC 1369).
3. The right to humane treatment in prison. (Sunil Batra vs. Delhi Administration (1978) 4 SCC 494: AIR 1978 SC 1675 and Sunil Batra (2) vs. Delhi Administration (1980) 3 SCC 488 AIR 1980 SC 1579.
4. The right not to be handcuffed, fettered or put in solitary confinement. (ibid.).
5. The right to live with dignity. (Francis Coralie Mullen, AIR 1981 SC 746).
6. The right against custodial violence (Sheela Barse vs. State of Maharashtra (1983) 2 SCC 96 AIR 1983 SC378.
7. The right against unauthorized intrusion into the home. (Kharak Singh vs. State (1964) I SCR 332 AIR 1963 SC 1295).
8. The right of effective appeal. (M.H. Hosket vs. State of Maharashtra, AIR 1978 SC 1548).
9. The right to bail without economic restrictions. (Hussainara Khatoon vs. Home Secretary, AIR 1979 SC 630).
10. The right to shelter (Sontistar Builder vs. Narayan Khimalal Totama, 1990, 1 SSC 520 AIR 1990 SC 630).

Right to life—now also means free legal aid in Khatri vs. State of Bihar, the Supreme Court has held that the Magistrate or the Sessions Judge before whom an accused appears must be held under an obligation to inform the accused that if he is unable to engage the services of a lawyer on account of poverty or indigence, he is entitled to obtain free legal services at the cost of the State (1981) 2 SCR 408 AIR 1981 SC 928). The protection of Human Rights Act in India has ratified and acceded to the following International Covenants which came into force from the dates mentioned below:

(i) International Covenant on Economic, Social and Cultural Rights of 1966 (3rd January, 1976). Adopted and opened for ratification and adopted by UN General Assembly.

(ii) International Covenant on Civil and Political Rights (Adopted by L.R. General Assembly on 16th Dec. 1966) (Entry into force on 23rd March, 1976).

The Concept of "Security Forces" and Their Leadership Problem

"Security Force" is a broad term to refer to armed forces of the Union and include Central Police Organisations like Central Reserve Police Force (CRPF), Border Security Force (BSF), Central Industrial Security Force (CISF), Assam Rifles, National Rifles, National Security Guard (NSG), and other armed forces of the Union and the State Armed Forces. Generally, in terrorist infested areas and insurgency areas army along with National Security Guards assist State Police and other Central Police Organisations for certain specific anti-terrorist and anti-insurgency operations. Their leadership generally consists of Commissioned Officers of the armed forces. Leadership of Central Police Organisations like CRPF, BSF, CISF, NSG at the top level generally consists of Indian Police Service (IPS) Officers who come on deputation to these organisations for a flexible tenure of three to seven years. Directly appointed Subordinate Officers and Gazetted Officers generally stagnate middle levels. Thus, the leadership of Central Police Organisations at the top level consists of mainly deputationist Indian Police Service Officers. Most of the IPS officers having leadership of security forces spend their maximum efforts and energy for "(a) surviving on the post, (b) keeping the powers that are pleased, (c) dealing with the dead burden of routine paper work and (d) making arrangements for post-retirement jobs and supplementing their incomes."[5] Among common failing of police leadership is its obsession with creating a coterie of favourites who are given the most forward treatment in all matters.[6] According to the Sixth Report of the National Police Commission, two Central IPS Cadres should be constituted, one for the paramilitary organisations like the BSF, CRPF, ITBP and the other for such organisations as the IB, CBI and RAW. Such cadres could be constituted within the frame of Article 312 of the Constitution.[7] Experience of the last four decades has proved that Central Police Organisations cannot entirely depend on IPS cadre for field postings, particularly in difficult insurgency infested or terrorist effected areas and therefore, CPO personnel policy needs review.[8] Senior Police Officers have failed to inspire and enthuse the members of the Police force and could not cope adequately with the challenges facing the organisation.[9] Indeed therefore, a time has come for senior leadership of the Police/Security Forces to go in for some self-introspection and make a dispassionate stock-taking.

Human Rights Violations by Police and Security Forces: An Analysis

Despite an increase in Human Rights awareness among the police and security forces in the recent past, there has been an increase in the report of cases of violations of human rights. As many as 444 custodial deaths were reported in the country during April 1995 to March 1996 within Bihar alone accounting for 75 such cases.[10] The figures are more than double for what was reported during 1994-95 when 162 people had died in police and judicial custody. During the first three months of 1996, 157 custodial deaths were reported in the country. Maharashtra, which had registered only 36 deaths since 1993 recorded an alarming increase in death in custody during the first quarter of 1996 with the State accounting for 25 deaths. While Bihar reported the highest number of 75 deaths. Andhra Pradesh recorded 55 deaths, followed by West Bengal 51, Delhi 40, Uttar Pradesh 37, and Maharashtra 34. Jammu and Kashmir reported 15 deaths in police custody. According to National Human Rights Commission, a permissive approach to the use of third degree methods in investigation led to serious violations of the Human Rights and that it was wrong to believe that such practices were necessary for the success of investigation of cases. The Commission's concern in the matter is heightened by the awareness that most of the victims of custodial deaths and brutality belong to sections of society that are economically poor or disadvantaged.

Violations of human rights by the police and security forces, State-wise admitted by the National Human Rights Commission from 1/4/94 to 31/3/95 are given in attached Table No.1. There were 111 custodial deaths in police custody and 9 in custody of security forces. 3 cases of custodial rapes were reported during this period and 55 cases of disappearance were reported. There were 114 cases of illegal detention and 497 cases of other police excesses during the reported period. There were 69 cases of indignity to women. Uttar Pradesh had 104 cases of police excesses, followed by 85 cases in Punjab, 47 cases in Bihar and 62 cases in Tamil Nadu.[11]. Police excess include third degree methods, abuses and torture by the police personnel. During 2000-2001, there were 127 cases of custodial dealth in police custody, 54 cases of disappearances, 1257 cases of illegal detention or arrest and 3947 cases of other police excesses. These cases generally belong to civil police of various states.

The Extent of Violations of Human Rights by the Police and Security Forces and Related Problems

The Supreme Court has itself only admitted that "it is heart-rendering to note that day in and day out, we come across with the news on blood curdling incidents of police brutality and atrocities, alleged to have been committed, in utter disregard and in all breaches of humanitarian law and universal human rights as well as in total negation of the Constitutional guarantees and human decency."[12] The police and security force personnel have come to treat themselves as law unto themselves, sometimes even above the law. Policemen and security force personnel stepping out of the legal boundaries is not new; but the frequency and the freedom with which they trample on the rights of the citizens are frightening. (Dhananjay Sharma vs. State of Haryana (1995) 3SCC 757).

The annual report of the National Human Right Commission (1994-1995) has given the following illustrative cases for violations of human rights.

1. Alleged custodial death of Madan Lal in Delhi.
2. Alleged death of Korra Satya Rao, a tribal, in Visakhapatnam district, Andhra Pradesh as a result of police mis-treatment.
3. Alleged killing of civilians in Ukrul town, Manipur, in cross firing between 20 Assam Rifles and NSCN.
4. Alleged death of Mohd Akbar Sheikh in armed forces custody, Baramulla district, J&K.
5. Alleged death of Allen Kuki of Kholijang village, Manipur, incustody of the armed forces.
6. Disappearance of Shri Harjit Singh since April 1972 (Arrested by Punjab Police on 29th april 1992).
7. Alleged rape in custody by an Assistant Sub-Inspector of Delhi Police.[13]

National Human Rights Commission Annual Report 2000-2001 received 109 cases reported as alleged fake encounters out of which 68 cases were from U.P., 14 from Andhra Pradesh, 9 from Maharashtra 6 from Bihar and 4 from Uttaranchal.

In a telling indictment of the politicisation of the police the Supreme Court on May 3, 1995 sentenced three police officers, two of them of senior IPS rank, to prison terms of two to three months on contempt charges for illegally detaining a business rival of the son-in-law of the then State Chief Minister, Mr. Bhajan Lal, on trumped up grounds.[14] In their separate but concurring judgements Dr. Justice A.S. Anand and Mr. Justice Faizannuddin said: "this case was perhaps one of the most unpleasant episodes in the history of the police force which has been exposed in the portals of the highest court of the land which has plunged the members of the force and its reputation to a new low probably out of a frantic zeal to please someone best known to the officials concerned." In the present case, the court discharged the then Director General after accepting his apology and passed severe strictures on the Haryana Home Secretary.

Mr. Sibtey Rezi told the Parliament that 52 allegations of excesses committed by the paramilitary personnel were received during the last two years. The details of actions taken in these cases were: appropriate penalties imposed in two cases after departmental proceedings, court of inquiry proceedings in progress (two cases), departmental enquiry in progress (one case), cases in which police investigation are in progress (30 cases) and filed as untraced after investigation were eight cases.[15] Making available statistics of complaints of human rights violations for the first time, Army sources said "it had received a total of 351 complaints against troops in Kashmir since 1991 for which it had punished 41 soldiers including 15 officers. However, only 21 complaints have been found true out of the 322 cases investigated so far. The remaining 29 complaints were still under investigation.[16] At the first ever news conference on "Human Rights Record of the Indian Army", Additional Director-General (Discipline and Vigilance) Maj. General S.G. Vombatkere said that 170 complaints of human rights violations against the army had been received from the north-eastern states, of which only five complaints involving 15 soldiers have been found correct. This puts the total number of Army soldiers published so far to 66 including 17 officers. Currently, 31 complaints pertaining to the North-East were still under investigation. Between 1990 and 1994, 245 cases have been registered against the Border Security Force and 39 against the Army. While admitting that "Human Rights violations could never be eliminated but can only be minimized, Major General Vombatkere said that technically speaking even search and cordon operations were human rights violations. But these are minor violations, and major violations in army parlance constituted rape, murder, beating, extortions and custodial deaths.

The security forces are obviously not required to act illegally in order to meet the situations created by separatist and terrorist movements since the black laws have provided them with ample powers.[17] Section 19 of the Protection of Human Rights Act, 1993 has prescribed special procedure with respect to armed forces which is as under: "19. Procedure with respect to armed forces - (1) Notwithstanding anything contained in this Act, while dealing with complaints of violation of human rights by members of the armed forces, the Commission shall adopt the following procedure, namely: (a) it may, either on its own motion or on receipt of a petition, seek a report from the Central Government,: (b) after receipt of the report, it may either not proceed with the complaint, or, as the case may be, make its recommendations to that Government, (c) The Central Government shall inform the Commission of action taken on the recommendations within three months or such further time, as the Commission may allow."

Why incidents like Bijbehara, Sopore and Kupwara occur? It is partly due to poor and ill-trained top leadership, partly due to a lack of clarity at the political level; administrative errors in deploying inappropriate forces to deal with violent political movement; lack of proper training and mental preparation of the security forces to deal with the violent movements; and the stress factor operative on the security forces.[18] There is need to rationalise the deployment of police and security forces and this should be task-oriented and determined by well-informed professional leaders. There is a tendency to flood an area with security forces without a clear objective and generally the emphasis remains on quantity rather than quality. As regards the North-Eastern states, 52 complaints were received by National Human Rights Commission during 2000-2001 alleging the violations of human rights by the army and security forces.[18a]

The record of the CRPF, with regard to protection of human rights, has been so far excellent. The CRPF officers and men have shown highest respect for human rights. During the last four years (1990-94), three officers, one Inspector, five Sub-Inspectors, 5 HCs, 4 NKs, 3 LNks and 46 Constables making a total of 67 have been punished for violation of human rights. Prompt and adequate punishment to the defaulters has enabled CRPF to maintain a very high level of discipline in the Force. In CRPF, the details of violation of human rights for the period (1991-93) are as under :

Year	*Total No. of Cases*	*Allegation found false*	*Allegation Confirmed*	*Cases decided*
1991	51	26	4	29
1992	9	5	4	1
1993	1	-	-	-

A Casestudy of Violations of Human Rights Firing by Security Forces in Bijbehara, Jammu & Kashmir

On Ist November, 1993, the National Human Rights Commission suo moto, took cognizance of press reports in and around Bijbehara in Jammu and Kashmir as a result of firing by security forces operating in the area and called for reports from the Ministries of Defence and Home Affairs and also the Government of J & K. While the Ministry of Defence clarified that the army was not involved, the Ministry of Home Affairs sent a report to the Commission on the basis of the Magisterial Inquiry ordered by the State Government into the incident and the Staff Court of Inquiry ordered by the BSF authorities. On examination of the report, the Commission felt that perusal of copies of evidence given by the witnesses was necessary and accordingly called for additional material viz. the evidence given by the witnesses. That evidence having been made available to the commission and considered by it, together with the report and material provided earlier, the Commission made the following observations/ recommendations.

(a) The Commission noted that disciplinary proceedings had been initiated under the Border Security Force Act against 14 members of the Force, and further that, on the basis of a Magisterial Inquiry steps may be initiated to launch prosecutions. The Commission expected that the dual proceedings would be pursued to their respective logical ends and that it would be kept informed about the action taken against those found guilty.

(b) Payment was recommended of interim compensation on a graded scale.

(c) It was recommended that a thorough review should be undertaken by Government of the circumstances and conditions in which Units of the Border Security Force are deployed and expected to operate in situations involving only civilian population.

These were communicated to the Central Government and the commission has since been informed that the recommendations made by it have been accepted.

The J&K State Government has disbursed ex-gratia relief of Rs. 1 lakh each to the next of kin of the 31 civilians, who were found by the Magistrate to have been killed in the incident. An amount of Rs. 25,000/- each has been paid to 44 injured persons, Rs. 5,000/- each to 26 persons and Rs. 1,000/- each to 5 persons. The Commission has taken note of the fact that as against the recommended sum of Rs. 10,000 for each of the injured person of the second category, smaller compensation has been disbursed.

The Central Government has specially directed the DG BSF,

notwithstanding the extremely complex and difficult environment in which the BSF personnel were required to operate in the State, to take all necessary steps to ensure that no Unit/formation of the BSF resorted to indiscriminate use of Force. The DG BSF has since communicated that as the terrorists are mostly operating from the urban/built up areas and are mixed with the civilians, the BSF, while tackling the militants, cannot avoid involvement with the civilian population. In this context, the following steps have been/are being taken by the BSF to ensure proper safety of the civilian population.

(i) The training syllabus emphasises respect for human rights/humanitarian laws and how to deal with the public, particularly with the elders and ladies/children.

(ii) Whenever cordon and searches are conducted, the services of the Magistrate, Civil Police and lady police are requisitioned to help during such operations.

(iii) The number of the supervisory level officers is being increased and special emphasis is being laid on their interaction with the men.

(iv) Efforts are being made to increase the motivation of the troops to develop respect for human rights; among other things, a series of training films bringing out this aspect have also been developed.

(v) Careful detailment is being made of supervisory officers of proven integrity and efficiency for Internal Security (IS) Duty Battalions.

(vi) Strict instructions have been issued to ensure adherence to the principle of minimum use of force.

(vii) Immediate action is taken for removal of the units from the area of deployment when they are found involved in such incidents, besides taking strict disciplinary action against the defaulters.

(viii) The troops are being changed/rotated after every two years to avoid stresses and strain which may lead to over-reaction by the troops while dealing with such situations.

(ix) Pre-induction training is given to each Unit for a period of 4 weeks, before its actual deployment on Internal Security duties.

(x) To create a rapport with the public and secure support of the civil population, the following actions have also been taken by BSF:

(a) establishment of a number of dispensaries in the areas of their deployment to provide medical aid to civilians.
(b) assisting the reactivation of schools by providing them stationery items; and
(c) distribution of essential commodities like kerosene oil, sugar, etc. to the needy population in areas of deployment.

The Central Government has indicated that because of the extremely complex and serious ground situation difficulties would continue to be faced by personnel of the Central Government paramilitary forces deployed in J&K and elsewhere in the country.

Responsibilities, Duties and Obligations of The Police/Security Force Leadership - A conceptual Frame

Obligation refers to duty, responsibility or promise. Obligation is primarily a moral concept. Obligations are inherently action-guiding directions to guide human conduct in a given society.[19] Leadership is a constant and continuous process of stimulating, influencing and inspiring subordinates towards cherished goals, aims and objectives, which the society demands at a particular time. Indian police has produced many leaders all along at all levels from the junior most to the highest who could compare with the best anywhere else in the world and who have done our country proud. The present day police leadership has a responsibility to usher the Indian Police out of its traditionally accepted image of being an instrument of repression.[20] It is the function of a good leader to inspire the force with the correct attitudes. [21] In the modern day context leaders of the police/security forces are entrusted with the responsibilities of spreading human rights literacy and human rights culture among the police/security force personnel. The ultimate objective of these obligations should be one of inculcating human rights culture by orientation, briefing, training and effective supervision. The obligations of the police/security force leadership is to bring positive attitudinal change in the police/security forces. Following obligations are very important in this context:

1. Leadership of the Police/security forces should ensure functional autonomy of the police/security forces by isolating it from political interference; and police/security force carry out their duties in a professional manner.
2. Police leaders should make all efforts to bring professionalisation and modernisation with emphasis on

human rights culture. Lie detectors' should be used for interrogation and modern interrogation and investigation techniques should be encouraged by the leaders.

3. Human rights training for all ranks in both basic and in-service courses should be ensured by the leaders of the police/security forces.
4. Better working and living conditions for the police/security forces with a view to protect their own human rights should be provided by the leaders.
5. In-built system to redress grievances and prompt disciplinary action when cases of violations of human rights are reported/noticed. Leadership of the police/security forces must ensure a very high level of discipline and prompt action against those who violate human rights. During the past four years (1990-94) the BSF had taken disciplinary action against 440 personnel and of them 30 were suo moto action where no complaint had been lodged against the BSF personnel.[22] To prevent custodial deaths senior gazetted officers should be made responsible to ensure that no person or suspect is detained unnecessarily in a police station and there is no torture.
6. Fair and just personnel policies in the police/security forces so that all personnel get rotation of duties from hard duties to relatively softer duties.
7. Police and security force leadership should ensure that internal security operations like search and cordon, raids, ambushes and patrolling in disturbed areas should be carried out by their personnel under their close supervision so that there are no allegations of violation of human rights at large stages. The senior leadership should not allow the following :

   (i) Arbitrary and unlawful arrests.
   (ii) Arbitrary and unlawful searches.
   (iii) IIlegal detentions in custody.
   (iv) Custodial violence.
   (v) Fake encounters and disappearances.
   (vi) Use of third degree methods of interrogations.

8. Effective dialogue and pressure on the governments to implement the various recommendations of the National Police Commission. Leader should implement at their own levels

wherever possible useful recommendations of the National Police Commission.

9. Leadership should take up case for the complete re-organisation of the police/security force to keep pace with the changing internal security scenario and to ensure that better quality of life is granted to the police/security forces.
10. They should utilize the services of the psychologists in large personnel with time of recruitment/in-service courses with a view to identify sadists and personnel with mental disorder and to keep them out from the police/security forces.
11. They should arrange to supply regularly Supreme Court and High Court judgements relating to human rights at all police stations and other organisational levels with a view to spread human rights culture.
12. They should adopt a bold and clear cut policy of not accepting and orders from politicians and civil servants which are likely to infringe human rights of the people. Police leadership should cultivate correct, cordial and healthy relationship with the mass media so that problems of police in protection of human rights can be properly highlighted. Police leadership must also build up rapport with the various human rights organisations and must project their problems, dilemma and limitations so that human rights leaders understand their viewpoint. Public appearance of police leaders on TV and Radio can help in seeking cooperation of public in discharge of their duties.
13. Ensure and implement police Code of Conduct as laid down by the 106th plenary meeting of the United Nations on 17th December, 1979 which has the following 8 Articles and also basic principles on the use of force and fire arms by law enforcement officials as recommended by the seventh United Nations Congress on the Prevention of Crime and the treatment of offenders held at Varenna, Italy in May, 1986. Article 2 of the United Nations Code of Conduct of Law Enforcement officials categorically lays down that "in the performance of their duty, law enforcement official shall respect and protect human dignity and uphold maintain and the human rights of all persons.
14. Leaders of police/security forces must themselves keep abreast of all the laws, international Covenants and

Constitutional provisions related to human rights and ensure that the police/security force personnel are briefed and informed about these latest developments in the field of human rights literature.

15. Establishment of monitoring cells at district headquarters, range headquarters and force headquarters to constantly watch performance in the field and respond effectively and immediately for increasing the commitment of the police/security forces for the human rights. To prevent custodial violence it is necessary for senior officers of the force to make clear to the subordinates that use of third-degree methods against persons in custody will not be condoned and swift and deterrent action will be taken against the perpetrators of such offences.[23] Experienced senior police officers should frequently talk on the television and radio and may contribute articles in the leading journals/newspaper explaining how the police function, what are the limitations and difficulties of the police and how the community could assist the police in the performance of their functions.[24]
16. Police / security force leadership has an obligation to design a "Human Rights Curriculum of Police Academics" so that all ranks of the police/security forces undergo training at various stages of their service in human rights. Dr. Upendra Baxi has already suggested a comprehensive curriculum for police personnel.[25]
17. Police and security forces, particularly in the disturbed areas such as Jammu & Kashmir and North Eastern States are undergoing serious emotional and occupational stress. Life in CRPF, BSF, and other security forces in very tough, demanding and stressful today. The rigours of a hard life, being away from families and children, not getting adequate educational facilities for their children, all add upto the psychological stress.[26] Leadership of the police and security forces have to take stock of various problems faced by the personnel in the police/security forces and have to provide adequate relief, compensation and stress-coping opportunities to them. In November, 1992, a CRPF Constable shot dead his Deputy Commandant (105 Battalion) because he has been refused leave. Excessive deployment of the police/security forces round the year, inadequate leave and compensatory

allowances has increased psychological stress that finally finds a violent outlet. Emotional stress was in evidence in Kupwara when the army opened fire killing 19 civilians. Sopore and Bijebehara incidents of BSF all are indicative of the problem. In the rush to fly out CRPF and other security forces from one troubled spot to another what the police leaders and the MHA forget is that the men in fatigue are not only tired but also slowly reaching the breaking point. Police and security force leadership must not only understand their psychological and personal problems but should effectively project these problems to the highest echelons of the MHA and Government of India.

18. Leadership of the police and security forces should not connive or patronise fake encounters and disappearances. Amnesty International has recorded 80 disappearances, from January 1990 to October 1993. According to the Human Rights Trust, 263 people were killed in 166 encounters between 1 January 1991 and 24 February 1993. 71 people disappeared in the 15 months between 7th March 1992 and 20th June 1993; for the same period there are 60 documented instances of people escaping from custody during encounters while not a single police/army officials were injured in any of these incidents. Leaders of the Police /security forces have an obligation to ensure that such violations of human rights are not allowed to occur again. Leadership should develop a new culture in the police / security force which should be sensitive to the human rights of the people.

19. Leadership of the police /security forces have an obligation to ensure that their subordinates are allowed their "human rights" Dr. Upendra Baxi states that the police remain on "exploited, neglected and despised minority" who are denied the most basic minimum working conditions and who are subservient to the rulers rather than responsive to the people." The police/security forces are poorly paid, suffer difficult working conditions, lack adequate housing facilities and even denied the right of association under the police forces (Restriction of Rights) Act, 1996. Undoubtedly many of the excesses committed by them are due to a tremendous degree of frustration in the lower ranks of the force. Leadership of the police/security forces have an obligation to their organisation

for ensuring that the men under them should get their human rights in ample manures. Safeguarding and protecting the human rights of the police/security forces is one of the most important obligation of the leadership.

20. Conscious efforts are to be made by the leaders of the security forces and the civil administration to bring the people and the security forces together through "cultural events", "provision of medical facilities", "reconstruction work", etc. Security forces can relate to the youth well and earn their friendship. These would call for imaginative action on the part of the local Unit Commanders. Police and security forces must develop cordial and friendly relations with the public. Any improvement in the situation can be brought about only if the higher police officers and State Governments take the initiative to improve the attitude of the police towards the people.[29] Positive attempts must be made by the leaders of the police/security forces to improve police public relations so that the police earn the respects and confidence and eventually the friendship, of the people among whom they work.

Type of Police Leadership - and Their Role vis a vis Human Rights

Police leadership in India can be broadly divided into three kinds of authority at work:-

1. The authority of position - job title, badges of rank, appointment;
2. The authority of personality - the natural qualities of influence.
3. The authority of knowledge - technical professional and human beings.

The Gill Model

Punjab's turbulence created by terrorism and violence has thrown up "the Gill - model of leadership" Shri K.P. S. Gill (IPS 1957) served two tenures as Director General of Police Punjab - from April 1988 to December 1990 and again from November 1991 to December 1995. "His name conjured up contradictory images. To the militants, he instilled fear and awe. To the common person, he was either a saviour or a cold killer."[30] He in generally even accused of spearheading a "counter-terrorist outfit". Many accuse him of inventing "personal legislation's" to subvert the due process of law. One human rights activist said: "The success against terrorists came not because of Gill's policies but because of the indiscriminate killings sanctioned by him." His leadership style of giving out of turn promotions in the Punjab Police to help build up a cadre that was loyal to him, his recruitment of unemployed young men in the villages as special police officers, his delegation of authority to his commanders in the field to get their complete involvement in anti-terrorist operations and his total lack of concern for police excesses and violations of human rights, has created history by almost eradicating terrorism from Punjab and has made Shri KPS Gill a real "Super-Cop". There are many young admirers of this leadership style in police today. Shri K.F. Rustamji, retired Director General BSF and former member of N.P.C. has observed: "A new attitude has filtered down to the district officers. It is common to find officers openly advocating unorthodox methods. Their excuse (which has some justification) is that the support from the judiciary in the administration of justice is no longer possible and therefore crime can not be kept under control except by rough and ready methods. Their superiors, they say, want results. And they are satisfied even if the results are fake ones, as long as they delude the public into believing that something is being done. ". [31] The "Super-Cop" leadership is an unprecedented phenomena in India built up by conditions of internal insecurity and deification of same in strategic positions. The cult of the Super-Cop can provide quick results and counter-response to the terrorists and armed Naxalites (or insurgents) but it can mean demoralization in the law abiding conscientious police officers. The more fundamental argument against the cult however, is the political mind set it can create.[32]

The Vijay Karan Model "Vijay Karan, as Commissioner of Police Delhi started a campaign for eliminating third degree and torture in police stations. After one year of campaign he came to the conclusion that it has neither resulted in an increase in crime nor in the decrease of detections. It is men like Shri Vijay Karan who show the true quality of leadership and prove to the world that Indian Policing has the right leaders."[33]

Opportunist and Careerist Leadership model The 20th All-India police Science Congress held in November, 1986 at Calcutta arrived at the consensus that there has been a careerism in the leadership of Indian Police. Opportunism and Careerism practiced by senior officers act as examples and incentives to compromises at the lower levels of the police. Some of those who masquerade as leaders at different levels in the present times are in effect bullies in their roles as commanders and are pitiful self-seeking sycophants in their relationships with their departmental and civil service superiors and the politicians who are in a position to throw crumbs to and at them.[34]

Research Study on Leadership

A syndicate study carried out by XXXIX Senior Officers Course at

SVP NPA Hyderabad has given the following findings: (1) No study about the types of leadership being followed in the police organisation and their corresponding effects had ever been undertaken. (2) There was strong evidence of the prevalence of rather authoritarian style of leadership in the police organisations and there is total lack of participation by the middle and junior leader of the police. (3) Police leadership was considerably diluted because of the abuse of the concept of unity of command and introduction of several irksome executive controls. (4) Survey of leadership styles conducted with the help of managerial grid (developed by Blake and Mounton) instruments show an overwhelming concern for tasks than for people.[35] Police leadership is seriously impaired by the fact that between the local politicians and subordinate police officers, particularly at levels of police station, a nexus has developed circumscribing there by the role of senior officers in the transfer, posting and disciplinary control over the staff.[36]

Challenges Before the Leadership of the Police

General erosion of moral values, gradual shrinkage of public cooperation to the police, fast growing cynicism and indiscipline in police ranks are serious challenges to the leadership of the police. The obligations of the police/security force leadership in the context of protection of human rights can only be fulfilled provided leaders develop "the breadth of vision, perspective or motivation to do what must be done".[37] Police and security force leadership have to bring our organisational re-structuring , so that personnel are better trained and motivated to protect the human rights. "They have to be better educated, qualified, extensively trained, and should have meaningful understanding of the nature and purpose of the law in the society....they will have to display considerable sensitivity and discretion in the matter of law enforcement.[38] Frequent transfers, lack of right type of training, uncertainty of tenure, IAS-IPS feuds and lack of commitment at the higher leadership in police are some of the reasons why police leaders are not ready to accept their obligations towards protection of human rights. "We have never understood the type of leadership, good policing requires".[39] Failure of the Indian Police Service (IPS) officers to give correct leadership to the force and their inability to combine in a proper esprit-de-corps and service discipline is of the foremost cause of steadily increasing violations of human rights by the police. "The play safe policy" adopted by most of the senior police officers results in "Crisis of leadership" in police and Central Police Organisations. This attitude of avoiding responsibility is the result of lack of police professionalism, weak and poor top leadership, unsatisfactory work culture, lack of courage in police leader and the lack of commitment to the rule of law.[40]

Training and Orientation of Police/Security Forces in Human Rights

Section 12(h) of the Protection of Human Rights Act, 1993 sets before the National Human Rights Commission, the responsibility to spread human rights literacy among various sections of society and promote awareness of the safeguards available for the protection of these rights through publications, the media, seminars and other available means, "The 1978 UNESCO International Congress on Teaching of Human Rights which was convened in Vienna developed the reasons for teaching human rights and suggested various strategies. It is of utmost importance that training syllabus at each level of police functionaries are given adequate theoretical input of human rights.[41] In Kishore Singh vs. State of Rajasthan, the Supreme Court has held "the State must re-educate the constabulary out of their sadistic arts and inculcate a respect of human persons - a process, which must begin more by example than by precepts if the lower rungs are really to emulate". (AIR 1981 SC 625). In all training institutions of the police and security forces, training in human rights is being imparted to all ranks both at the basic training level and during in-service training courses.

The real task before all of us is and it is in fact a very heavy task, to ensure human rights to large section of the society, who are suffering from untold hardship and misery on account of massive deception and exploitation and who cannot live as ordinary human beings with basic human dignity.[42] Effective leadership and close supervision can definitely promote human rights in disturbed situation like those prevailing in J&K and North Eastern States. Lack of leadership can play havoc, as BSF realized soon enough, when its force panicked and opened fire, killing 39 people in Bijbehara in October, 1993.[43] Senior leadership of the police/ security force must constantly take stock of prevailing stress and strain of the men under their command and see that their operations are closely monitored. Junior and middle level leadership have very important obligation to control the tempers of their subordinates in the field areas. Police reforms and restructuring of the security forces need to be brought about for not only bringing about professional competence, organisational efficiency and behavioural changes but also for promoting human rights.

The challenges before the Government and the people today are to search for effective institutional arrangements under which while the police force can be allowed operational freedom to do the professional job expected of democratic accountability is ensured to public authorities and the judiciary. In order to project the human rights of the people, people's participation through advisory bodies and civilian control boards should

State-Wise Statement of Category of Cases Admitted By National Human Rights Commission For Disposal From 1/4/1994 to 31/3/1995

Name of the State/Union	Custodial Deaths PC* JC* Os*	Custodial Rape	Disapp-earance	Illegal Detention	False Impli-cation	Other Police Exceses	Indignity to woman	Terrorist Naxalita-violation	Others			Total
(1)	(2)	(3)	(4)	(5)	(6)	(7)	(8)	(9)	(10)	(11)	(12)	(13)
Andhra Pradesh	6	-	-	-	-	11	-	28	2	9	40	96
Arunachal Pradesh	-	-	-	-	-	-	-	1	-	-	-	1
Assam	14	4	-	-	-	2	-	9	1	3	5	38
Bihar	17	-	-	-	2	3	1	47	7	2	51	130
Goa	1	1	-	-	-	-	-	1	-	-	1	4
Gujarat	-	-	-	-	-	1	-	6	-	-	2	9
Haryana	2	-	-	-	1	-	-	23	-	-	22	48
Himachal Pradesh	2	-	-	-	-	-	-	1	-	-	5	8
Jammu & Kashmir	-	-	3	-	-	6	6	12	3	8	46	84
Karnataka	1	-		-	-	-	-	10	2	1	17	31
Kerala	3	-	-	-	-	-	-	4	1	-	27	35
Madhya Pradesh	2	8	1	-	1	-	-	8	2	-	22	44
Maharashtra	2	-	-	-	-	4	2	21	1	-	20	50
Manipur	2	1	-		-	-	-	2	1	-	6	12
Meghalaya	3	-	-	-	-	-	-	1	-	-	1	5
Nagaland	1	-	1	-	-	-	-	1	-	-	-	3
Orissa	3	1	1	1	2	1	1	15	6	-	23	54
Punjab	10	2	-	-	44	39	-	85	2	41	53	276

(Contd.)

(Contd.)												
Rajasthan	10	-	-	-	-	1	-	14	6	-	30	61
Tamil Nadu	7	-	2	1	2	37	7	62	12	-	116	246
Tripura	1	-	-	-	-	-	-	-	-	-	1	2
Uttar Pradesh	5	-	1	-	2	5	2	104	19	-	85	223
West Bangal	14	1	-	-	-	3	-	8	2	-	12	40
Chandigarh	-	-	-	-	-	-	-	-	-	-	3	3
Delhi	5	33	-	1	1	1	2	31	2	1	75	152
Lakshwadeep	-	-	-	-	-	-	-	1	-	-	1	2
Pondicherry	-	-	-	-	-	-	-	2	-	-	1	3
Total	111	51	9	3	55	114	21	497	69	65	665	1660

PC - Police Custody JC - Judicial Custody OS- Others Oincludes third degree/method/abuse/torture in the oustody of security forces/Assam Rifles/ Forest Deptt. Source - National Human Rights Communual Annal Report (1994-95) become a working reality all the way down in the police work. The protection of human rights in a democratic society requires a vigilant/dedicated police leadership, a free mass media, dynamic criminal justice system and a strong sensitive human rights conscience throughout the country. The time has come when police leaders must accept their responsibilities and obligations for the protection of human rights with dedication and full commitment. A new leadership in police and security forces, brave, soldierly, dedicated, committed and disciplined will have to arise which will usher in an era of police - culture where human rights of all are protected and promoted.

References

1. Dr. Upendar Baxi (ed) - "The Right to be Human" India International Centre, New Delhi, 1987.
2. S. Vasudeva Rao - "Human Rights - Police role undefined" - *The Hindu*-OPEN Page Tuesday August 22, 1996, p. 25.
3. Dr. S. Venugopal Rao; Human Rights, Police and the Nation. SVP NPA Journal; Jan - June 1994, p. 15.
4. Dr. Krishna Mohan Mathur - *Management of Internal Security* and Related Issues - Gyan Publishing House, New Delhi, 1995, p. 227.
5. Sixth Report of the National Police Commission, Government of India, 1981, p.3.
6. Jaspal Singh - "Aspects of Negative Leadership in Police" - *The Indian, Police Journal* No. XXVIII No. 3 January - March 1982, p. 187.
7. Dr. K.M. Mathur - *Police in India - Problems and Perspective* - Gyan Publishing House, New Delhi, 1991, p. 187.
8. Dr. S. Subramaniam - CPO Personnel Policy Needs Review - *Hindu* - June 18, 1993.
9. Sankar Sen - "Police Leadership" *SVP NPA Magazine* Vol. 39, No. 2 July - Dec 1989 - Also see Management Concepts and Effective Police Administration, *SVP NPA*, Hyderabad 1993, p. 66.
10. 444 Custody deaths reported to HNRC, Bihar accounts for 75 - *Times of India*, 17 September 1996.
11. Annual Report 1994 - 95 National Human Rights Commission, p. 64.
12. Karan Singh vs State of Punjab (1994) 3 SCO 569 at 711.
13. For details of various cases, see Annual Report 1994-95 of the National Human Rights Commission.
14. Supreme Court sends top Haryana Cops to Jail, *Indian Express*, 3 May 1995.
15. *The Hindustan Times* - Parliament Questions, 8 December 1995.
16. Army got 471 Rights Complaints since 1991 - *Times of India*, 8 December 1995.

17. V.M. Tarkunde - Police and Human Rights. *The Hindustan Times*, 29th April 1992.
18. S. Subramanian - Issue of Internal Security - *The Tribune*, 31 May 1994, Chandigarh.
18a National Human Rights Commission, New Delhi Annual Report 2000-2001. p. 18.
19. Dr. Krishna Mohan Mathur - *Indian Police - Role and Challenges,* Gyan Publishing House, New Delhi, 1994, p. 13.
20. P R Rajgopal - *Violence and Response* - Delhi, Uppal, 1988.
21. Padam Rosha - Communal Riots, a failure of Governance- *SVP NPA Magazine* Vol. 47, No. 2 July - Dec 1995, p. 13.
22. Plan to increase Rights Awareness - *The Hindustan Times,* 25 June 1994.
23. Sankar Sen - Custodial crimes, *SVP. NPA Journal* Vol. 46, No. 1, Jan.-June 1994, p. 11.
24. Dr. K.M. Mathur - The Problems of Police in a Democratic Society-R.B. S.A. Publishers, Jaipur, 1987, p. 193.
25. Dr. Upendra Baxi - *A Human Rights Curriculum Designed for Police Academies - Police Training Problems and Perspectives* - Edited by Sankar Sen and A.K. Saxena.
26. Harinder Baweja - Security Forces, Excessive Pressure - *India Today* - March 31, 1994.
27. Amnesty International India, 1992.
28. S. Subramanian - Issue of Internal Security - *The Tribune,* Chandigarh - 31 May 1994.
29. V.M. Tarkunde - "Custodial Crimes and way to Curb them" in *Perspective on Human Rights* - Edited by Vijay K. Gupta - Vikas Publishing House, New Delhi, 1996, p. 189.
30. Kanwar Sandhu - "Butcher of Saviour? The Legacy of K.P.S. Gill" - *Express Magazine* - January 14, 1996. p. 1.
31. K.F. Rustamji - The Wrong Tests of Policing - 22 *Denouement* - January -Feb 1991.
32. J.Shri Raman - "Cult of the Super Cop" - *The Hindustan Times,* 17 July 1993.
33. K.F. Rustamji - The wrong test of Policing 22 - *Denouement* Jan - Feb. 1991.
34. P.R. Rajgopal - *Violence and Responses,* - Delhi, Uppal, 1988. Chapter 5.
35. Syndicate Report on Leadership Styles in the Police - Chairman, A.R. Sharma, *SVP NPA Transactions*. Vol. 26, 1978. pp. 3 - 86.
36. Sankar Sen - Police Leadership. *SVP NPA Magazine,* Vol. 39, No. 2, July - Dec 1987.
37. A.C. Germann - Changing the Police - The Impossible Dream. *Journal of Criminal Law, Criminology and Police Science* 62 (1971) p. 417.

38. Sankar Sen - Policing in the 21st Century - Paper presented at XXI All India Police Science Congress, Bangalore Feb 1988, p. 87.
39. K.F. Rustamji - The wrong Tests of Policing, 1991.
40. Krishna Mohan Mathur - *Police, Law and Internal Security* - Gyan Publishing House, New Delhi, 1994, p. 348.
41. Krishnn Mohan Mathur - *Indian Police Role and Challenges* - Gyan Publishing House, New Delhi, 1994, p. 106.
42. P N Bhagwati - "Human Rights and Democratisation of Remedies". *Indian Bar Review,* Vol. 10(4), 1983, p. 584.
43. Harinder Baweja - Security Forces Excessive Pressure - *India Today,*

9

Policing in the 21st Century—Challenges and Agenda for Reforms

"When law-makers turn law breakers; there is no respect left for the rule of law. Then police becomes powerless." (D.P. Ojha-D.G.P. Bihar) Management, according to Peter Drucker, has no choice but to anticipate the future, to attempt to mould it and to balance short range and long range goals. Managers therefore need to be skilled in making decisions with long futurity.[1] Management experts like Peter Drucker, Prahalad and Hamal have very useful messages for the police planners and manager. "Competition for the future is competition to create and dominate emerging opportunities to stake out new competitive space. Creating the future is more challenging than playing catching up."[2] Peter Drucker said "What to do is increasingly becoming the Central challenge before management that would steer them into the 21st Century." Police managers must attempt "a redefinition of strategy" for building core competencies for facing the challenges of policing at the dawn of the 21st century with confidence and courage. Political cohesion of the Indian state has become quite weak, and it has affected state's capabilities to meet the emerging challenges of nation-building for 21st century.[3] Indian society has been moving towards the direction of fragmentation and there is an internecine warfare among the various functionaries because of casteisation, communalisation, criminalisation and regionalisation of the society. How can we prepare and equip our police system to enter the 21st century in the present dismal scenario? Are present police structure, training, equipment and motivation, its basic concepts, value system and procedures, still relevant for the 21st century. Due to our federal structure, it is little wonder that we have a highly differentiated and heterogeneous police structure. On 11th and 13th May 1998, India conducted its nuclear tests. Nuclear tests, Globalisation and Liberalisation have thrown many new challenges for all, more specially for the public service organisations. India is on its march towards the 21st century, acquiring global perspectives and demanding a pro-active responses from various organisations. The decade of 1990's symbolized the spirit of "Perestroika" and unprecedented changes all over the world. More recent researches have demonstrated that monolithic organisations designed for repetitive transactions and routine activities were inadequate to cope up with the futurechallenges.[4] Any exercise to look at the future is a hazardous attempt because futurology involves an extrapolation of the past into the future with intelligent guesses. However there are too many imponderables which can make guess work redundant, however it has to be done for anticipating events. Strategic planning and effective preparations in terms of recruitment, training, equipment and technology are required to prepare the Indian Police for the 21st century. The challenges and problems of Police in the 21st Century are likely to be more difficult, complex and demanding. Only a highly motivated, trained and well-equipped police and law enforcing agencies can tackle political, economic, technological and social challenges of the 21st century. A new generation of enlightened and trained policemen, committed to the ideals of democracy, social justice, secularism, human rights and dignity will be needed who at the same time are well-equipped to deal with newer types of crimes, social disorders and internal security challenges. The volume, methods and patterns of crime will be changing faster than police organisations can keep up pace with and there is a great need to revolutionize the methodology and operational techniques of the police.[5]

For a developing country like India, its population explosion will be confronted with an uphill task of challenges in providing food, education, housing and medical care on a massive scale in 2010 AD. As such, the 21st century would be the greatest challenge for human survival, vegetation, forestry and wildlife in a world wide perspective.[6] What challenges, opportunities, uncertainties and tasks for Indian police would it bring? If we only know what the twenty-first century holds for us, we could prepare ourselves for it.[7] Nothing would seem to be more important than thinking and planning about the police administration for the 21st century. There is an in-built time lag between the challenges of the 21st century and the needed infrastructure of the innate conservative police system. A large mass of police personnel live below poverty line, without proper accommodation, without required training and even minimum infrastructure today. Being a non-development department, its available resources are always most inadequate and unsatisfactory. Police Management Information System, police station records, investigation of cases, traffic management and challenges of crime and internal security all need and demand vast resources and political will to make police administration really equipped and motivated to face the challenges of

21st century. Without ameliorating the living and working conditions of the police personnel at the ground level, any amount of modernisation is unlikely to improve the situation. The role and responsibilities of the Indian police have become most complex, variegated and challenging at both the individual and institutional levels due to unprecedented changes. The socio-economic and political scenario of the twenty-first century would be greatly influenced by the following factors:-

1. The population explosion and the drift towards urban areas.
2. Sociological changes due to modernisation and urbanisation.
3. Spread of literacy and political awakening among masses.
4. Criminialisation of politics and the growing nexus between politicians, criminals, bureaucrats and administrators;
5. Growing clamour of human rights, human dignity and equal rights.
6. Increasing terrorism, insurgency and other forms of violence.
7. Scientific and technological developments in a market economy.
8. Globalisation, privatisation and growing influence of corporate world.
9. Increase in crime and violence against women and girls.
10. Growing impact of communalism casteism, regionalism and their impact on law and order.
11. Increasing indiscipline and erosion of values among police personnel.
12. Political instability and Unstable Governments.
13. Near collapse of criminal justice system and demand for victim oriented justice system.
14. Paradigm shift in power centres.
15. International terrorism and trans-border organised crimes.

"We live at a moment when the entire structure of power that held the world together, is now disintegrating. A radically different structure of power is taking form. And this is happening at every level of human society.[8] Future scanning and anticipatory management common in other countries is still somewhat alien in India in all organisations. Police in India must take the lead in this field and thoroughly prepare it in all respect to meet the emerging challenges of the next century. Knowledge is the key to growth in the 21st century. Winston Churchill once said, "Empires of the future are empires of the mind." As explained by Alvin Toffler, in the twenty-first century, barring nuclear holocaust or technological cataclysm, electronic money will proliferate and drive out most alternatives, precisely because it combines exchanges with real time record keeping.

Changing Role Perception of Police

There is no denying the fact that at present the public image of the police at all levels has reached its nadir. Time and again, questions have been raised about the imperviousness, wooden-headedness, obstructiveness, brutality, corruption, and arrogant attitude of the police. Frequent violations of human rights by the police, criminal-politician-police nexus, lack of professionalism and undemocratic style of functioning are well-known ills of Indian police today. Before entering 21st century, all efforts need to be made to bring about drastic changes in the role and responsibilities of the police. Politicisation and communalisation of the civil police, dereliction of duty, lack of motivation, failure to ensure efficiency are some of the specific ills of the Indian police which need to be looked into if police of the 21st century has to be different from the present day police. Changing role of the police has to be analysed in the content of following factors:

(a) Changing dimensions of crime and criminality.

(b) The inadequate and incomplete nature of the police organisation in respect of recruitment, training, living conditions, transport, logistics, legal handicaps and lack of support from the public.

(c) Perpetual shortage of resources in terms of manpower and resources as against increasing demands for various duties and responsibilities.

(d) Social responsibilities of the police and its limitations.

(e) Changing social development and social conflicts.

(f) Political processes requiring police involvement like elections, Assembly meetings and VIP/VVIPS visits.

(g) Changing economic scenario including developmental programmes requiring police involvement, and

(h) Increasing social legislation demanding enforcement from the police.[9]

(i) Allegations of fake encounters-During 2000-2001, there were 109 cases reported to National Human Rights about fake encounters from various states as given below-Andhra Pradesh-14, Bihar 6, Gujarat 2, J&K 1, Madhya Pradesh 1, Maharashtra 9, Tamil Nadu 2, Uttar Pradesh 68, Jharkhand-2, Uttaranchal 4. Such alleged fake encounters spoil the image of the police. (NHRC Annual Report).

(j) Change in force deployment-Jammu & Kashmir has seen following trends in police deployment.

Crime in Delhi

Year	*CRP*	*BSF*	*ITBP*	*J KAP*	*India Reserve Police*
1996	33 coys	6 Bus	-	-	6 coys
1997	33 coys	6 Bus	-	-	5 coys
1998	23 coys	6 Bus	2 coys	2 coys	5 coys
1999	23 coys	-	1 BN	1 BN	5 coys
2001	23 coys	-	4 coys	1 BN	-

Police have an important role as social service agency, committed to act as social change agent. Policing will face serious challenges in metropolitan cities and over-populated cities in the 21st century. Policing in the 21st Century will demand a reidentification of its role not only as a social service agency but also as people's police. Police will have to act as agents of social defence and national integration. Limitations of police role need to be explained to the public which expects too much from police without providing it necessary manpower, resources or training. There is an urgent need for a national debate to evolve a consensus about the changing role of police in India. In the 21st century India's metropolitan and large cities would become polluted with the excessive growth of automobiles. In fact the large-scale emission of automobiles would give rise to the innumerable pollutants like carbon dioxide and carbon monoxide, etc. innumerable water borne diseases are likely to threaten the health of urban inhabitants and cause a grave threat to their existence.[10] Megacities like Delhi, Mumbai, Kolkata and other metropolitan cities are becoming more ugly, more polluted and more congested everyday. Blighted by slums, pollution, unhygienic conditions, diseases, political agitations social unrest, destitute and urban crime present the most difficult challenges for policing. Managing the ever-growing mega-cities is one of the most critical and complex problems of Indian policing "The problems of Police in 2010 AD are not likely to be uniform all over the country. The problem faced by the police in Bombay today may be faced by Delhi in another five years and by Bangalore, Hyderabad and Lucknow in another fifteen years. The problems faced by cities like Lucknow, Allahabad and Tiruchirapalli may be faced by numerous smaller cities by 2010 A.D. Accordingly, no single model can be applicable to the whole country although certain essential features would have to be common all over the country because of improved means of transport and communication available to criminals.[11] Domestic crimes are likely to increase all over the country by the 21st century due to breakdown of close family ties, ineffective social control systems, erosion of moral values, growing sub-culture of violence, sex and western norms, heavy density of population and thickly populated slums, and poor household livings. Dowry deaths, sexual abuse of children, wife beating, abuse of elderly parents and other forms of domestic crimes are likely to increase in near future.[12] Police has to be trained to deal with ever-increasing domestic crimes. In a random criminological sample study of complaints received against husbands, engineers and doctors ranked very high among professionals on cruelty to wife list.[13] Dr. U.N. Biswas of C.B.I. said that the police were mostly found to be ineffective in controlling crime against women as they lacked training. To deal with crimes against women, at least 25 per cent of the police force should consist of women police. More women police stations should be opened in all states. For handling women agitations, for investigating oftencess against women, more women need to be inducted in state police organisations. Training to handle domestic crimes should be made mandatory and policemen after being trained should be properly assessed for their attitudinal orientation. A research survey by S.S. Sen Gupta observes: Power and authority is the base of police organisations and the lower rungs of the police-Inspector/sub-Inspectors enjoyed the fruits of power and influences while senior officers are reported to have failing of powerlessness and even erosion in their formal power. (Indian Police Journal Oct. 1990-March 2000). Perceptions make attitudes and from attitudes flow action as Stephen tells us in his famous treatise "Seven Habits of Highly Effective Men." Indian police need to radically change their perceptions about themselves to be able to alter the bad image they have earned in the eyes of the citizens. The Indian Police of the 21st century must have a much cleaner image—an image of a democratic, humane and professional policeman. Police is bound to face more economic offences and organised crimes during the 21st century and therefore specialised units to deal with such offences have to be established. By 21st century, the following economic offences are bound to increase in India.

(i) Hoarding, smuggling and black marketing in essential commodities.
(ii) Narcotic drugs trade by the mafia gangs.
(iii) Defalcation and misappropriation of public money including bank scams and frauds.

(iv) Evasion of taxes, violations of foreign exchange regulations, offences under the Customs Act, The Central Excise Act.

(v) Corruption, manipulation of stocks and shares, profiteering.[14]

(vi) Dacoities, high way robberies, extortions, murders kidnapping and lawlessness are all socio-economic problems. Due to political pressures, polices are unable to fulfil people's expectations and people have begun to distrust and even hate police.[14a]

Organised crimes derive the major portion of its power through money laundering, loan sharking, Narco terrorism and corporate corruption. All possible efforts should be made by the criminal justice system to seek citizens participation in crime control. Police has an important role in National Security and internal cohesion. A recent survey carried out by India Today May 19, 2003 has ranked the various states from law and order perspective and has the states in the following ranking. 1. Kerala 2. Tamil Nadu 3. Delhi 4. Himachal Pradesh 5. Rajasthan 6. Gujarat 7. Karanataka 8. Madhya Pradesh 9. Goa 10. Maharashtra 11. Andhra Pradesh 12. Haryana 13. Orissa 14. Punjab 15. Jammu and Kashmir 16. West Bengal 17. Uttar Pradesh 18. Assam and 19 Bihar (India May 2003).

The Problems of Police Resources and Working Limitations

At a time when the global community is reviewing the human rights reports cards of each country at Geneva, India has reported[191] custodial deaths in 1997-98 as against 127 deaths in 2000-2001. National Human Rights Commission has reported state-wise reports of Police custodial deaths as given below:

Police Custodial death since 1998-2001

S. No.	*State*	*1998-1999*	*1999-2000*	*2000-2001*
1.	Uttar Pradesh	20	18	10
2.	Bihar	10	7	19
3.	Maharashtra	20	30	19
4.	Andhra Pradesh	25	11	2
5.	Tamil Nadu	14	9	4
6.	All India	180	177	127

(*Source:* National Human Rights Commission Annual Report 2000-2001.)

Indian Police have to build up a new police sub-culture of human rights respects and sensitisation to the various human right issues. Failure of the Indian Police Service (IPS) officers to give correct leadership to the police force is one of the foremost cause of steadily increasing violations of human rights by the police. The time has come when police leaders must accept their responsibilities and obligations for the protection of human rights with dedication and full commitment. The XXVII All India Police Science Congress held at Guwahati highlighted the need for in-house cleaning on the part of the police by taking disciplinary actions against those who violate human rights or have developed nexus with criminals. The training syllabus at each level of the police functionaries should give adequate input of human rights and inculcate a respect for human persons—a process which must begin more by example than by the precepts if the lower ring are really to emulate.[15] As a preparation for 21st century, Indian police must adequately train is personnel for safe guarding and protecting human rights. The most urgent needs of the police organisations can be briefly summarised as under:

(i) Improvement in the quality of manpower along with increase in quantity with reference to crime and population : the ratio of women police should be at least 25 per cent of police force.

(ii) Strengthening the middle and lower levels of policing by providing them basic needs and a sense of higher quality service commitement;

(iii) Creation of a police sub-culture of respect for human rights and recognition of democratic values and norms.

(iv) Provision of adequate equipment, training, transport and other infrastructure required for pro-active strategy.

(v) Strengthening of the intelligence system at all levels and providing adequate motivation for staff working in intelligence agencies.

(vi) Recognition of the hazardous and difficult role played by Central Reserve Police Force and other Central Police Organisations.

If the present trends continue, the world in 2010 will be more crowded, more polluted, less stable ecologically, and more vulnerable to disruption than the world we live in now. Barring revolutionary advances in technology, life for most people on earth will be more precarious in 2010 AD than it is now—unless the nations of the world act decisively to alter current trends.[16] By the beginning of the 21st century, there will be a greater need to prevent further degradation and depletion of nation's natural resources and life-support systems of land, water, vegetation and animal kingdom by effective environmental protection. Special environmental law courses should be started for police officers of various ranks.[17] Police should become a service, not a force and more public cooperation should be sought for prevention of crimes.[18]

Indian states must start special units for enforcing environmental laws and educate by bringing awareness among law enforcement officers. The Environment (Protection) Act 1986 and Supreme Court directions in the famous M.C. Mehta vs Union of India (AIR 1987 SC 965) need to be effectively enforced. Government of India should constitute a special law-enforcement unit for enforcing various laws relating to environment.

Need for Coordinated Action Plans for Tackling Naxalites, Insurgents and Militants

On 15 June 1998 Shri L.K. Advani, Union Home Minister had convened a meeting of representatives of the four contiguous states of Andhra Pradesh, Madhya Pradesh, Maharashtra and Orissa and a concerted strategy had been drawn for coordinated action plan for tackling the Naxalite menace. The concerted plan included the preparation of a development and security plan, upgradation of technological skills and tightening of the laws. The coordination meeting would be held every month and review meetings by the Union Home Minister will be held at least twice a year.[18] It has been suggested that each state should formulate its own appropriate laws on the lines of the Tamil Nadu Prevention of Terrorist Activities Act 1998. On similar pattern, problems of insurgency in north-east and militancy in Kashmir should be effectively tackled. There is an urgent need to draw a comprehensive action plan for reorganisation of the state police and central police organisations with a view to reduce the deprivational factors and to bring effective leadership, operational efficiency, a high degree of motivation and morale of the personnel. The human factors need to be recognised and duly compensated for deprivations. Police organisations should offer stress management courses for police officers at all levels and should organise stress alleviation programmes at organisational levels. A new police culture should be developed, based on the values of a democratic polity, secularism, social justice, human rights and pro-active service to the community with a deep human dimension of concern. The sovereignty of government will be seriously undermined if the regulator does not possess the ability to regulate.[19] Nation must exercise effective control over militants, insurgents and other anti-social elements at all costs. National security can not be sacrificed on the altar of human rights.[20] The increasing level of technological sophistication among terrorist groups is creating genuine fears about the spread of WMD (Weapons of mass destruction) terrorism. The risk of nuclear, chemical and biological weapon blackmail poses a real threat to democratic countries like India. The wisdom lies in recognising the danger and allocating adequate resources for developing a practical plan of action to cope with the menace.[21]

Challenges of Computer Crime in 2010 AD

By the end of the present Century, computers are likely to be used extensively in industry and business, by public authorities, banks and other financial institutions. While their versatility is a great boon, computers are easy prey to the manipulations by criminals with technical expertise who may steal vast sums from the banks and may commit other computer assisted crime. The chances of a computer crime being detected is one in ten thousand. It is very easy for an expert computer criminal to commit the crime without leaving any tell tale traces, which makes the investigations and subsequent prosecution extremely difficult complicated and uncertain. Computer technology has many security threats which include the following:

1. *Viruses*—Computer programmes are replicated and it damages files.
2. *Worm*—Programmes move through and between system.
3. *Trojan horse*—Secret programmes are hidden in regular programmes.
4. *Data didling*—Illegal entry to a computer and altering its data.
5. Trap door—Secret entries in computer system.
6. Time bomb—Computer internal clock triggers file damage.
7. *Super zapping*—Programmes to over side the standard security system.
8. *Salami slicing*—Bank fraud where sums of money are removed.
9. *Hacking*—Unauthorised entry to computer through a modem.

Latest computer technology has to be utilized by the 21st Century Police. The C-view image communication system offers the facility to capture on P.C full colour photographic quality images, drawings and data to any remote location and transmit it world wide in just 30-40 seconds via standard telephone or Fax line or satellite communication system.

This system provides rapid, accurate multi-user access on a PC to images, drawings and data via LAN or WAN Net-works. Latest technology like Optical Mark Readers (OMRS), Vigilante Prokit, Photo-phone, MAPINFO, PAFEC GIS, Astra guard Surveillance system, Physical security Devices for computers like floppy disk drive lock, security cable system ALS Mobile Computing System, DRS INFO SCAN, RAM Mobile Data Network and Watch IT (automated computer telephone system, should be adopted for police work to meet the challenges of 21st century.[22] Combating computer crime will be one of the most challenging tasks of the police in the 21st century. There will clearly be a role to be played by police computers in future particularly in the field of crime information, criminal intelligence and even in the management of police manpower.[23] *The Business Times* of 28 November 1994 reported that experts forecast the real cost of computer net work crime to be close to roughly 15 billions annually in the USA.[24] The various dimensions of computer crime can not easily be understood by a lay man. Therefore a special police computer crime unit will have to be formed to investigate and prosecute those involved in computer crime and other specific economic offenses. It is definite that computers are going to play an increasingly important role in police operations in the foreseeable future and would have to be integrated as part of the over all growth of the police.[25] Majority of the computer crimes can be prevented effectively if a well structured crime-prevention strategy is in-built in computer technology and various administrative and procedural physical controls are organised.

Gujarat State bruilds Separate Intelligence Cadre

On the recommendations of the R.C. Mehta Committee on June 6, 2002, Gujarat state has set up an exclusive cadre of Intelligence officers and 25 percent of their posts will be filled by direct recruits. Their jobs will be non-transferable and will have fixed tenure of officers.

Focus on Performance

The Delhi Police Commissioner B S Gupta clainned to have focussed on performance and 74% cases have been solved. The figures are as under:

1.	Heinous Cases registered	726-upto April 02	626 upto April 03
2.	Non-heinous cases registered	14, 377 upto April 01	13255 "
3.	Heinous cases worked out	67%	74%
4.	Preventive arrests	5646	6886

(Times of India 11/5/2003 New Delhi)

Need for Restructuring Indian Police

Indian police can be broadly divided into following categories:

1. Unarmed civil police, particularly at the police station level,
2. Armed state police
3. Central Police Organisations like CRPF, BSF, STBP, RPF, SSB, and NSG.
4. Central Bureau of Investigation and other enforcement agencies.
5. Central Intelligence Bureau and Research and Analysis Wing.
6. Home guards, village volunteer force and community service agencies.

There is an urgent need to redraft the police act to assign specific tasks and responsibilities to each type of police organisation—Civil police, as the basic unit of policing needs an over-haul and effective restructuring from the top to the bottom and it should not remain top heavy. Civil Police should have good public-relations and the ratio to growth of population and area to be policed needed to the taken care of. Various recommendations made by the National Police Commission (Dharm Vira Committee) Government of India in eight volumes of report need to be implement immediately. The solutions and remedies to the long standing ills and deficiencies of the Indian police will have to be basic and sweeping. Any patchwork of temporary remedies will not serve the purpose. For meeting the challenges of the future, police planners must consider the following basic issues and work out adequate requirement for each issue:-

1. What structural, organisational and functional changes are required in Indian Police to meet the needs of 21st century?
2. What will be the qualitative and quantitative requirements of police manpower and what will the requirements of each police organisation?
3. What will be the requirements of arms, ammunition, transport, wireless equipment, computers and human resource development to meet the challenges of 21st century.

The real dilemma of police reforms in India is the lack of strong political will to bring reforms and reorganisation of the civil police. However unless the entire criminal justice system and the criminal law reforms are carried out, simultaneously police reforms cannot be sustained in isolation. The working and living conditions of the CRP and other police organisation need to be improved immediately. Indian police as a whole in having a lot of maladies such as leadership failure, lack of clear cut goals, rampant corruption, nepotism and adhocism, communications break down lack of proper human resource development and personnel management. For meeting the challenges of the 21st century Indian police not only needs an over-haul but also modernization, better living conditions, adequate equipment, training, motivation and leadership. Modernisation of police should include not only improved facilities for communication, transport, computerisation but also better housing facilities, better pay packets, better training motivation and organisational development programmes. An effective and dynamic police leadership will be required to cope with the challenges of the 21st century. The challenges of the future will require new skills in personnel management and a much higher level of professional knowledge, competence and leadership from the senior officers in the police.[26] We should build up a future oriented think-tank to enable us to keep up with the developments in various sphere. Future planning should be followed by concrete action plans to implement the various recommendations and suggestions made by the planning department. Goal emphasis, social perception, work, facilitation, supportive relationships, conflict resolutions and deeper commitment are some of the essential factors needed in police leadership for their effectiveness.[27] Police officers can play a critical role in Environmental protection by utilizing powers granted under the Forest Act and Wild-life protection Act by acting in a pro-active manner.[27a]

Human Resource Developments in Police for the 21st Century

Since the levels of political, social, economic and technological awareness and expectations of the people will be higher in the 21st century police organisations will have to embark on a well-planned human resource development strategy. The police organisations should established an organisational development task force which should be responsible for:

1. Sensing and predicting the pace and directions of change of the 21st century,
2. Creating and maintaining human resource development strategies that will prepare the police personnel to cope with the new challenges of 21st century.
3. Identifying and proposing new structural arrangements for getting people's voluntary cooperation and building a good image of the police.
4. Identifying performance gaps and restructuring training to over come performance discrepancies by bringing required attitudinal

changes.

5. Making the Indian policeman more professional more honest and effective as a "friend, philosopher and guide" to the people in general.
6. Building a culture of respect for human rights, democratic values and high integrity.
7. Improving police image by soliciting peoples voluntary cooperation and assistance.

Police administrators of the future will have to reckon with what Toffler described as "the dizzing disorientation brought on by the premature arrival of the future" and HRD programmes drawn up for future should necessarily need to equip them for this role.[28] Indian police have to train and indoctrinate its special tasks forces and groups to perform various internal security duties. Intelligence agencies have to gear up the intelligence work at field levels and provide timely and accurate intelligence to the special commando troups, anti-terrorist squads, Rapid Action Force and the specially trained troops dealing with various internal security challenges of the 21st century. The police station personnel need to be imported regular refresher and vertical interaction courses on police-public relations, investigation, scientific methods of interrogation and crowd control techniques. All managerial level officers should be imparted training in Behavioural science, management techniques and strategic management of personnel and resources. All techniques and methods of human resource development should be utilized to improve the core competencies, skills, techniques and behaviour of senior police officers. CRP, IB, National Security Guards, BSF, ITB and Railway Protection Force have specialised tasks to perform. CRP is the most versatile, multidimensional force to deal with various internal security challenges. Central Reserve Police Force has developed enough experiences and professional expertise to deal with problems of communal violence, extremists naxalite movement, insurgencies, terrorism and other serious law and order problems. The central government has a very important role to play in planning, evaluation and coordination of Central Police Organisations, particularly in respect of training, equipment, modernisation and financial assistance.[29] To improve police communication, latest available video-projectors, VHF/UHF portable radios, stero-micto cassette surveillance recorders, Micro-wave communication systems, Digital Cameras, interview recorders, photo-phone XD, photo wallet, and the watsonline telephone connectors should be procured for the police. For improving training FATS (Fire Arms Training simulators, and Indoor range training equipment, should be provided to all police training institutions and district headquarters.[30] Latest inventions and equipment available in the field of forensic science, traffic and investigation should be made available to the police organisations.

Police Computer Network for Meeting Challenges of Inter-State Crime

For meeting the challenges of 21st century the Government of India has sanctioned the proposal of police network (Polnet). Police force functioning of 32 states and union territories has been standardised on the basis of a pre-devised format to achieve uniformity in investigation and to ensure information is properly shared by them. Over 600 police districts in the country are connected through Polnet. Seven Input forms have been devised to ensure that data in terms of case histories and investigation, information about criminals, their background, previous records and other crime related details. This project is being implemented through the Delhi based National Crime Record Bureau. A data bank of fingerprints of convicts across the country would be accessible on the screen. According to Sharda Prasad, Director N.C.R.B. "this would help in verifying members of inter-state gangs and those who may have shifted their states for carrying out crime". While 23 states and four union territories are already in the process of adopting the form, other states are reportedly waiting government clearance and financial sanctions.[31] There are a number of problems and working limitations for this ambitious project but it is hoped to be functional in all states before the beginning of the 21st century. Police profession in India has to develop dynamism and viability to cope with the changing needs of the modern society.[32] Unless both Centre and State Governments remove the difficulties and financial constraints on the police system and bring out necessary reforms, professionalism and law and order situation of the country would have to face the next century with the type of decay that has occurred in Indian policing system. Democracy, social justice, and human rights can be effectively safeguarded in the country only when Indian police is modernised, reorganised and provided adequate human resource development. Mind sets of the Indian police need to effectively cope with the various tasks and responsibilities of the 21st country. To prepare police for the 21st Century, it is the malady and ailments of the police, rather than the system, which need to be addressed on priority basis at both central and state levels. Major role has to be played by the states because police is a state subject Chief Ministers of various states should adopt a time-bound programme to reorganise the state police after amending police Act 1861 and bringing adequate financial and administrative support to implement the reorganisation of the state police. Central Government have to provide necessary financial and administrative support. The National Human Rights Commission in its annual report for 1996-97 tabled in the Rajya Sabha by Union Home Minister L.K. Advani has suggested the insulation of the investigating wing of the police; constitution of a five member Police security and integrity commission at the state level, improvement in the mode of appointing prosecutorial personnel at all levels, amendment in Indian Evidence Act 1972 and need for judicial reforms. Stressing the need for restructuring of the police system, former home minister Indrajit Gupta suggested that states address themselves to issues relating to the dilution of command structure, system of selection of Police Chief, undue emphasis on crime statistics and the need for toning up the prosecution machinery.[33] We need to seriously implement the various useful and important recommendations of the National Police Commission in a time bound programme and must modernise, sensitise and train Indian Police for meeting the various challenges of the 21st Century. Police must enjoy full autonomy in matters of investigation and prosecution of cases at all levels and it must develop accountability and pro-active responses to various challenging situations. Community policing with emphasis of peoples active participation in crime prevention and crime control is one of the most important imperatives of the 21st century. Police can build up core competencies through communication, involvement and a deep commitment to working across organisational boundaries. During the last fifty years, Indian Police has been a victim of serfdom, of object subservience to the political and administrative executives, who misused and abused the disciplined police force for its selfish, partisan and narrow political objectives. The Shah Commission in its interim report observed: "The Government must seriously consider the feasibility and the desirability of insulating the police from the politics of the country and employing it scrupulously on duties for which alone it is by law intended." Police must enlist people's support, and corporation. "In the absence of citizen assistance neither more manpower nor improved technology, nor additional money will enable police to shoulder the burden of combating the 21st century crimes." (The U.S. National Advisory Committee Report 1977).

Will Agenda for Police Reform Ever be Implemented and Who Will Do It?

The real dilemma of police reforms in India is the existence of a paradoxical socio-political situation wherein reforms are essential as well as impossible simultaneously. "Those who can reform the system do not want to attempt it and conversely, those who really wish to reform, just have no power or capability to do it."[34] There is lack of political will to bring police reforms. It is unfortunate that there is no public demand or pressure for police reforms. Unless there are also reforms in criminal justice system and criminal law reforms, reforms in police organisations cannot be even sustained in isolation. Police organisations require strong political will and public support for drastic reforms in police system which can be possible only when Central Government and state Governments together agree to bring revamping of the system. But unfortunately such a possibility is very remote in the near future. "Perhaps it is time for the nation to re-evaluate the goals and objectives, policies and procedures, methds and techniques of police organisations in order to prepare it for the 2010 A.D. It is high time for all the people to observe, experience and judge policing at close range and suggest suitable remedial measures to reform and restructure the police organisation".[35] The question arises why all desirable reforms and modernisation have not been so far carried out and who are all responsible for the failures of Indian Police to restructure itself according to the needs and demands of the time. The crying need is to awaken people's consciousness so that those who determine the destiny of the nation, are forced to redefine the charter of police duties and bring about much wanted modernisation, reorganisation and professionalisation in the Indian Police System. Modernisation, depoliticisation and reorganisation of the Indian Police are overdue and are the most urgent needs of the day.[(36)] The Indian police must assume national security connotations, dealing with terrorism, subversion, economic offences, espionage trans-border crimes and criminal fall outs of globalisation and liberalisation.

References

1. D.P. Ojha-D.G.P. Bihar Times of India (25 May 2003).
2. Gary Hamel and C.K. Prahalad – "Competing for the Future" (Harvard Business School, 1994). pp. 10-20.
3. C.P. Bhambhri – The Indian State: Journey from Intervention to Liberalisation – *Indian Journal of Public Administration,* July-September, 1997, Vol. XLIII, No. 3, p. 304.
4. C. Handy, The Age of Unreason, Boston (MA), Harvard Business

School, 1998; R.M. Kanter, 'When Giants learn to Dance New York (NY), Simon and Schuster, 1987 pp. 20-21; A Morita, Edwin M. Reingold: Mistsuko and Shimomura, Made in Japan, New York, E.P. Dubton, 1986; Kohmae, 'Beyond National Borders, Homewood (iii), Dow Jones Irwin, 1987; R. Pascale, Managing on the Edge, New York (,), Simon and Schuster (1990): T. Petery Thriving on Chaos, New York (NY) Haper and Row, 1987, PR Singh and Bhabderkar. 'Corporate Success and Transformational leadership' New Delhi. Wiley Eastern (1990): A. Toffler, Adaptine Corporation, New York, Bantam Books, 1998. A. Toffler 'Power Shift' New York, Bantam Books 1991. P.R. Singh and Bhan Barker. Also see Krishna Mohan Mathur–Indian Police-Role and Challenges—Gyan Publishing House, New Delhi, 1994. Chapter 10, pp. 240-296.

5. K.M. Mathur– *The Problems of Police in a Democratic Society*–RBSA Publishers, SMS Highway, Jaipur, 1987, p. 21.
6. Gopal Bhargava (editor) '*India in 21st Century-challenges and opportunities*, Publications, New Delhi, 1993. p. (ix).
7. K.M. Mathur–*Management of Internal Security and Related Issues*-Gyan Publishing House, New Delhi, 1995, p. 63.
8. Alvin Toffler–*Power Shift*, p. 5.
9. K.M. Mathur, *Police in India Problems and Perspectives,* Gyan Publishing House, New Delhi, 1991, p. 298.
10. Gopal Bhargava in his preface to the book *India in 21st century challenges and opportunities,* edited by Gopal Bhargava, Anmol Publications, New Delhi, 1993.
11. Eight and the concluding Report of the National Police Commission, (Dharmvira Report) Government of India, May 1981, p. 23.
12. Dr. Krishna Mohan Mathur–*Crime Human Rights and National Security,* Gyan Publishing House, New Delhi, 1996, pp.1-51.
13. Engineers, Doctors ran high on cruelty to wives list, Biswas—*The Times of India*, Monday, New Delhi, 15 June 1998, p. 1.
14. For further details see Dr. K.M. Mathur *Crime, Human Rights and National Security*; Gyan Publishing House, 1996, New Delhi, Chapter 2, pp. 58-97. Also see *U.P. Police Patrika* June 1997, pp. 27-48.

14a. D.P. Ojha-Bihar's Super Cop. *Times of India,* New Delhi. 25th May 2003. p. 16.

15. Kishore Kumar vs State Court-AIR 1981 SC 625.
16. Gopal Bhargava in his book- *India in 21st century-challenges and opportunities*, Chapter- Indian economy scenarie 2001 A.D., p. 134-135, Anmol Publications, New Delhi, 1993.
17. Krishna Mohan Mathur- *Police, Law and Internal security* Gyan Publishing House, New Delhi, 1994, p. 72.
18. *The Times of India*-16 June 1998, New Delhi, Edition.
19. Donald F. Ketti-*Sharing Power: Public Governance and Private Markets*: Washington D.C. Tere Brookings Institution 1993, pp. 208-9.

20. Human Rights Newsletter - May 1998, Vol. 5, No. 5. Published by National Human Rights Commission, New Delhi, p. 4.
21. Ved Marwah- The Emerging Threat of Super-terrorism. *The Times of India*, New Delhi, 26 June 1998.
22. For further details see *Police Research and Development Journal* October-December 1997, See pp. 33 to 38. Brief description of the product and name of address of the manufacturing companies have been mentioned against each. Bureau of Police Research and Development-MHA GOI-Oct.-Dec. 1997, Quarter IV.
23. Dr. Krishna Mohan Mathur-*Internal Security Challenges and Police in a Developing Society*-RBSA Publishers, Jaipur, 1989, p. 221.
24. Private Security in Asia Towards the year 2000. Paper presented by Major N.S.P. Kalastree WSO CSSD e II at secusafe 94, Baroda Reported in *The Times of India,* New Delhi, 29th April 1995.
25. Sixth Report of the National Police Commission (Dharam Vira Committee) Government of India 1981, para 58: 1 p. 74.
26. DharmVira Report- Sixth report of the National Police Commission, Government of India, March 1981, p. 1.
27. Krishna Mohan Mathur, Indian Police- Role and challenges - Gyan Publishing House, New Delhi 1994- p. 245.

27a Nikhil Jai Prakash Gupta and S.S. Vagal, Environmental Protection and Law: Critical analysis of role of Police—The Indian Police Journal. Vol. IL No. 1. January March 2002. pp. 24-30.

28. Dr. Krishna Mohan Mathur - *Concerns and Constraints in Administration,* RBSA Publishers, Jaipur, 1991, p. 70.
29. Dr. Krishna Mohan Mathur—*Internal Security Challenges and Police in a Developing Society*- RBSA Publishers, Jaipur, 1989, p. 317.
30. For further details see *Police Research and Development Journal* October-December 1997, Quarter IV Published by Bureau of Police Research and Development, New Delhi, p. 39-50.
31. Vinay Tewari - Computer Net work will link Police Force in different States - *The Times of India,* 15 June 1998, New Delhi, Edition.
32. Dr. Krishna Mohan Mathur—*Administration of Police Training in India,* Gyan Publishing House, Delhi, 1987, p.361.
33. *The Times of India*, New Delhi - 31 August 1997. Restructure Police System-Indrajit.
34. Dr. P.D. Sharma, Dilemmas and Dimensions of Police Reforms- in India-*Indian journal of Public Administration* - July-September, 1985, Vol. XXXI- No.3, p. 788.
35. Dr. Krishna Mohan Mathur "Planning For Future Policing - Some Reflections:" Paper presented at XXI, All India Police Service Congress Banglore, Karnataka 25-27, February, 1988, p. 27.
36. Dr. K.M. Mathur - "Indian Police After 50 years of Independence - A Reappraisal" *Indian Police Journal,* Jan-June 1998, Vol. XLV, No. 1 and 2- B.P.R & D, New Delhi, p. 72.

10

Challenges to National Security

We are in a new era. We spend a lot of time thinking about how to secure our homeland even further.

George W. Bush

"National Security can be defined as part of the government policy, having as its objective the creation of national and international conditions, favourable to the protection or extension of vital national values against existing and potential adversaries". Security of a nation-state demands an examination and analysis of the political and security environment of the region in which it is located, the nature of relations with and its attitude towards its neighbours and vice versa, the military doctrines, force deployment postures, weapons system capacities of countries in the region and above all, the inter-play of defence and foreign policy objectives of the countries in the area. Modern nation-states are facing challenges of globalisations and collapsing borders in the political sphere. National-Security today includes military and non-military connotations including human dimensions.

National Security in general terms would include:

1. Preserving the territorial integrity of the country against external threat or aggression.
2. Preservation of constitutional and political order.
3. Maintenance and development of the economic system.
4. Promotion of national core values.
5. Protection of legitimate national interests and internal values.
6. Preservation and protection of plural multi-religious society.

National Security of a country depends on some of the following factors:-

(i) Geographic and geo-strategic conditions including location, extent, physical confirmations, climate, weather of the national territories and their vulnerability in terms of security and defence.

(ii) Human and material resources available and their extent of optimum utilization.

(iii) Industrial, material and economic development of the nation and its potentials for future development in relation to other countries of the worlds.

(iv) Political conditions including national policies, political structure, level of national cohesion and level of national consciousness.

(v) National power in terms of air power, naval power and military power and their effectiveness and level of national preparedness.

(vi) Socio-cultural conditions including level of social cohesion and solidarity.

(vii) Security from all internal and external threats to the vital national values and legitimate national interests.

(viii) Maintenance and preservation of political, economic and social structure that the nation has given to its citizens."[1]

National security requires the willingness and capability of a nation to secure itself from all unwanted foreign domination and fulfill the following criteria:

1. The over-all national capability to manage the domestic process of economic development and national integration.
2. The capacity to resist outside penetration.
3. The capability to deter outside states (especially superpower and regional powers) from lending support to its hostile neighbours.
4. The capacity to preserve and protect national interests, values and core ideals.
5. Capability to ensure safety and security of all its citizens from trans-border crimes, illicit narcotic trade and terrorism.
6. Capacity to protect its citizens from all crimes and attacks and to protect its national property and property of its citizens.
7. The capacity to provide psychological assurance of a good quality of life free from all dangers and attacks.
8. The creation of conditions which will contribute to its politico-economic and social consolidation and its territorial integrity, transcending strategic and military factors.

9. Safeguarding the freedom of options and capacity to live as an independent sovereign power in the international community.
10. National security today is closely linked to good governance. The nation needs to cater for its own security and the security of its individuals which has acquired equal, if not greater significance with the passing years.[1a]

Main components of Internal and External Security are as under:

INTERNAL SECURITY CHALLENGES :

	1.	Secessionist movements.
N	2.	Parochial and regional aspirations.
A	3.	Religious fanaticism.
T	4.	Revolutionary activities.
I	5.	Casteist aggression.communal conflicts
O	6.	Espionage and sabotage.
N	7.	Corruption at the upper reaches of power and authority.
A	8.	Economic offences and operations of Mafia gangs.
L	9.	Refugees problems.
	10.	Political agitations.
	11.	Other miscellaneous agitations.

EXTERNAL SECURITY CHALLENGES :

S	1.	Military aggression by neighbouring nations.
E	2.	Limited territorial violations, air volations.
C	3.	Low intensity conflicts, proxy wars, Insurgency.
U	4.	Economic aggression and economic sanctions
R	5.	Politico-diplomatic offences by foreign countries.
I	6.	Religious aggression Islamic fundamentalism.
T	7.	Subversion and sabotage.
Y	8.	Demographic aggression by refugees/infiltrators.
	9.	Border skirmishes.
	10.	Air space violations.
	11.	Cultural invasion through mass media and other means.
	12.	Intelligence operations and subversion.

In the operationalisation of National Security, the following instruments are commonly resorted to in practical policies:-

(i) Strategic defence plans and military measures.
(ii) The police measures.
(iii) The secret service operations.
(iv) Economic measures.
(v) Political measures.
(vi) Socio-psychological operations and thought-control measures.
(vii) Diplomatic and international pressures.
(viii) People's voluntary support for national security.
(ix) India needs a dynamic, forward looking pro-active national security policy which can take care of all internal and external challenges and make India a powerful nation.

Internal Challenges to National Security

India's first security concern is to cope with a more complex and competitive international situation. India's national security faces serious internal threats from the following factors:

1. Problems of federalism and Centre-State relations with different political parties at the Centre and in the State.
2. Collapse of criminal justice system and rule of law.
3. Erosion of state authority and state of anomalies as happened during Delhi Riots in 1984 and after Ayodhya aftermath in 1992.
4. Collapse of constitutional institutions like Parliament and their subversion by foreign agents and saboteurs.
5. Crisis of the polity due to political horse-trading and nexus between criminals and politicians in power.
6. Social, ethnic, cultural and religious conflicts arising out of plural nature of Indian society.
7. Terrorism and organised violence on a large scale due to easy availability of small arms and hi-tech explosive devices.
8. Corruption at various levels in political, bureaucratic and social institutions.
9. Insurgency and separatist movements under the pretense of right of self-determination.
10. Trans-border smuggling and organised crime by mafia.

National security planning requires institutionalised arrangements for in-depth analysis of economic, political, social and international issues and their macro-level complexities.

Espionage Activities of the Foreign Agencies

Espionage activities of the foreign intelligence agencies and subversive activities of explosion are serious threats to national security. According to the latest statistics available till 1994 December out of a total of 247 individuals arrested for spying, 61 were convicted and 73 were yet to face trial.

Hostile and Unfriendly Neighbourhood

Fifty years after independence, India still has unresolved land and maritime boundary disputes with its neighbours, beset with numerous disagreements over jurisdiction, cross border smuggling of weapons, explosives and narcotics.[2]

India shares borders with the following six countries:

1. Bangladesh	-	4,096 kms
2. China	-	3,917 kms
3. Pakistan	-	3,310 kms
4. Nepal	-	1,752 kms
5. Myanmar	-	1,458 kms
6. Bhutan	-	587 kms

India shares 3310 kms borders with Pakistan. India has faced 3 Wars from Pakistan - 1948, 1965 and 1971 and the threats from Pakistan continues to be a serious threat to the national security. There are 38 terrorist camps/centres in Pakistan where recruits/militants were regularly trained and sent on Jihad missions to Kashmir, Bosnia, Palestine and some African countries. Disputed border with Pakistan are:

1. Line of control.
2. Siachen Glacier.
3. Sir Creek.

Kargil conflict was an undoubted victory for India. The crisis of the Line of Control (Loc) cannot be discussed without considering the Kashmir issue which again can not be dealt in isolation but only in the context of overall Indo-Pakistan relations. India-China war happened in 1962 and the border dispute continues from 1964. China carried out its nuclear explosion in 1965 and stepped up its relationship with Pakistan. In 1971 witnessed both US and China brow beat and the threat from China cannot be overruled. Disputed border with China can be enumerated as under:

1. McMohan Line.
2. Aksai Chin
3. Road in Aksai Chin linking Tibet with Sinkiang.

The Chinese threat manifested itself in three broad patterns:

(a) Military strategic threat.
(b) Threat to India's power and influence position at the regional and contiguous level.
(c) The threat resulting from China's support to the insurgency problem in North-Eastern India. Viewed broadly, it was a challenge to India's democratic institutions and the values associated with it.

Not a bullet has been fired across the high Himalayan Frontiers between China and India in the last three years" said Defence Minister on 11 May 2003. Both China and India want tranquility along Indo-China borders.

Though the Chinese ideology does not retain the same harsh and abrasive edge and frenzied fanaticism that it did during Mao's lifetime, the Chinese will to power can be ignored only at peril to the security of the country.[3] The great Himalayas are more of a strategic liability than natures gift of a barrier against aggression for India. For China and any other power in control of Tibet, the Himalayas are a strategic asset against India. In May 2003 Defence Minister George Fernandes visited China to build up cordial relations with China. Indian Prime Minister is likely to visit China in June-July 2003 to keep eastern and north-eastern borders "trouble free" by establishing cordial relations with China.

Threat from Nepal

We cannot allow that barrier to be penetrated because it is also the principal barrier to India. Therefore, much as we appreciate the independence of Nepal, we cannot allow anything to go wrong in Nepal or permit that barrier to be crossed or weakened because that would also be a risk to our security.

Threat from Bangladesh

Bangladesh also became the recipient of Chinese arms during the days of Gen. Zia-ur-Raham. According to the Stockholm International Peace Research Institute, during 1977 Bangladesh received 10 (out of an order of 50) Shenyang fighters from China and during 1978 another 14 fighters (of the same Shenyang variety) were delivered to Bangladesh.

Disputed border with Bangladesh are as under:

1. 78 km in West Bengal.
2. 3 km in Assam
3. 8 km in Mizoram
4. 38 km in Tripura
5. New Moore/ South Talpathy Island.

India's concern resulting from increasing border skirmishes about the danger of its security in the eastern sector was reflected in its decision to deploy five divisions of its Armed Forces on the Indo-Bangladesh borders.

Threat from Sri Lanka

The dispute over the ownership of the island of Kacchativu - a legacy of the British rule - had eluded solution for a long time. The agreement, while recognising Sri Lanka's sovereignty over the island, make it clear that the fishing, navigation and pilgrimage rights of the two countries in the island would remain unaffected.

Disputed border with Sri Lanka - Kacchativu Island
(Area of 6 sq. kms)

With Sri Lanka, tension exists over the Kacchativu island in Palk Straits, covering an area of 6 sq. km, located around 19 km from the Indian coast and 17 km from Sri Lanka. India and Sri Lanka also agreed to explore and divide whatever mineral wealth was available in the area. The LTTE problem has not been solved and the assassination of Shri Rajiv Gandhi our former Prime Minister was a result of our policy towards Sri Lanka.

Though at present islamic fundamentalism is only providing indirect support to the terrorists in India and certain civilian trained nationals are fighting the security forces in Kashmir.

Pakistan Funding Kashmir Militants

There are 110 Terrorist Training Camps in Pak Occupied Kashmir (POK) North West Frontier Province (NWFP) which are being funded and monitored by the Pakistan's Inter-Service Intelligence (ISI). There are being run by terrorist outfits like the Hizbul Muzahdeen the Lashkar-e-Taiba and the Jaish-e-Mohammad.[3a]

A mind boggling Rs (Pak) 2.40 crore per month has been spend by the Pakistan Inter-Services Intelligence to sustain militancy in Jammu and Kashmir. A RAW (Research and Analysis Wing) report noted that militancy has become a business proposition for both fundamentalist organisations and valley-based secessionist groups. "The ISI's contributions are presently classified under militant operations' and 'social welfare work' (an euphemism for aiding the militant groups)".

Details of ISI Funding to Kashmir Militants

Organisation	*For Militancy*	*For Social Welfare*	*Total*
Al-jihad	Rs. 30	Rs. 20	Rs. 50
Hizbul Mujahideen	Rs. 36	Rs. 20	Rs. 56
AL-Barq	Rs. 24	Rs. 20	Rs. 44
Muslim Mujahdeen	Rs. 20	Rs. 20	Rs. 40
AL-Umar	Rs. 02	Rs. 20	Rs. 22
Jammatul Mujahideen	Rs. 10	-	Rs. 10
Ikhwanul Mujahideen	Rs. 10	-	Rs. 10
Harmatul Mujahideen	Rs. 07	-	Rs. 07
Tehreekul Mujahideen	Rs. 05	-	Rs. 05
(Total in lakhs in Pak. Rs.)	Rs. 144	Rs. 100	Rs. 244

(Ruppes two hundred and forty-four lakhs in Pak. Rs.)

According to one report there are 1200 to 1500 trained militants of various terrorist outfits waiting to infiltrate into J&K. Another additional 3,000 to 3,500 militants are lodged in various Training Camps.[3b]

Another report claimed that Pakistan currency is valid in certain areas of state and in few areas it is only Pak currency that is in usage.

I.S.I. Infiltration Route Through Nepal

The Inter-Services Intelligence (ISI) of Pakistan has sent in highly-trained Pakistani and Arab terrorists into Indian territory via Nepal to establish a "country-wide network and support system of subversion and terrorism". The bomb explosion at Delhi airport on June 25, 1991 and later on December 1, when bombs were found Delhi to London and New York, was also the handiwork of these terrorists of ISI.

Should India Sign the CTBT (Comprehensive Test Ban Treaty)

The demand of the Big-5 is hypocritical. After conducting 2,045 tests between 1945 and 1996 they had no "moral standing" to ask anyone else to desist from nuclear testing. An attitude of one-upmanship has no place in foreign policy, and certainly not in international treaty negotiations. We can't compromise our national security.

Globalisation and National Security

There need not necessarily be conflict between indigenisation and globalisation, provided we are careful to maintain our independence in formulating policies that serve our national interests and do not subject ourselves to the dictation and domination of more developed and industrialised countries. In a message to the Ninth U.N. Congress on prevention of crime, Former Secretary General Boutros Boutros Ghali observed: "powerful international criminal groups now operate outside national or international law. They include traffickers in drugs, money laundering, the illegal trade in arms—including trade in nuclear materials—and the smuggling of precious metals and other commodities. These criminal elements exploit both the new liberal international economic order and the different approaches and practices of the states"[4] Any euphoria over globalisation and the World Trade Organisation will not be beneficial to us as we must be realistic in dealing with this phenomenon so that our cultural and national identity and our people's interests are not jeopardised. Visit of Defence Minister of India to China from April 21-28, 2003, after an 11 year gap is likely to restore amicable high level political contact between the two Asian giants and is a small leap forward.[4a]

India's Foreign Policy—Need for Caution and Long-Term Perspective

In the field of foreign policy, now India cases a challenge as well as an opportunity to play its due role. It can be done in a positive manner provided India sticks to its basic principles of foreign policy which were evolved during our struggle for freedom and in the first decade of our independence, such as non-alignment or the independence of judgement and action bridging the gulf between developing and developed countries on a fair, just and equitable social, economic, cultural and communications world order where all cultures and countries can retain their identity and benefit from inter-course with others. India's stand on the NPT and the CTBT is an example of how Indian can stand alone, if necessary, to uphold its independence of judgement and action not only in its own interests but in the larger interests of the people of the whole world. India must safeguard actual LOC. Ensuring the inviolability of the LOC requires two things political initiative such as honouring the Delhi Agreement of 1952 and the revival of the draft agreement of 1988 that envisaged a pull-back and demilitarisation of Siachen. The policy on

Kashmir needs a thorough review and strategic long term perspective during indo-Pak Negotiations

India's emphasis on complete nuclear disarmament and rejection of such gimmicks as nuclear weapon free zones which exclude nuclear weapon powers and allow them to retain their monopoly of nuclear technology is praiseworthy. India in this matter represents perhaps the wishes, hopes and aspirations of all the people of the world who do not want to risk self-destruction through a nuclear holocaust and would like to see the world free from war and nuclear weapons.

Need for Adequate Budget Outlay for Defence

The Rs. 35,620 crore budget oulay for defence for 1997-98 registered an increase of about Rs. 6,600 crore over the 1996-97 revised outlay. The provision includes 3,620 crore for implementing the recommendations of the Fifth Pay Commission. The 20 per cent increase is only on paper, however, over the last year's revised estimates. In actual terms it is only five per cent. The Indian Army has got a significant increase in the budget which is Rs. 19,205 crore compared to last year's revised estimate of Rs. 14,166 (14,166) crore. However, again in real terms this increase is not much because the Army is to convert the present 7.62 mm self-loading rifles (SLRs) to 5.56 mm rifles. The Army's shortage of equipment could also lead to a crisis situation. Though India has, 3,400 MBTs (Main Battle tanks) compared to 2,000 that Pakistan has, many of them are outdated. We have 800 Russian T-55 tanks (1955) and 1,200 Vijayant (1965) which should have been phased out long ago. The T-72 tanks are also becoming outdated and need to be upgraded before they become obsolete. The long awaited MBT Arjun is yet to take off. Since the Arjun is expected to cost Rs. 12 crore, money will have to be allocated to produce a minimum of 100 tanks if at all it goes into production by the end of the century. The Indian Air Force (IAF) outlay is Rs. 4,814 crore, up from 3,911.84 crore. Again, the Rs. 902.16 crore increase is significant though a major chunk of the Rs. 8,907 crore capital outlay on defence services goes to the IAF. The IAF has to pay Rs. 7,000 crore for Sukhoi-30 twin engine, multirole aircraft to Russia. It has to cover up the loss of 89 aircrafts due to accidents in the last three and half years. The Light Combat Aircraft (LCA) has been in the Pipeline for many years. There is a need for adequate budgeting for national security.

Some Alarming Issues - 34 Cases of Air- Space Violation

There were 34 instances of violations of the Indian airspace in 1995 and 1996 by aircraft of other countries, including 25 violations by those belonging to Pakistan. While Pakistan aircraft violated Indian space on 16 occasions in 1995, there were nine violations by them the next year. These airspace violations cannot be considered as mere mistakes of the Foreign Aircrafts but need our careful attention. In 1997, the Indian Air Force shot at an intruding Pakistani Remote Controlled pilotless Aircraft (RPV) near Bhuj in Gujarat on January 16 following a series of violations of Indian air-space by similar spy craft in the South Western Sector.[5]

Surplus Arms Flooding World Market

A recent survey published by Herbert Wulf - the Director of the Bonn International Centre for Conversion (B.I.C.C.) report that ranked top among the main exporters of weapons between 1990 and 1995, the United States sold 7,123 armoured vehicles, 827 military air-crafts, 72 Navy ships as well as artillery radar and guidance systems. Other nation exported 3972 armoured vehicles, 256 air-crafts, 98 ships and other military equipment.

Purulia Arms DROP

As discovered after the Purulia arms drop of December 17-18, 1995 detection is hardly possible unless the gun runners make mistakes. In case of the AN-24 which was used for the Purulia drop, the pilot, Peter Bleach, had turned double-agent and deliberately left a trail. He had even sent prior information to India via British Military Intelligence and landed at Calcutta airport for "refuelling" hoping the police would be waiting for the plane. But the Indian Home Ministry was caught napping.

Mysterious Aircraft over Tripura Raises Doubts

According to a news in *Indian Express* on 24-4-97 the sighting of a mysterious aircraft sans any markings, which flew at a height of under 3,000 feet. at Mandai in Tripura twice during the night of April 19, 1997 has made security experts sit up and take notice. The question uppermost in the minds of the Army is : was this an other Purulia? The plane had probably dropped its consignment to the recipient quite successfully. And in the insurgency prone North East, they could have been meant for any of the hard-core underground groups now waging a desperate, back-to-the wall fight against the Indian Army, what with Bangladesh, which was so far their principle source of support, funds and arms, no longer being reliable. Army Intelligence sources at Fifth Corps headquarters believe Summer night conditions are excellent for flying in arms and ammunition to underground rebels. "We believe that the seizure of a ship at Chittagong port in early March by the Bangladesh Navy has unnerved gun runners and perhaps they were prompted to use the air route in order to keep commitments", they said.

Integrated Defensive Policy Needed

India should develop Supervisory Control and Data Acquisition System (SCA DA) to safeguard and protect electricity grids, power distribution systems, dam controls, barrage controls as part of integrated defensive policy. India's banking sector, stock exchanges, telecom and internet networks should also come part of integrated defensive policy.

Review of Our Options Regarding the Chemical Weapons Conventions

India has now formally informed the Preparatory Committee that "We will have to review our options" regarding the Chemical Weapons Convention (CWC) which will come into force from April 29. This has been interpreted by some to mean that India might withdraw its retification before the treaty comes into force. India obviously cannot accept the situation where the weapon states (and its neighbours) do not subscribe to a binding the treaty obligation to forego chemical weapons. The treaty has clause permitting withdrawal after a 90 days notice, and notifying the members, the UN Secretary General, and the Security Council, India has already indicated its intention to review its participation if the weapon states do not join the treaty.

Need for a National Security Apparatus

National security management requires integrated thinking and coordinated application of the political, military, diplomatic, scientific and technological resources of the state to protect and promote national security goals and objectives.

When assessing the security concerns of any country, the normal approach is to examine the political and security environment of the region in which it is located, the nature of relations with and its attitudes towards its neighbours and vice versa, the Military doctrines, force deployment postures weapons system capacities of countries in the region and above all, the interplay of defence and foreign policy objectives of countries in the area. Ensuring the security of India implies, *first,* the creation of conditions which will contribute to its politico-social consolidation and its territorial integrity, *secondly,* the sustaining of these conditions, guaranteeing its existence, its survival and *thirdly* safeguarding the freedom of options and capacities of India to survive in a volatile internal environment. In any case, in a parliamentary democracy like ours, a "National Security Council" has to be a committee of the council of ministers chaired by the Prime Minister. The Prime Minister will always have (and is likely to exercise) discretion in the composition of such a committee although ministers of defence, home, external affairs and finance are obvious, almost inevitable members. The crux of the issue, therefore, is not the council, but the supporting system, and processes for it to take appropriate decisions.

This is apparently the basis for the recommendation of the Standing Committee on Defence (1995-96) in its Sixth Report and the Government should urgently come up with formal institutional mechanism with adequate support structures to monitor the states of our defence preparedness. Government of India in its decision of January 4, 2003 has accepted the doctrine of no-first-use recommended by the first national security advisory board after a six-month intensive deliberations devoted entirely to the nuclear doctrine.

Need for Crisis Management Group

To start with, a culture of shared information and evaluation of alternatives has to be strengthened. Similarly, greater emphasis will be needed in scenario-building and crisis management techniques and processes. A future oriented assessment and policy evolving process is required. Crisis management action group is needed not only to initiate but also to monitor various action.

Call for Setting up National Security Council

The National Security Council has to deal comprehensively with external security, security threats involving atomic energy, space and high technology, trends in world economy, internal security, patterns of alienations emerging in the country, trans-border crimes and intelligence coordinating.

The appointment of a national security advisor has been a major departure from the current set up, it is vital for ensuring national security within the framework of foreseeable threats and national resources. The setting up of an NSC and the appointment of a national security advisor would be a permanent solution to all defence-related problems.

The Institute for Defence Studies and Analyses (IDSA) should together form think-tanks and pressure groups. The two should together undertake to :

1. Suggest measures ensuring efficient handling of issues relating to national security, beneficial for the Armed Forces and the country in general.
2. Long-term planning for defence, from which should emerge the five-year plans duly supported by committed resources.
3. Make representations to the powers that be, with respect to the main issues, so that they are sympathetically considered,

and if found acceptable, ensure their implementation to educate those who are policy makers, namely the political leadership.

4. To advocate enhanced expenditure on research.

I.B. and Raw Should Work in Coordination

The recent exposure of Shri Rattan Seghal case has created an alarm regarding our security conscience and exposed our weaknesses. Counter intelligence over our intelligent apparatus and periodical verifications of assets of Senior Officers working in these organisation needs to be carried out. India requires a highly professional intelligence agency which could excel the CIA, KGB, Mossad, Stassi and ISI so that moles can be unmasked before they can damage national security.[6]

Need for Checking NATO

NATO—a military body expressly directed against the former Soviet Union—is an artifact of the bipolar division of the world and should have no place in the post-Cold War dispensation. That is what common sense dictates. The "Evil Empire" has melted away, the USSR has itself imploded and the present occupant of the Kremlin had his last election campaign underwritten by the IMF. Surely the US is on the roll and its soldiers in Europe can pack their bags and head homeward, along with their nuclear missiles and other weapons of war. Presence of NATO can be a threat to the National Security of India.

Andaman Arms Seizure Confirm PLA Nexus

The recent illegal arms seizure of the People's Liberation Army (PLA) of Manipur by the Royal Thai Navy confirms the nexus between Naga, Manipur, Assam Rebel Groups as well as Sri Lanka's Tamil Tigers gun-running through the Bangladesh ports. Ten men were arrested in mid March when their 16M vessel was intercepted by the Royal Thai Navy patrol boat following a chase in the Andaman sea, off the Southern Thai port of Ranong. The Thai Navy personnel recovered two RFG launchers, two recoil less guns, 20 American assault rifles, four M79 grenade launchers and more than 10,000 rounds of rifle ammunition. The Indian authorities have for long suspected presence of some Naga, ULFA and PLA rebels in Thailand and their using some remote Thai ports to sneak in clandestine arms from Thailand Cambodia and Laos.

Strategic Management Needed for National Security

The main stages of Strategic Management are as under:

1. Target setting.
2. Gap analysis - Forecast future performance of current

strategies and identify gaps between forecasts and targets.

3. Strategic appraisal - it calls for external (environmental) appraisal and internal appraisal, identification of competitive advantages of various action plans and strategies and redefine the targets in the light of the strategic appraisal.
4. Strategic formulation demands (a) generation of strategic options, (b) evaluation of various strategic options (against targets and internal/external appraisal and then formulation of final strategic decision for action.
5. The fifth stage is strategy implementation by drawing up action plans and budgets and monitoring and control of the operations.
6. The sixth stage is mid-path corrections to meet the difficulties and problems faced during implementation of strategies.

No Need for Pessimism However Eternal Vigilance Needed

Although national security needs external vigilance of the people, there is no need for pessimism due to the following main factors:

1. Mature political wisdom of our people.
2. Our people's faith in electoral processes and their wisdom in exercising their right of voting.
3. Sense of oneness and unity in diversity which assert itself in the face of external threats.
4. Our defence forces, civil and police services and our steel-frame bureaucracy.
5. Ancient culture having resilience and capacity to assimilate new trends and emerging forces.
6. India's foreign policy based on the principles of "Panch Sheel" and coexistence.

However there is need for modernisation, expansion and better training of State Police, Central Police Organisation and the Army, Navy and Air Force to remain in a state of full alertness to safeguard our national interests both during low intensity operations and proxy wars by foreign nations and also combating internal security challenges.

There is no scope for complacency if we can learn from India history. We must build up cordial, strong relationship with friendly countries. We must constantly review and monitor our foreign policy in the national interest.

Responsibility for national security lies with the Centre. If a situation arises in which the country's security is threatened, the President can, under the Constitution, enforce Emergency in a part or whole of the country. It is also the Centre's responsibility to protect citizens against external aggressions and internal disturbances and any state which is not being administered in accordance with the Constitution can be subjected to Central Rule. There is need to sensitise senior government officials and bureaucrats as well as our politicians and leaders about the need to take precautionary measures to safeguard national security. National security should be kept above party politics. People's role in detecting illegal aliens, foreign agents and fifth columnists should be sought through mass media and by "educating the masters". Since the intelligence and the police agencies have the mandate to safeguard national security, they should be made accountable for protecting sensitive organisations from the depradation of foreign intelligence agencies. We must build up a vision - a vision of building democratic, secular, socialist republic, a self-sufficient developed nation, a mighty nation-mighty in thoughts, mighty in action, mighty in culture and mighty in peaceful service to humanity. Political leadership and all political parties have to develop a conscious approach to the national security problems. Shri L.P. Singh former Governor and home Secretary to the Govt. of India once issued a cantionary note that it is important to guard against the tendency that equates national interest with the interest of the party in power and with central power politics. There is back of strong political will to translate their strong words of waging war against proxy war of Pakistan and peace efforts are always given utmost priority. India has worked out the entire road map for the peace process.[7] However one has to remember that preparation for war is the best guarantee for peace and eternal vigilance is needed:

> "Know the enemy and know yourself and
> you can fight a hundred battles with
> no danger of defeat".
>
> -Sun-Wuzi, 5th Century B.C.

References

1. Dr. Krishna Mohan Mathur, *Crime, Human Rights and National Security*, Gyan Publishing House, New Delhi, 1996, p.307.

1a. Security and Governance in South-Asia, Monohar 2001. pp. 25-30.

2. Rahul Bedi - Not so Friendly Neighbourhood, *Indian Express,* May 17, 1997.
3. T.N. Dhar - *Society and culture in the Himalayas.*

3a. Bisleshwar Mishra-Times New Network—About 110 terrorist camps in ROK—*Time of India,* New Delh—12 May 2003.

3b. *Time of India,* New Delhi—12 May 2003 — Time News Network.

4. *Hindustan Times*, June 18, 1995.

4a. Uday Bhaskar, C-Small Leap Forward—A smooth Passage to China—*Times of India,* 13 May 2003.

5. *United News of India* - New Delhi, May 29, 1997, Indian Air space most violated by Pakistan. *Indian Express,* May 30, 1997.
6. Surinder Puri—India Needs an Agency Like CIA—*The Times of India*, February, 1995.
7. Sinha—Peace Road map is ready—Times of India New Delhi 13 May 2003.

11

Strategic Management and National Security

"National Securıty can never be hundred per cent fool-proof. The Supreme reality of our time is our individuality as children of God and the common vulnerability of this planet".

—John F. Kennedy

"After ascertaining the strengths and weaknesses of powers, place and time . . . losses, gains and troubles, of himself and of the enemy, the conqueror should march if superior in strength, otherwise stay quiet".[1] Kautilaya in his Arthashastra has thus introduced the concept of strategic warfare and became the founder-father of strategic management. He was a pioneer of "highly successful state craft.[2] The term "Kutayuddha" in Arthashastra refers to strategic warfare only.[3] "Strategic Management" is now-a-days not a task, limited to the elite top level political masters but also heads of various organisations. It is a set of managerial skills that-has to be mastered and used by all managers at various levels. In strategic management, there is a fine blending of strategy and management. In the context of national security, general management concepts of planning, organizing, staffing, directing, coordinating, reporting and budgeting are most relevant but strategy takes care of safeguarding and promotions of national interests and achieving national security with multiple-time horizons perspective. It addresses the following questions:

(a) What are the objectives of national security?
(b) What contributes to national security?
(c) What are the organisations dealing with national security?
(d) What are the good strategies for safeguarding and promoting national security and national interests?
(e) What infrastructure is now available and what are the ideal features of needed infrastructure?

There are many such related questions which need to be analyzed in strategic management. Strategic management of national security takes care of national values, aspirations, core competencies and managerial orientations of the leaders in the determination of organisational, economic, social, cultural and political structure of the nation. Environment, Technology, and international scenario are the contextual factors that are given due consideration in strategic management. Strategic Management of National Security is one of the most important subjects in which all citizens, all politicians, all generals and all enlightened countrymen must take adequate interest. Eternal vigilance is the price of freedom and therefore there should be no complacency as far as national security is concerned. Strategic Management sets the major directions for the nation, i.e., mission, environmental analysis, strategic planning, strategic options and strategic implementation of policies and decisions relating to the safety, security and unity of the nation. Strategic management is a stream of decisions and actions which can lead to the development of effective strategies to help achieve comprehensive long-term national security. The constitution of a new national security council to carry out a Strategic Defence review and decide on security options by the Vajpayee Government has been widely welcomed as a step in right direction.[4] One should not equate national security with "Defence", one should believe in the centrality of strategy and of seizing opportunities as well as confronting dangers for planning, coordinating and integrating various strategic policies and their implementation in a holistic perspective.

The Contents of Strategic Management

According to Lorsch—Strategy can be defined as "the stream of decisions takes over time by the top managers, which, when understood as a whole, reveal the goals they are seeking to achieve and the means/ used to reach these goals.[5] Strategy basically refers to long-term goals sought to be achieved through a set of decisions and actions aimed at gaining sustainable growth advantage. Strategy was originally a term applied to warfare and has been defined as the art of planning and directing larger military/police movements and the operations of war against a hostile country. Louis Pasteur rightly said "Chance favours the prepared man". Strategy is the broad programme for defining and achieving an organisation's objectives and complementing its mission keeping in view a broad time horizon.[6] There are five major characteristics of strategy that distinguish it from general types of planning.[7] *Firstly,* strategy is used to describe activities that involve an extended time horizon. *Secondly,* the eventual impact of a given strategy is significant. *Thirdly,* an effective strategy requires concentrated efforts and focus on chosen activities. *Fourthly,* strategy requires a series of certain types of decisions made over time and a consistent supportive pattern of decisions. *Fifthly,* a strategy embraces a wide spectrum of activities ranging from resource allocation process to day to day operations and large number of simultaneous activities to reinforce the strategy at various levels. When we combine the best of the concepts from general management and strategy, the result is strategic management. In the context of national security, strategic management implies strategic analysis, strategic formulation and strategic implementations of those policies, decisions and strategic interlinking of strategic planning and process that will ensure safeguarding and protecting of national interests and national sovereignty. National leaders and statesmen like President of India, Prime Minister, Defence Minister, Home Minister, Finance Minister and even Chief Ministers of the States and other Minister must develop a strategic vision of national security, and national development. The strategic vision involves:

(i) The ability to solve most complex and complicated problems relating to national security; country's defence, nations survival and national interests, Keeping long-term perspective.
(ii) The knowledge and competence to be more anticipatory in perspective and approach.
(iii) The willingness to develop strategic options for the future.
(iv) Ability, willingness and capability to formulate, implement and monitor strategic policies for the security of the nation.
(v) A holistic perspection of strategic management of national security and ability to formulate and implement strategic integrated planning keeping long-term perspective in view.

Harry S. Truman held that National Security does not depend only on an army, a navy and an airforce . . . It depends on a sound economy, on civil liberties and human freedoms[8]. Strategic management of national security would mean those strategic decisions and policy implementations which would ensure:

(i) Preserving the territorial integrity of the country against external threats or aggression;
(ii) Preservation of constitutional and political order;
(iii) Maintenance and development of the economic system;
(iv) Promotion of national core values.

(v) Protection of legitimate national interests and internal values over a long period of time and

(vi) Preservation and protection of a plural multi-religious democratic society.[9]

National security strategy requires institutionalized arrangements for indepth analysis of economic, political, social and international environment and their macro-level complexities.

i) Strategic analysis ii) strategic choice and iii) strategic implementation with a proper monitoring system. Strategic analysis is concerned with understanding the strategic internal and external environment in which national security is to be secured and preserve. Strategic choice is concerned with the formulation of possible courses of action, their evaluation and the choice between them keeping in view long range perspective of national security Strategic implementation is concerned with the execution and translation of general directions of strategic planning and policies into action with a proper monitoring system for mid-path corrections.[10] India must identify its national interests and spell out national strategic objectives for formulating a comprehensive security plan.

The Three Modes of Strategy Making

Henry Mintzberg has described three modes of strategy making; entrepreneurial, adaptive and planning.[11] In the *entrepreneurial* mode one strong leader, like Smt. Indira Gandhi Former Prime Minister of India, makes bold, risk-taking decisions more or less intuitively, relying on personal judgement by experience, motivated by an over-riding goal. Strategy making is dominated by an active search for new opportunities with choices guided by the leaders plan and intuitive decisions. The *adaptive* mode is called "the science of muddling through" wherein leaders' only react to each situation as it arises generally in a series of small disjointed timidly moved steps. It tends to react defensively to the actions of others without proper planning.[12] The third mode of strategy making Mintzberg terms "the *planning* mode. It provides the guiding framework and strong sense of direction and follows a systematic procedure that requires them to analyze the internal and external environment and the organisation that can develop a strategic plan to move into the future. In planning mode, choices are systematic and structured and based on a rational estimate of opportunities and threats in the environment and are tailored to fit the overall mission. Strategists need ideological inspiration and motivation for working out a plan of action. Macridis Roy C. (1980)

has defined ideology as "a set of ideas and beliefs through which we perceive the outside world and act upon our information. It is the medium through which we try to learn and comprehend the work but it also generates emotions which hold people together.[13] National Security ideology provides guidance to the defence and security specialists to work out an action plan and envision a strong, secure and socio-economically self-sufficient, growth-oriented nation, having good governance. Ideology involves collective effort and action to strengthen national security, stability, unity, integrity and good governance with self-accelerating growth.

An integrated planning process comprises of three elements—strategic plan, operational plan and Results management. Operational plan includes operational analysis, key result areas, indicators of performance, short-term objectives, action plans and budgets. Results management covers control systems and corrective actions[13a].

Strategic Planning

Strategic planning is the formalized long-range planning process which has five components:

(a) basic questions—objectives, goals, mission
(b) frame today's decisions—immediate operational decisions
(c) long-time frame—5 to 30 years perspective
(d) focuses energies and resources and
(e) has top level involvement and commitment to strategic planning analysis and implementation.

Strategic planning is the process of selecting an organisational goals, determining the polices and programmes necessary to achieve specific objectives enroute to the goals and mission and establishing the methods necessary to assure that the Policies and strategic programmes are effectively implemented and monitored. The characteristics of strategic planning are:

(a) Formalized long term planning process to achieve goals and basic objectives
(b) Framework of day to day decisions.
(c) Long-time frame, and top down approach.
(d) Focuses energies on resources and energies on high priority activities.
(e) Top level involvement and commitment of people.
(f) It provides guidance and boundaries for operational

management.

(g) It enables managers to prepare for a deal with rapidly changing environment.

Strategic planning is analytical thinking and commitment of resources to action. It deals with the futurity of present decisions, it is a frame work for carrying out strategic thinking, direction and action leading to the achievement of consistent and planned results for a long-term time-frame. It is a continuous process of making present risk-taking decisions systematically and with the greatest knowledge of futurity, organising systematically the efforts needed to carry out these decisions and measuring the results of these decisions against the expectations through organised, systematic feedback.[14] National security needs strategic planning by leaders of vision and transformational leadership qualities with a team of dedicated workers. The Indian subcontinent is basically characterised by diversity in geographical setting, environment, ecology and demographical factors. For strategic management, a geo-strategical and geo-resource analysis is needed so that the nation may maintain a proper equilibrium and ensure environmental protection. Today India is facing a crisis of ideology (socialist democratic republic becoming globalised and liberal), crises of political system and crisis of national security alongwith governability. In such a scenario, national security needs strategic management with a strong political will to reassure survival, development and peace in the nation. Strategic management of intelligence operations is necessary because intelligence production, analysis and assessment are three important functions of the national security set up. An intelligence coordination apex under the chairmanship of the national security advisor is quite appropriate and it would ensure a coordinated flow of all intelligence of strategic important to the right receivers.[15] An important segment of the security road map is the National Security Council (NSC) itself, comprising of the Prime Minister and his Cabinet colleagues in charge of strategic ministries whose function is to decide strategic options. In 1998 Atal Behari Vajpayee Government showed the political will - lacking in earlier regimes - to establish the National Security Council (NSC) to formulate well-considered strategy options to deal with various national security threats and to ensure effective strategic management of national security. Once a decision is taken a strong institutional mechanism such as the core group headed by the Cabinet Secretary should come into play to ensure the implementation of the strategic decision. Figure

1 shows the matrix of strategic management of national security. The strategic management of national security must be geared to the new economic, social, political and security realities of the 21st century. National Security Council must guide a top down strategic planning process and that process should be linked to the adequate allocation of resources, equipment and logistics.

Figure 1- The Matrix of a blueprint for Strategic Management (SM) of National Security.

1.	S.M. of Intelligence Operations/counter-intelligence	14.	The Awareness of National Issues and Response Programme.
2.	S.M. of Human Resources /Equipment/logistics and other resources.	15.	National Security Action Plan Internal and external strategies.
3.	S.M. of International Borders and perceptions International L.O.C	16.	Strategic Management of Media Policy
4.	S.M. of Disasters and crisis situations.	17.	Recapitalizing Nation's Strength in science and human resource development
5.	S.M. of Low Intensity conflicts and proxy wars.	18.	Strategic reappraisal of changing environment for institutional redesign
6.	S.M. of Internal Security Analysis and Operations.	19.	National Security Threat listing and analysis.
7.	S.M. of Defence Forces and other security org.	20.	Strategic Management of economic espionage.
8.	S.M. of National Security Structures and nation's building	21.	Reappraisal of National Security doctrines/policies.
9.	S.M. of Foreign Policy and International Diplomacy.	22.	Pro-active Management of good governance and security.
10.	Strategic appraisal of external environment.	23.	Strategic Management of security budget, finances, economic social and political policies.
11.	Strategic Appraisal of Internal Environment.	24.	Institutionalised coordination between Home, Defence and External Affairs under appropriate political guidance on regular basis.
12.	Strategic Management of Public Opinions and People's Morale.	25.	National Security and citizens fundamental duties.
13.	Strategic Management of human rights issues and cases.	26	Management of Nuclear deterrence and doctrines

In National Security, there are strategies which are critical for the safety, security and promotion of national interests and national sovereignty. Such tasks must be performed exceedingly well for the strategy to succeed. Each strategy rests on a set of key success factors. In the context of national security, the key to effective strategic management is to ensure that leadership at various levels and occasions runs like a uniform thread through all functions of management to integrate them into a culture of excellence. India must restructure its security structure, taking a holistic over view, identifying vital national interests, examine the options avoidable and accordingly spell out national strategic objective and formulate a comprehensive national security plan.[14]

The Process of Strategic Management

Strategic Management (SM) starts with defining mission, scanning of environment conditions, evaluating strengths and weaknesses of the organisations, development of future objectives and formulation of strategic planning. It is done with the help of SWOT Analysis - analysis of Strengths, Weaknesses, Opportunities and Threats. Strategic formulation demands:

(a) generation of strategic options;
(b) evaluation of strategic options against targets and internal/ external appraisals and the
(c) then the formulation of strategic decision for action.

Strategy consists of the common threads of thoughts for facing risks and uncertainty, seizing the opportunity presented by the environment and using the distinctive competence of the resources of the organisation. Strategic Management ensures policy decisions which provide guidelines and framework for subordinates decision-making. Strategic management starts with goal-formulation and identification of the mission of the organisation and then proceeds to formulate realistic strategies having a long-term perspective with a scope to adjust to unpredictable opportunities with the help of "SWOT" analysis on a regular basis. The hierarchy of strategic intent includes five types of elements ranging from: (1) a broad vision what the organisation should be, to (2) the organisation's mission to, (3) specific goals that are operationalised, (4) various strategic objectives to be reached by acting according to specific (5) plans. The elements of this hierarchy set forth the ideals and the ideas that serve to unify the energy and the forces scattered throughout an organisation.[17] In strategic management, vision refers to the category of intentions that are broad, all inclusive and forward-thinking. A vision becomes more tangible in the form of a mission-statement. Strategic programming can be defined as strategy formulation, strategy implementation and feedback of results over long terms. Planning is the essence of, strategic programming. Strategic programming's greatest contributions centre around its role of facilitating communcation about strategic issues and achieving integration across organisation levles and functional specialities.[18] Various steps in the formulation and implementation of strategy are as follows:

1. The strategic planning as a hierarchy of strategic intent with vision, mission, goals, objectives and plans.
2. Identification of current objectives and strategy - Target setting and strategic programming.
3. Environmental Analysis.
4. Resource Analysis: Organisational strengths and weaknesses - profile, skills and resources.
5. Identification of strategic opportunities and strategic appraisal.
6. Gap analysis: Determine extent of change required in current strategy - new goals and objectives.
7. Strategic planning and decision-making - develop alternatives, evaluate alternatives and select alternatives.
8. Strategy implementation by drawing action plans and budget and monitoring of operations.
9. Measurement and control of progress - feedback and monitoring.
10. Required mid-path corrections and changes to achieve intended results and to meet the difficulties and problems faced during implementation of strategy.[19]

National Security needs strategic planning and strategic management for the survival and growth of the nation state. These steps have been slightly modified from the concepts of Andrew. National Security is to be secured through various internal and external strategies. Internal strategies will aim at the safe guarding of internal security through the complete spectrum of socio-political and socio-economic policies and various other nation building strategies. External strategies would include defence and diplomatic strategies, United Nations strategies, economic, trade and aid strategies, special interest group strategy for coping with external military threats and coercive diplomacy.[20] The role of the state is to strengthen our internal and external security through multidimensional strategies and international diplomacy by adopting non-alignment policy of peaceful coexistence.

Strategic management in a democratic country like India is tempered by the popularly accepted models of public administration. Scholars have drawn the following models.[20 a]

1. *Empire Model*: In this model the role of Government is viewed in terms of expanding its economic empire in terms of creating public infrastructure and providing commanding heights to the public sector. It is also called welfare state model.
2. *Umpire Model*: In this model the Government adopts a laissez faire policy and envisages the role of an umpire to a provide level playing field to economic players. It implies metaphorically laying down the proper pitch for fair market play. Liberalisation of economy envisages this type of role for the Government.
3. *Development Partnership Model*: In this model, role of state in development is to act as a development partner and take care of basic infrastructure and social sector. In this model Government and industry relationships are viewed as complementary and symbiotic.
4. *Empowerment Agency Model*: It highlights the life saving role of public institutions and state is viewed in terms of institution building for empowerment.
5. *Constitutional Welfare National Security Mixed State Model*

The Constitution of India has established a welfare state and has also enunciated an activist state through positive action for promotion of welfare of weaker sections of the society including Scheduled Castes and Tribes for achieving social justice. According to Gunnar Myrdal, the state planning and control of the economy is required in order to :

1. Squeeze and twist consumption and thereby to enhance capital formation and productive investment;
2. Keep out non-essential imports;
3. Invest in social and economic over-heads;
4. Eliminate speculative activities and monopolistc practices;
5. Obtain loans from the Government and private organisations of other countries; and
6. Ensure that the drive for private practice does not result in gross inequalities.[21]

National Security Strategy, formulation and evolution can be summarized in the Figure given on the next page. The basic duties of a sovereign state are:-

1. Preservation of territorial integrity of the country.
2. Protect citizens from external aggression and internal disturbances.
3. Provide stable conditions by protecting socio-economic, cultural ethical and political structures.
4. Carry out promotion of national interests, national policies, national goals and analyze various threats.
5. Ensure peaceful and cordial relations with neighbouring nations in order to find out new markets for its products.

Exhibit - 1

Matrix of National Security Strategic Plan

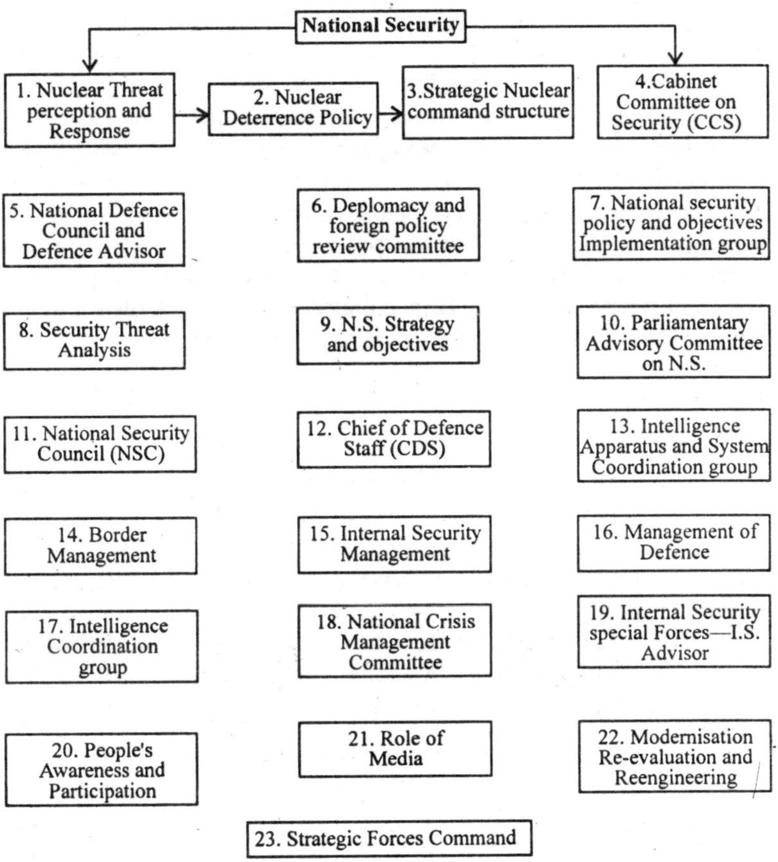

National Security Strategy

Implementation, Formulation and Process. National security analysis must take care of nuclear threat perception, nuclear deterrence policy and control command for critical decision making and implementation of nuclear command structure. National Security muct include development of nuclear command structure. National security must include development of defence objectives and broadly various alternative plans and strategies related to nuclear deterrence. Matrix of proposed national security strategic plan is given on previous page :

4. Environmental Analysis and Strategic Gearing through forward Engineering

The concept of "forward engineering" provides a foundation premise for the strategic gearing of organisations keeping in view its existing and new capabilities with respect to current and an ticipated challenges. By "forward engineering" we imply creative, proactive and responsive actions in the context of continuously changing competitive environment. It involves creative imaging, envisioning, anticipatory witnessing and mind pooling for creative solutions. Forward engineering is an overarching construct and a guiding principle for total management approach to forward movement of organisations in competitive world "environment and it starts with backbone analysis" coupled with core strengths, capabilities and competence analysis. A large number of analytical tools are now a days available for forward engineering as given below:[22]

1. BOW Analysis - An analysis of Barriers, Obstacles and Weaknesses.
2. CINE Matrix - A matrix of Controllable, Internal, Non-controllable, External factors influencing a decision situation.
3. SW-SW WINDOW - An analytical window to compare one's strengths and weaknesses with that of competitors.
4. FATE Analysis - An analysis of Future Anticipated Trends and Events.
5. SPOT Analysis - Space and Pace of Opportunities and Threats.
6. MIND-Pooling - A methodology for pooling collective institutional, wisdom leading to intuitional visioning.

In the context of national security, for purpose of clarity, it is necessary to provide a conceptual framework of forward engineering which is given in Exhibit 2 as follows:

Exhibit-2

National Security

Reach Out
Forward Engineering

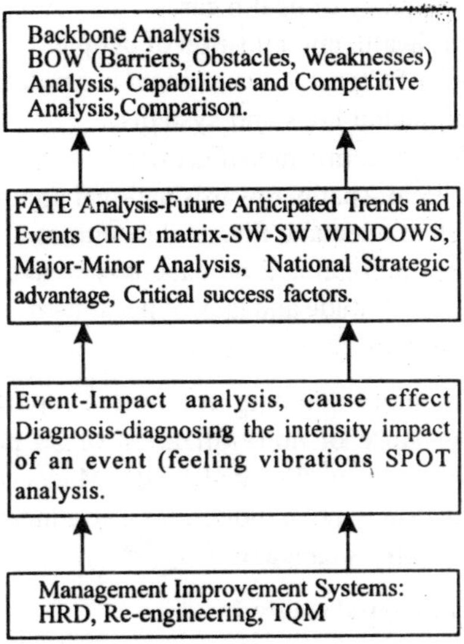

In the context of national security BOW analysis for forward engineering can be indicated below:

Exhibit-2

National Security - BOW Analysis

Barriers	Obstacles
1. Large border with a number of countries	1. Terrorism/Proxy war
2. Different climatic condition	2. Low intensity conflicts and insurgency.
3. Too many illiterate Unskilled workers	3. Political interference.
4. Lack of adequate mechanization.	4. Environmental degradation.
5. Inadequate Research and Development System.	5. Law and Order and Internal Security problems.
6. Lack of proper defence structure.	6. Corruption.
7. Lack of National Security awareness in people.	7. Level of professionalism.
8. Poor intelligence Infrastructure	8. Plural multi religious society.
9. Reactive approach to security.	9. Illiteracy and poverty
10. Poor leadership	10. Lack of political will.
11. Poor Infrastructure of roads etc.	11. Lack of strategic planning

Weakness: Indian National Security System has following main weaknesses:[23]

1. Lack of vision.
2. Low level of motivation of staff.
3. Inadequacy of health care.
4. Poor health and nutrition of people.
5. Lack of Career Advancement in services.
6. Antiquated laws and systems.
7. Poor economic rate of growth.
8. Political Apathy towards national security.
9. Lack of adequate financial resources.
10. Constitutional and bureaucratic weaknesses.
11. Selfish attitude and lack of patriotism.
12. Conservative social system.

A parliamentary standing committee report pulled the defence ministry for the lapse of non-utilization of 30 percent of the capital expenditure and lapse of allocated funds. Madan Lal Khurana was the Committee chairman which reported for a continuous lapse of budgetary grants for the ministry's capital out lay.[23a]

External Environmental Analysis

There are six broad dimensions of external environment assessment as given below:[24]

1. Demographic - ethnic composition, aging of the population, regional changes in population growth and decline, Density of population.
2. Political/Constitutional/Legal Constitutional Laws, Deregulation, Environmental protection laws, Political System, Changing profile of political parties and politicians, changes in government regulations.
3. Technological - Bio-technology, Consumer electronics, television technology, process innovations (e.g., robotics, minimills) Information Super highways, industrial disasters, computer technological.
4. Global environment - Unipolarity, Third World debt problems, powerful economic alliances, acquisitions and mergers consumer tastes and preferences.
5. Macro-economic environment - Interest rates, budget deficits/ surplus, trade deficit, inflation rates, saving rates.
6. Socio-cultural - multiple income families, health and fitness

awareness, educational standards, use of addictive drugs, competitive environment.

Above factors often overlap and developments in one field may influence other areas. National security planning requires institutionalised arrangements for indepth analysis of economic, political, social and international issues and their macro-economic complexities.[25] The year 1991 witnessed the end of the cold war and emergence of an unipolar world with the United States of America as the unchallenged leader of the nations. Major threat to India may emanate from China, Pakistan, Sri Lanka, Bangladesh, Nepal and even USA while from the American point of view, geopolitical reality has become messy and murky. The Indian strategic thinkers and policy makers will have to redefine India relationships with various nations and maneuover for it a position of advantage. Various irritants do exist even in Indo-US relationship and India must strive to establish strong ties with the major-players of various regional sub-systems both at multi-lateral and bilateral levels. Political and geo-strategic development in our neighbourhood, unabated missile development and technological transfer and nuclear proliferation in the region pose serious external threats to our security.[26] Recent international developments indicate that USA may resume nuclear testing and in the future the USA and China may discuss resuming underground tests if they are needed to assure the safety and reliability of their arsenals (*The Times of India*, New Delhi, September 4, 2001). From junking the Comprehensive Test Ban Treaty (CTBT) to unveiling the National Missile Defence Plan to slowly moving towards physically testing nuclear weapons, the international political scene has undergone drastic change. Two important policy decisions, according to J.N. Dixit, taken by India now become subject to doubts in the context of the likely revival of nuclear and missiles test by the USA (*Indian Express,* New Delhi 6th Sept, 2001). India has to safeguard and protect its territoral integrity. China occupied about 38,000 sq. kms in Jammu and Kashmir while Pakistan illegally ceded about 5120 sq. kmsof Indian territory in Pak-Occupied Kashmir to China. (External Affairs Statement in Lok Sabha on March 10,1977) There were 34 instances of violations of the Indian air space in 1995 and 1996 by air craft of other countries including 25 violations by those belonging to Pakistan. While Pakistan aircraft violated Indian space on 16 occasions in 1995, there were nine violations by them by June 1996. Diplomatic protests were, of course, lodged by India Government. Central Intelligence Agency of USA (CIA) has recently analysed the implications of world demographics on US security over the next thirty years. It sees India having to cope with environmental problems (*The Times of India,* 7th Sept, 2001, New Delhi). The change in the security paradigm demands every nation in the world to review and reevaluate afresh its own national security parameters. With the collapse of the Soviet Union and end of the cold war, Russian defence capability is now a fraction of US capability and former Soviet Republics Ukraine, Georgia, Tadgikistan, Uzbekistan and Kazakistan have entered into military and arrangements with the United States, Pakistan nuclear and missile capabilities are now of major concern to India.India is developing defence cooperation with US and western Europe-Russia continues to be a friend and supplier of sophisticated military technology. Pakistan and other enemies of India like Al Qaida and Taliban have been targetting India's secularism and multi-culturalism and have been carrying a compaign to fragment India. India has to be a member of international coalition against terrorist and support US policies.

Internal Environmental Analysis

Every internal analysis must evaluate the assets, capabilities and competencies of the organisation and also its critical success factors. India as a nation, is the second most populous and the seventh largest country of the world. The main internal security challenges before the nation can be briefly enumerated as under:

1. Terrorism, proxy war and secessionist movement in Kashmir sponsored by Pakistan.
2. Insurgency and low intensity conflicts in North-Eastern States of India.
3. Communal violence and communal virus and disturbances in different parts of the country.
4. Criminalisation of politics and politicalisation of criminals.
5. Narco-terroris, border smuggling and border crimes in border areas.
6. Corruption at all levels of administration and in all fields of life.
7. Economic offences, organised crimes and security scams.
8. Deteriorating law and order situation and almost collapse of criminal justice system.
9. Atrocities on weaker sections of society and gang wars resulting in emergence of private armies and senas in different parts of the country.
10. Problems of soft state and non-functional society with crimes of violence, kidnapping for ransom and indiscipline in police organisations.

11. Violations of Human Rights and particularly against women and childern.
12. Refugee problem.
13. Booth capturing, electoral violence and regional unrest created by caste wars in rural areas.
14. Environmental degradation and reoccurrence of natural disasters like floods, earthquakes.
15. Espionage, intelligence work and subversion of outside force.
16. Proliferation of weapons, ammunition and explosives and clandestine activities of fifth columnists.
17. According to C.I.A. report on the impact of demographics on politics, India will face serious environmental problems over the next 30 years. The 1984 Union Carbide accident in Bhopal caused nearly 3000 deaths. In India nuclear power reactors are already contaminating surrounding soil with dangerous levels of uranium. Management that tolerates poor operating practices and measures the level of success in terms of building new projects rather than running existing ones' supports the notion that contamination will most likely continue.
18. Starvation, mal-nutrition of children, pregnant mothers and poor people are serious challenges to our security management. There is a huge mass of its citizenry chronologically hungry and many die due to non-availability of food for mere survival. The phenomena of hunger is a complex one both in terms of perception and concept.
19. The internal situation of the country has been most unsatisfactory and promoting internal security by the use of police forces alone is a fools errand. For the last fifty-four years the internal security of the country has been handled in a manpower intensive approach on ad hoc policy basis. In the new era, sharp distinction between external and internal security, between foreign aggression and domestic armed disturbances, no longer apply. National security is no longer to be equated with "defence". We do not believe in the centrality of strategy and of siezing opportunities as well as confronting dangers.[27]
20. Few countries are free from the scourge of political corruption. India is targeted by an adversary sworn to its disintegration. Therefore the nexus of narcotics, organised crime and money laundering needs to be thoroughly probed from the point of

view of India's national security interests.[27a]

Operational Level Strategy at Various Theatre of Operations

Strategic Management approaches have been used for national security by all nations of the world and this envisages the deployment of scientific and intellectual methodologies which include: Forecasting, Planning, *Programming and Budgeting, MIS (Management Information System)* and operations research. As the theory of strategic planning attains greater maturity of content and universality of acceptance, the role of various factors and constituents of strategic management are expected to improve in their total effectiveness. Strategic magagement continues to utilize the classical functional management functions of planning, organising, controlling, staffing, directing and coordination as developed by Henri Fayol. Time horizon, eventual impact, concentration of efforts, pattern of decisions and all pervasiveness are the five major characteristics of strategy that distinguish it from general types of planning. In the month of May, 2001, Union Home Minister L.K. Advani released the report of the Group of Ministers (GOM) on reforming the national security system. Both the effort, focused on the overhaul of the nanagement of defence, intelligence, internal security and the country's borders and the release of such a sensitive report is the first in the country.[28] The GOM, headed by Advani had been set up in April, 2000 and comprised of Finance Minister, the Defence Minister and the External Affairs Minister. The report, aided by four specialised Task Forces, was released and report covered subjects of defence, internal security, border management and intelligence organisation. Regarding operational level strategy there is no mention of any evidence of an intelligence of an integrated operational strategy to deal with problems of Kashmir, insurgency in North-Eastern States or fighting intruders on international borders. In the above mentioned reports there is no integrated operational strategy nor an integrated Command Headquarters for various operations in Kashmir or elsewhere. Insurgency in North-Eastern States is still being fought in an ad hoc manner. India has dedicated and committed security forces, capable of fighting terrorism, insurgency and low intensity conflicts but they have to work under different political, bureaucratic and other legal pressures under most difficult circumstances. No country in the world including established democracies like the USA, UK and France have been able to combat insurgencies and civil wars without facing charges of gross abuse of human rights.[29] Unfortunately policy makers particularly home Ministers generally develop a singularly monochromatic vision and do not provide clear cut operational strategies to deal with problems like Kashmir and

North-Eastern States. Shri K. Subramanyam says, "We had recommended a draft nuclear doctrine but have not heard anything about it. .... It has received more attention outside India than within. Neither Parliament nor the media has debated it at all". Public memory is proverbially short-but granting safe passage to militants in Kashmir. (At Hazratbal shrine about 8 years ago and recently in Shopian) indicates that no operational level lessons have been learnt from the past blunders. An operation like Black Thunder at the Golden Temple in 1986 would have done Kashmir a world of good because it would have demonstrated to the outside world who was desecrating the mosque. Sadly this was not even attempted.[30] Security forces engaged in counter insurgency operations in the North Eastern States also find no operational plans and carry out operations on ad hoc basis with conflicting political pressures and uncoordinated government instructions from time to time. "Kargil showed poor border management. Kandahar was a shame. And Kohima has been a disaster;[31] writes Prakash Singh. The Home Ministry has botched up negotiations with Naga rebels by accepting cease-fire in the Naga inhabited areas in the whole North-Eastern States of India. The operational strategy of hiring vigilant type groups in the police force to help in the counter-terrorism battle is both dangerous and ethically questionable."[32] For dealing with terrorism, an operational policy need to be evolved at three plans: Psychological, Political and Administrative.33 An operational strategy has to be worked out "for winning the hearts and minds of the people". As an operational strategy of involving people and media representatives in fighting terrorism, there should be a well-trained, highly motivated, corruption free and contented security forces who enjoy goodwill and confidence of the people. The operational strategy of involving people and media representatives in fighting terrorism and insurgency can succeed only if there is a fuller and enlightened media participation and political will to deal with the problem. Useful lessons can be learnt from the operational strategies developed in the USA. and Britain and special programmes for controlling terrorism should be made. The crisis management committees at various levels must be formed to deal with developing situations in terrorist infested areas.[34] For developing operational strategies for various national security threats, think-tank should be created for suggesting strategic policy. Constant research and training on conceptual and operational aspects of the national security problems are essential for developing operational suitable strategies and policy options. For each theatre of operation, the operational strategies depend on the following factors broadly:

1. Terrain and topography of the area;

2. Nature of problem and its various ramifications;
3. Educational and cultural background of the people of the area;
4. Level of popular support for the cause and the well of the people;
5. Political, economic and social under currents in the problem;
6. Type of police and Central Police Organisations deployed, their training and operational background.
7. Intelligence network available and their time lag;
8. Level of political will and bureaucratic commitment to solve the problem;
9. International factors in the problem and its ramifications;
10. Historical and geographical factors related to the problem;
11. Demographic, ethnic, religious background of the trouble-makers and their age group and level of involvement of younger age people.

For each theatre of operation, above factors decide how the problem originates, is sustained its various under-currents. Accordingly to K. Sundarji, "Terrorism and insurgency demand that counter-terrorism and counter-insurgency planning must be jointly done by the various agencies of the Ministers of Home Affairs and Defence under appropriate political guidance. In the event of foreign country sponsored terrorism or insurgence the Ministry of External Affairs has also got to come in. We have no institutionalised system for doing this effectively and on an ongoing basis and we must create one without further delay.[35]

Internal Security - the Biggest Challenge

The internal security scenario in North-East especially in Assam, Nagaland, Manipur and Tripura continues to be a matter of great concern. The increased use of IEDs/explosives by the North-East insurgents is a serious development.[36] Proxy war of Kashmir, insurgency of North-Eastern States, economic crimes and scams all over India and activities of organised criminal gangs indicate that Internal Security needs strategic management and should be treated as the biggest challenge.

Hunger Deaths Call for Drastic Action and Strategic Management

In India a huge mass of its citizenry is chronically hungry (over 200 million at least count). While on one hand, there are surplus stocks of foodgrains, on the other hand there were reported deaths due to starvation in Orissa. On September 3, 2001. The Supreme Court, in a bench, comprising Justice B.N. Kirpal and Justice Ashok Bhawan, expressed shock over the manner in which state Governments have handled starvation deaths. Centre and State Governments particularly Orissa, Bihar, Tamil Nadu, West Bengal, Assam, Goa, Tripura, Manipur, Uttaranchal, Nagaland, Arunachal Pradesh and Union Territories of Delhi, Pondicherry, Chandigarh and Lakshadeep were to identify the below poverty line (BPL) families and arrange speedy supply of foodgrains from the Food Corporation of India (FCI) godowns to the public distribution system. The Governments food for work scheme should be implemented in draught prone and flood prone areas. This scheme has not achieved even 20 per cent implementations rate by September, 2001. The Government claim of self-sufficiency in foodgrains should have stopped starvation deaths. State Governments must act swiftly.

Prime Minister of India Shri Atal Behari Vajpayee has reiterated the Govt's commitment of ensuring food security and creating hunger free India. Shri Vajpayeeji says, "we have sufficient stocks of foodgrains. No one need go hungry in the country. We are guided by the commandment of the Upanishads. "Annam Bahu Kurirta". It means—Multiply food production many fold ensure an abundance of food all round. (*The Times of India* - New Delhi, 9th September, 2001). Government has promulgated the Public Distribution System (Control) order 2001on 31, August, 2001 PDS is the joint responsibility of the central and State Governments. The Central Government procures, stores, transports the foodgrains upto FCI depots in the States. Actual distribution to the beneficiaries through the network of fair price shops is the responsibility of the State Governments. Central Government is implementing food for work programmes in eleven states in order to mitigate the hardship of the people affected by the droughts and floods.

Organisational Responsibilities, Specialisation and Coordination for National Security

National Security is the supreme responsibility of the Central Government and National Defence Council with Group of Ministers have direct responsibility for it. Defence forces of India including Army, Navy and Airforce have the primary responsibility for the security of the country. In the area of national security, the Ministers of Defence, Home, External Affairs and Finance have to coordinate their activities on a to-day-to-day basis. Today even so called peace is complicated by the instant gymnastics involved in dealing with activities such as coercive deplomacy, nuclear deterrence, and adversary states using inspired insurgency and terrorism as tools for the advancement of foreign political objective.[37] There is urgent need for institutional arrangements for planning and handling it, if and when we are at the receiving end of coercive diplomacy. Terrorism and insurgency demand that counter-terrorism and counter-insurgency planning, deployment and resources - mobilization should be done jointly by various agencies of the Ministry of Home Affairs, Ministry of External Affairs and Defence, under a unified command with appropriate political support and guidance. So far we have no institutionalized system for doing this effectively. Required intelligence back up is always a vital component for effective strategy. The recent change of control in the case of Assam Rifles to Home Ministry and I.T.B.P. to Defence is based on the GOM (Group of Ministers) recommendations to ensure the adoption of the principle of "one border one force". The Bureau of Immigration will now be under control of MHA instead of under Intelligence Bureau.

India today has the most advanced military technology base after China in the developing world though the Indian military complex is beset with many external problems. India's career bureaucrats dominate the national security decision-making process and the military plays a peripheral role in policy formulation. Not only is the Parliaments role weak in shaping national security policy but there is lack of independent overview of the defence complex.[38]

The Department of Personal and Training (DOPT) through appropriate career development strategies should enable officers of all services, and departments to branch off into different areas of specialisation after 10 to 12 years experience so that they may specialize in strategic management of national security. Human resource development of Defence services, Central Police Organisations and other State administrators must be ensured and proper career development should be ensured. Research and training on strategic management of national security must get due importance. Today, we must have at least a 25 year projection for research and development purposes and for strategic planning. We can ill afford poor planning that squanders money through sub-optimal expenditure on weaponry, logistics, equipment and basic infrastructure.

National Level Strategy—Policy Planning and Implementation

Policy implementation is a process of interaction between setting of goals and action geared to achieve it within a given time frame. The various inter-woven stages of policy making and implementation are given below:

i) Policy Formulation
ii) Policy Implementation
iii) Policy Evaluation, Assessment and feedback
iv) Policy Succession, Termination, Maintenance and mid course corrections

For successful policy implementation, political and bureaucratic support, availability of financial and human resources are key elements. Avoidance of conflict, enlisting of cooperation, and support of bureaucracy are fundamental conditions for effective implementation. It is necessary to provide a time framework within which projects should be planned, implemented and controlled. There are always some implementation gaps.

(i) Nuclear Tests

It is firstly important to recognize that India, like China, views the nuclear option as an essential component of national security and a symbol of its sovereignty.[39] A quantum jump has been made recently in the field of national security by India through the nuclear tests at Pokhran, Rajasthan. In the arcane world of security theology, India pioneered nuclear test ban signing without reservations the 1963 partial Test Ban Treaty, although it only prohibited atmospheric testing and India today is a nuclear power and has established strategic deterrence. The three underground nuclear tests conducted on May, 11 produced cavities which trapped all fission products. The subsequent tests two days later were of sub-kiloton range. India's reprocessing facilities have reduced the volume of nuclear waste to manageable levels. However management of nuclear waste would continue to pose complex environmental, economic and security dilemma for the country.[40] India has already declared its nuclear no first use policy to the world.[40a]

(ii) National Strategy

According to Gen. K. Sundarji, "National Strategy covers all aspects of a nation's life and living. It is composed of internal and external strategies. Internal strategies include the complete spectrum of socio-political and socio-economic policies and counters insurgency my operations. external policies would include diplomatic strategy, United Nation's Strategy, economic, trade and aid strategies, special interest group strategy for coping with external military threats and coercive diplomacy. The perspective time frame in which national strategy has to be considered must be long enough to be meaningful. A period of 20 to 30 years to generally preferred."[41] National strategy has to take into account various roots of conflicts and crises faced by the mankind throughout its history. These causes may be listed as under :

(i) The control of territory;
(ii) The gaining of basic necessities, food and wealth;
(iii) The control of another existing state;
(iv) The spread of an ideology; or religious fundamentalism and;

(v) The satisfaction of an individual pride (or megalomania) or the ambition's of a nation's ruling elite."[42]

(iii) Intelligence and its Utilisation

The first instance in recent history of "strategic information warfare" happened during World War II when German launched a propaganda campaign through posters depicting British solders in trenches while their women back home were flirting with American solders with open arms. This proved demoralising to the British troops.

"While national security management involves a host of issues, perhaps the most important single factor relates to the timely procurement of valid intelligence and its prompt and effective utilization.[43] There is a need for promulgating the charter of duties and responsibilities of various intelligence organisations and their timely evaluation by an apex organisation dealing with national security. Information warfare is important demand of any war situation.

(iv) Role of Defence Forces in National Security:

Defence forces including army, Navy, Airforce are the nation's ultimate weapons to Defend itself. Defence against external security is its primary secondary role. Currently the Army and Airforce have five regional commands each and the Navy three. The country currently spends an average of Rs. 70,000 crores per year on defence. During 2002-2003, defence ministry returned Rs. 6000 crores from its budget due to non-utilisation on training and modernisation. (*Times of India,* 19 May 2003).

(v) Responsibility for the National Security lies with the Union

The larger and ultimate responsibility for the National Security lies with the Union and the constitution provides that if a situation arises in which security of the country is concerned, the President can enforce emergency in part or the whole of the country.[44] Responsibility for the maintenance of the Internal Security essentially rests with the State. Failure of the State to maintain the Internal Security has been principally due to the serious decline in the attention denoted by the State Governments to the proper management of their police forces and lack of concern for their inherent responsibilities to maintain public order and internal security of the States.

(vi) National Security Needs Many Inputs

Ensuring national security involves political, economic, social, technological and even environmental factors as inputs. India has economic security concerns in a broad perspective in the context of structural readjustments and economic reforms. In the present scenario incremental trend of international regulatory regime is being put in place, governing activities in the sphere of technology, space exploration, nuclear energy, human rights and environment.[45]

(vii) Refugees can Create national Secutity Problems

The estimated numbers of refugees from neighbouring countries residing in India are as under:[46]

1. Tibet 80,000
2. Bangladesh 87,000
3. Myanmar 54
4. Sri Lanka 1,06,290

These were the figures in 1993. Illegal migration and influx of refugees from the neighbouring countries are being encouraged by some of our politicians in North-Eastern States to build up their vote banks and this is likely to affect social harmony, internal security and national interest.

(vii) India Must Rework its National Security Strategy by Learning lessons from Other Nations

We must learn from the examples of China and France who relentlessly pursue their strategic interest, undeterred by international opinion or pressure. US criticism on human rights issue or the threat to withdraw "The most favoured nation status has not made China stray from its chosen path.

(ix) Policy Implementation - Crux of Strategic Management

Lack of managerial knowledge, lack of political and bureaucratic support, lack of ability to change behaviour of people, passing of legislation without considering its practical implication, non-availability of adequate financial resources, internal rivalries and conflicting objectives, political pressures and pressures from powerful vested interests groups are main factors for delay or non-implementation of strategic policies.

International Level Strategy

National Security management is trilogy of foreign policy, defence policy and domestic policy.[47] International scenery has been moving in unpredictable directions and have been creating power-shifts in the balance of world power. Geo-politically the international order underwent fundamental changes with the end of the cold war. The task of assessment of international events in the increasingly complex world is not an easy task. "After all, even countries like the United States which have had far more sophisticated and well oiled national security machines had totally failed to forecast the collapse of their primary adversary and they have yet to reconcile to the altered scenario".[48] The interest and policy objectives of the great powers in country-specific and region specific terms from the strategic and military points of view have to be also considered. Concepts governing such approach are *first* intrusive political and likely military threat perception; *secondly* deterrence of such threats and; thirdly Defence aganist such threats if and when they become operational.[49] The world has become unipolar with US as the power Centre of the world. According to Gen. K. Sunderjee, nuclear deterrence is a politico-diplomatic-military exercise right from the planning stage and with total political control in peace time. In times of crisis, when hostilities have not occurred, crisis management though multi-disciplinary,will have politico-diplomatic preeminence. If deterrence has broken down, retaliatory action would be a political decision including targeting philosophy and scale of the second strike. Political decision would only delegate implementation authority to the military in small and monitored doses, with complete political control to stop military action which this is deemed to be best in national interest.[50] The right strategy for our foreign policy would be to look after our own national interest and watch the ongoing Sino-US interaction carefully. India must not rush to extreme stand on various international issues. The International scenario has changed and there will be great power consensus on important international issues in the United Nations under the leadership of the United States. However, western Europe, Japan, the Russian Federation, Pakistan and China cannot be written off as second class powers. In such a complex and competitive international situation India has to establish new political relationship, new strategies and fresh Defence equations are to be forged in the context of globalisation. India has signed 29 agreements negotiated in Uruguay round of negotiations in 1994 and has become a part of the process of globalisation of international economy.

On 9/11/2002, United States carried out commemoration exercises to pay tribates to those who become victims of terrorism on 9/11/2001 in the United States. For George Bush, it was an attack on democratic values. But why US President seems to be strangely unconcerned about the trampling of the same values in India and elsewhere in the world.

The Challenges of Change and Organisational Learning

Unfortunately strategy implementation skills are not easily mastered and experts generally find strategy implementation more difficult than stategic analysis or strategy formulation. Some of the important reasons for failure to implement strategies are as under:-

(i) Implementation is delegated to those in staff positions and-subordinate leadership.

(ii) The strategy implementation is generally partial because the staff in charge of the strategy implementation focus only on the range of issues under their direct control.

(iii) Generally a holistic strategy implementation is not carried out due to lack of political will, lack of commitment to national security and vested personal/political interests of the implementers.

(iv) Finance and resources are not made available in desired amount and scarce resources are also not properly utilized.

(v) In spite of failures in the past, many organisations don't learn lesssons from the past mistakes.

(vi) Legal, administrative and political considerations at time delay or block the implementations of strategy. At times government takes long time to take decisions on certain matters.

National Security becoming a Plaything of Politics

According to T. Ananthachari a matter of grave concern is the cavalier manner in which important issues that have a bearing on national security are being compromised for partisan political and individual benefit. The political system and the politicians who operate it, the administrative and bureauratic apparatus (which not only significantly influences the political authority but also in various ways shares power with it), intellectuals (collectively and individually) belonging to various shades of opinion - all these have in their own way contributed to this deterioration.[51] Allowing illegal migration of Bangladeshis from across the border is just only example. The identification of illegal immigrants as a source of social tension and threat to National Security, has not been touched even by the Group of Ministers who recently examined the national security requirements in the aftermath of Kargil conflict. Allowing a cease-fire in Kashmir for six months has enabled the terrorist groups to carry out new recruitment, establish informations and harboring centres and carrying out their recce of camps of security forces. The Central Government led by Vajpayeeji only realised its blunder after six months and by that time enough damage had been done to the national security.

Need for Updating Strategy, Weapons and Logistics to meet Challenges of Change

The six imperatives of changes - awareness, speed, innovation, flexibility, coordination in the face of complexity and involvement raise strategic issues for modern organisations because they so profoundly affect survival and growth.[52] Due to the complexities of change, strategic policies, weapons, and logistics have to be periodically reviewed. Organisations involved in security of the nation have to be learning organisations to keep pace with the rapidly developing changes. Intelligence failures have been central to the country's national security problems for the past 50 years, a point underlined by the Kargil affair.[53]

System Levers, Action Levers and Context Levers

Information resourcing systems, human resourcing systems, capital resourcing system and control systems are important implementation levers for national security strategies. Managing human resources is one of the most crucial implementation level for national security. Hundred per cent involvement and commitment of Defence and security forces alone can provide a secure strategic national security implementation. There is a continuing need for effective leaders to exercise power and influence over Defence and security. According to J.N. Dixit, Former Foreign Secretary, "When assessing the security concerns of any country, the normal approach is to examine the political and security environment of the region in which it is located, the nature of relations with and its attitude towards its neighbours and vice-versa, the military doctrines, force deployment postures, weapons system capabilities of countries in the region and above all, the inter play of Defence and foreign policy objectives of countries in the area".[54]

i) Need for Spending on Security

According to Defence analysts, "India spends a pitiful 2.5 per cent of GDP on defence, whereas Pakistan spends eight per cent and China six."[55] There is need for modernization of Defence forces, Central Police Organisation and the State Police with adequate funds for procuring required weapons, logistics and other equipment.

Sweeping Changes Planned in Defence

The Cabinet Committee on Security (CCS) in May, 2001 has decided to integrate three headquarters of the armed forces and set up an intelligence coordination group. Service headquarters will be integrated headquarters of the Ministry of Defence rather than attached officers.

Obstacles to Effective Implementation of Strategic Planning

The major reasons why strategic planning efforts are not effectively implemented are as under:

1. Formal planning is not accepted by all managers and administrators in various organisations.
2. Some aspects of formal planning are not understood in planned activities.
3. Managers and field functionaries at some levels are not included by planners.
4. Primary responsibility for planning is surrendered to staff and field experience is not given due weightage.
5. Long range plans are considered unchangeable.
6. An elaborate and expensive planning system is chosen.
7. Good practical plans are simply ignored.
8. Forecasting and budgeting are confused with planning.
9. Available information is inadequate.
10. Managers and planners get logged down in details.
11. There are errors in perception education and implementation.
12. Overall goals of strategic planning are ignored during implementations.

Once Indians would invest 11 per cent of their savings in the stock market; today it is barely 2 per cent. This is a no-confidence motion against the Finance Minister.[56] India's economic fundamentals are still largely not sound at all and needs strategic planning and implementation of various economic programmes. Corruption, lack of personnel involvement, and lack of properly trained staff generally cause mismanagement. The present work culture of India consisting of high absenteeism, general apathy for change, disproportionate concentration of authority, hydra-headed organisational structure, low appreciation of the collaboration nature of work and excessive status and obsessive authority consciousness are some of the reasons for economic mismanagement. G. Parthasarthy once said : "We have a defensive culture of waiting for aggressors, allowing them space within our territory (Panipat syndrome) and fighting every battle on Indian soil. This defensive culture goes well with our philosophy and commitment for world peace but strategically it is to our great disadvantage when the question of nation's integrity, unity and security is concerned, we must be pro-active and vigilant and must the war strategies with full confidence. We must adopt "a pro-active path to security and good governance" and must formulate and implement realistic, strategies. Amartya Sen has deplored the fact that India's strategic planning and management neglected the social sector (Education and health) and in the phase of liberalization, is neglecting the distributive aspects of food and goods.

Strategic Management of National Security in India - an Assessment of Past Performance

The present existing infrastructure in India for strategic management of our security is rather weak and faulty. It was the lack of such organisation for a closer politico-military consultations and geo-strategic assessment that led to a premature cease-fire in Kashmir and debacle in 1962 resulting in Chinese encroachment in the northern region, highly inadequate response to the aggressive Pakistan moves in 1965 and finally to the losing of peace after a military victory in 1971. Another example of its blunder is the unsophisticated handling of Sri Lanka problem and ultimately disgraceful withdrawal of Indian forces from Sri Lanka. The Defence Committee of Indian Cabinet has been defunct and was not use during several emergencies since the fifties. India's foreign policy and strategic management of borders have not been found successful at all.

In a large number of cases, national security is compromised because the politicians who finally approved the purchase deal may receive money/ gratification in kind from the dealers. The Bofors and HDW submarine deals fell into this category.[57] Recently the Defence Ministry has constituted a defence procurement board which includes representatives from the Ministry, Services HQRs, Finance DRDO etc. The present proposed Lok Pal bill must have both investigative and intelligence agencies to enforce corruption free transactions from politicians.

"Too many cooks spoiling the broth" is equally applicable to the strategic management of national security. Inconsistency is at the core of India's strategic management of security issues. In the connection of combating proxy war in J&K, each time the security forces succeed in consolidating their position through sustained counter-terrorist compaigns, the gains are frittered away through opportunistic, ill-conceived and unprincipled " political initiatives and attempts to play party politics. This has wasted the sacrifice of India's securitymen again and again. Intelligence agencies, Defence services, Central Police Organisations, Ministry of External Affairs, Ministry of Finance and Home Ministry - all have their respective roles for strategic management and at times there are problems of coordination and even ego problems of bureaucrats and politicians. India has miserably failed to evolve a responsive pro-active strategic management of national security due to various political, economic and diplomatic reasons. For strategic management, past lessons need to be learnt from history but this is not being done in India. We had wars with Pakistan and China and have we drawn suitable lessons from our failures, blunders and mistakes. In internal security operations have we learnt from our past mistakes committed in north-eastern States, Kashmir and even fight against terrorist in Punjab. According to Ved Marwah: " There is serious flaw in our policy planning and decision making system. It has resulted time and again in major blunders on important national security issues. With both the generalist civil servants and politicians depending on their intention to steer them through the complex problems, the chances of making major policy decisions on wrong premises become high because important inputs from the experts and those who have more experience and knowledge are frequently missing.[58] Strengthening of state police organisation by introducing police reforms recommended by National Police Commission reports is an important requirement for internal security. Civil Defence set up needs to be revamped to ensure effective citizen's participation in national security. On the lines of United States of America, the awareness of national security issues and response programme (ANSIR) should be immediately started in India. Constitution of India also enunciates fundamental duties of citizens to assist and give their support for national security duties.

Strategy and Leadership

Since the leadership is the very source of all planning and implementation of policies, the quality of strategic plans and the effectiveness of their implementation depend on the quality of leadership at all levels of managements. Leadership at various levels is the key to strategic managements and therefore there is a need to utilize some time-tested techniques for strengthening the universal inner, structure of effective leaders. A recent study by Standard Research Institute concluded that: "12 per cent of effective managements study is knowledge and 88 per cent is dealing appropriately with people."

The key to effective strategic management is to ensure that leadership runs like a uniform thread through all functions of management to integrate them into a culture of excellence. According to Lord Moran: "Leadership is the capacity to frank plans which will succeed and the faculty to persuade others to carry them out in the face of all difficulties." A good leader should be able to build an organisation into an energetic productive and pro-active one and can build a new culture of work. He has to understand and analyze various factors which affect national security as given in Diagram as on next page.

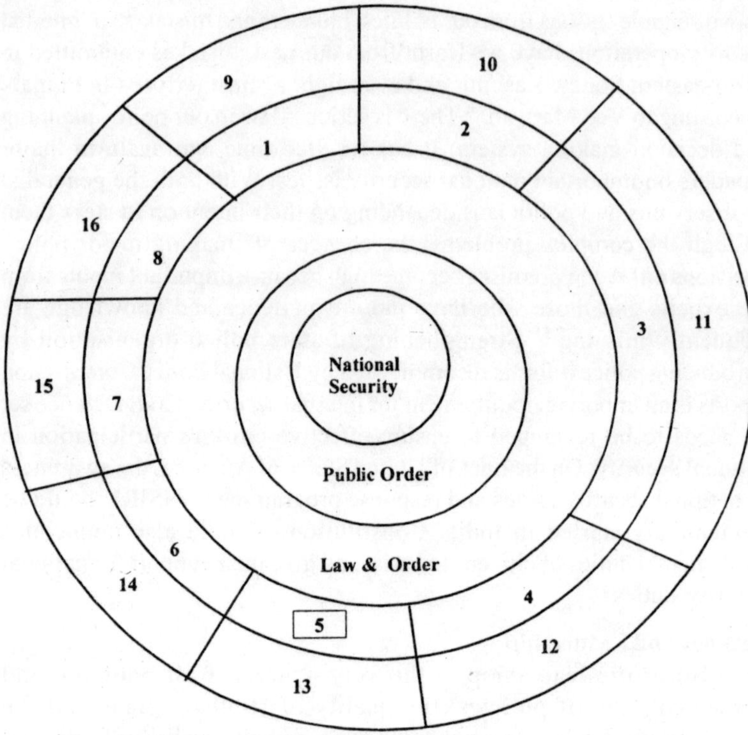

National and International Factors Affecting National Security

1. Environmental and Geographical factors/Geo-strategic positions
2. Political factors and Democratic aspirations—leadership
3. Economic factors and economic strength of the nation
4. Social and cultural factors
5. Constitution and Legal system—Administrative system
6. Historical factors
7. Level of Technology and scientific progress
8. Demographic factors. Age Group/Migration
9. Relations with Neighbouring countries—diplomatic, economic and cultural

10. Foreign Policy - Own and others
11. International Relations and Forums
12. Regional Economic Grouping
13. International trade and commerce
14. Changing World events and cosmic factors—natural calaimities
15. International Org. Balance of Power - International Law
16. Policies and Strategies of other nations

National security needs strong political leadership at the centre. A good leader must have four key characteristics of a transformational leader which are as under :

1. Charisma - Provides vision and sense of mission, instills pride and trust.
2. Inspiration - Communicates high expectations from others.
3. Offers challenge and stimulates energy motivation and sense of commitment.
4. Individualized consideration gives personal attention, coaches and advises.

A transformational leader performs both transactional functions such as policy-making, planning, developing systems, monitoring performance, coordination, rewarding, coaching and ensuring achievement of targets by maximizing efficiency, but also performs transformational functions including visioning, modeling, setting standards, building cultures and climates, boundary management, requirizing, searching and nurturing talents and finally ensuring organisational learning.[58]

Dramatic transformation can take place if armed and security personnel get committed leadership at various level of command. " The art of management is not confined to orchestrating the creation of a bold vision, a great plan or even one set of actions - that cause an organisation to face up the need for change. It must also encompass relentless follow - through (and) meticulous attention to detail ...[59]. Leadership for strategic management of national security, demands Role models who can provide inspiration, motivation and commitment to their subordinates for implementing the strategy. Power is the basic energy to initiate and sustain action translating intentions into reality, the quality without which leaders can not lead.[60]

Figure below shows sources and use of power and influence:

	Explicit	Implicit
Institution	Power and influence through commanding (orders given system change)	Power and influence through shaping (culture change)
Individual	Power and influence through persuading communication negotiation)	Power and influence through inducing (Role modelling

Leadership is exhibited through acts of charisma, providing a role model, acts of expertise negotiation and effective communication. For implementing the strategy, for national security, leadership is to be exhibited at various levels by their organisational leaders. Leaders have to play various roles - the role of administrator, problem solver, planner, strategist and transformer. A good leader must encourage leadership in others. The potential benefits of such "self-leadership" include increased employee commitment as well as innovation stemming from heightened motivation and unleashed employee capabilities. According to K. Subrarmanyam, it is now well recognized all over the world that India has not developed a tradition of strategic thinking. Our ancestors met in invader at Panipat only after he had penetrated several hundred miles into our territory instead of restraining him at Khyber Pars. Our political, bureaucratic and military establishments do not have the time, inclination or mechanism to think ahead, anticipate security threats and prepare the country to meet these effectively.[60a] Probably for the first time, Shri Atal Bihari Vajpayee and his Government at the Centre is providing the required political leadership to revamp the strategic management of national security but it will need effective leadership at various levels in the states particularly in the context of internal security because internal security is broadly the responsibility of the State Governments.

New Structures for Strategic National Management Needed

A holistic approach to national security demands multi-pronged measures. Some of the most important are as follows:

1. Timely procurement of useful strategic intelligence and its prompt utilization demands a coordinating agency at the apex level and all others levels of operations. What is called for is an integrated strategy encompassing intelligence as an effective instrumentality for pro-active operations and increased use of technology for surveillance and counter-intelligence. Intelligence should take care of espionage,

economic espionage and counter-intelligence. An apex intelligence coordination will be carried out under the chairmanship of National Security Advisor. It would ensure a coordinated flow of all intelligence of strategic importance to the night receivers.[61] Intelligence Coordination Group (ICG) is being set up to look after systemic intelligence oversight" at the apex level, presided by the National Security Advisor and would include the Cabinet Secretary and Chiefs of RAW, Intelligence Bureau, Defence Intelligence Agency and other agencies. The Cabinet Committee on Security (CCS) has approved the creation of a Technology Coordination Group (TCG) to be chaired by the National Security Advisor which will coordinate and regulate plans for acquisition of all new costly and major strategic facilities and equipment by the intelligence agencies and examine issues relating to allocation of funds for this purpose.

2. National Security structure needs revamping in view of the various recommendations of the task forces on defence, intelligence, internal security and the country's borders and accordingly overhaul of the management of defence and country's sensitive borders through thoroughly implemented reforms. Group of Ministers have recommended I.A.F. enhancement its surveillance capability and has disapproved deployment of border forces to deal with internal disturbances, law and order duties and counter-insurgency operations. Shri Brijesh Mishra has been appointed as National Security Advisor. Regarding the appointment of the Chief of Defence Staff to serve as a single point military adviser to the Government on strategic forces, the decision will be taken by the Prime Minister in consultation with various political parties at an appropriate time later. The Joint Intelligence Committee (JIC) which now doubles up as the Secretariat of the NSC. The three headquarters of the armed forces will be integrated. The service headquarters will be integrated headquarters of the Ministry of Defence.

3. An intelligence coordination group will be established for coordinating all intelligence agencies and it will be presided by the National Security Advisor. A Defence Intelligence Agency would be established to promote greater integration of intelligence collected by the intelligence directorates of the

three services. The DIA Chief would act as the Principal Military Intelligence Advisor (PMIA) to the defence minister, the proposed CDS and defence secretary. The integration of the service headquarters would lead to "progressive decentralization of decision-making and delegation of powers to service headquarters."[62] This type of exercise to revamp the national security system in its entirety has been taken for the first time after independence and needs to be worked out with commitment and sincerity. A holistic and integrated defence perspective plan will be prepared for 15 to 20 years and a defence procurement board will also be constituted shortly. On border management the Cabinet Committee on Security (CCS) decided that the principle of "one border one force" would be adopted to obviate problems of conflict in command and control and lack of accountability arising from multiplicity of forces on the same border. Border guarding forces would be exclusively deployed for border activities and will not be withdrawn for internal security maintenance. For ensuring sanctity of Indian air space procurement of additional low-level transportable radars and integrated air command and control systems would be undertaken. A specialized marine police would be raised in all coastal states. Air unified command for Andaman and Nicobar Island would also be established. A long term defence perspective plan will be envisaged by the national security advisor with the help of defence experts and professionals.

4. The defence revamp envisaged in earlier para will not in any way dilute the role of the Defence Secretary as the Principal Defence Advisor to the Defence Minister and as "Chief Accounting Officer." The Procurement Board for defence equipment will function under the Defence Secretary who will continue to control the purse strings. The Defence Secretary will enjoy an equivalent status vis-à-vis "the Chief of Staff". The proposed Chief of Defence Staff (CDS) will have no operational control over the strategic (nuclear) forces. Lt Gen. Pankaj Joshi on 1st October 2002 took over as the country's first Chief of Integrated Defence Staff (CIDS)

5. Between 1988 and today the Central Police Forces alone have grown from 406,000 (four hundred and six thousand) to 537,000 (five hundred thirty seven thousand strong). Almost one-

third of the million-strong Indian Army is involved in internal security duties.[63] India's internal security problem is that it has no organization to take a holistic overview of its internal security, identify vital national interests, examine the options available and accordingly spell out integrated internal security strategic objectives and formulate a comprehensive national security plan.[64] To start with, a culture of shared information and evaluation of alternatives has to be strengthened and similarly greater emphasis will be needed in scenario-building and crisis management techniques and processes. The over arching internal security staff is necessary to provide the necessary inputs for the political executives as nodal staff for inter-agency and inter-departmental coordination.[65] Recently on 19th July 2001, Union Home Minister L.K. Advani issued an order elevating Special Secretary M.B. Kaushal, in charge of internal security, to the rank of Secretary. Earlier, Advani Ji had appointed Former BSF Director General E.N. Ram Mohan, after he retired, as officer on special duty in charge of a task force on border management. Later he was sent as advisor to Manipur Governor Ved Marwah. Navy wants to go out of internal security duties although it was pressed into policing of the western coast following the March 1993 Mumbai Bomb blasts. At any given time the Navy has about 25 officers and 450 sailors spread over 22 detachments engaged in "Operation Swan". This involves patrolling, monitoring and maintaining close surveillance of the Gujrat and Maharashtra stretches of them western coasts from specially hired fishing travelers to prevent smuggling of arms and explosives by Criminal gangs sponsored by Pak ISI. Another 15 officers and 175 sailors spread over nine detachments are similarly engaged in "Operation Tasha" an anti-LTTE operation along the southern coast. For internal security duties, modernization training, deployment and task specialization of Central Police Organisation are immediate requirements.

The Concept of Human Security - An Intergral Part of National Security

The concept of human security in developing countries, like India, can be conceived in a positive sense in terms of maintaining a pattern of quality of life which consists of a number of indicators like food, health care, clothing, education, housing and supporting construction needs -

air, road, rail, sea, communications, women's progress and status, population growth, water energy, ecology and global interdependence, apart from eradicating (in negative sense) threats of hunger, disease, ignorance, repression, civil disorder and war, unemployment, homelessness and exclusion.[66] Internal national security strategies must be defined as a selective attack on the worst forms of poverty, i.e., progressive reduction and eventual elimination of mal-nutrition, disease, illiteracy, squalor, unemployment and inequalities.

Need for Public Awareness of National Security

National security needs to be understood by enlightened citizens national level politicians and senior bureaucrats. What is needed is a public debate based on a series of white papers on our national security threats, military and non-military measures to meet them and a clear enunciation of competing options.... The time has also come to redefine "security" and free it from its purely military - strategic connotations.[67] It is necessary to redefine national security and relate it to the broader agenda of development, progress, good governance and justice with democracy. National security must include personal security from violence fuelled by extreme and widening income disparities, social security through protective and promotional measures, environmental security through stopping degradation of our land, water, forests and other national resources and security of human rights and civil liberties. "Our concept of national security management must transcend limited objectives."68 Every enlightened citizen of India, our political masters, opposition leaders, bureaucrats, media and academia should be adequately educated about our national, security, challenges, our strategy, our options, our security structure and even nuclear strategy through various educational strategies at various levels. The ever increasing use of information technology in new weapons and revolution in military affairs (RMA) are inevitable for use by India to develop her security capabilites in the present nuclear age.

It is really high time to start educating every Indian about nuclear realities. The pronouncements of many of our ex-defence ministers and senior politicians have demonstrated how badly they are in need of education about our strategic management of national security and nuclear strategic wisdom. Unfortunately this country does not as yet have an adequate number of strategic national security thinkers to conduct a meaningful debate on the optimum strategy for India and its strategic options in the present international situation.

What India needs is a well thought out pro-active strategy for national security. Such an overall strategy formulation demands a massive political back up at both the central and state levels, complete voluntary support of bureaucracy at all levels, commitment and involvement of armed forces including Central Police Organisation, an intelligence back up with well analysed updated information, increased use of technology for surveillance and counter-intelligence, employment of advanced operational research units of defence research and development organisation and media support to build up favourable public opinion and a unified command group to executive strategic pro-active policy for protecting and safeguarding national security from its internal as well as external threats. This will need a motivated task-force involving the heads of the organisations concerned chaired by an eminent person with other experts appropriately co-opted to assist the task force unified command. Such a task force reports and assignments can be prepared periodically and then these could be considered by the Cabinet Committee on National Security and finally approved by the National Security Council promptly for implementation of strategy initiatives and strategic policy decisions. The present policy of adhocism and reactivism must give way to pro-active strategic initiatives. India faces an unprecedented opportunity to become world's technological leader and a world power with the help of a strategic pro-active policy of national security with constant research in bio-science and material science as well as information technology and scientific instrumentation. India must establish strategic diplomatic contacts with USA, China, Germany, France, United Kingdom and all the other nations of the world. China is likely to remain US's strategic competitor (not strategic partner) and this angers well for India. For India, China is well beyond the category of being a strategic competitor. Powell's straight talking with the Chinese on the issue of their suspected missile and weapons technology exports to a few countries is music to the ears. India is the US's new strategic partner in Asia and Vajpayee's Government deserve credit for getting off the blocks in their foreign policy enunciation. India has finally got off to a strategic doctrine: "Safeguard your own security and national interests first, and then move on to other strategic gains in the region and world wide." Shri Atal Bihari Vajpayee has said: "Our first commitment to the people is to give a stable, honest, transparent and efficient government capable of accomplishing all round development ...... Our system of administration is ill-equipped to fulfill our national objectives and the aspirations of the common man......My greatest concern today is in the area of (strategic) implementation ....where we fumble, however, is in implementing them in a manner that satisfies the people."[69]

Some Basic Issues

Every politician, every academician, every student and every citizen must understand and debate following issues:-

1. Is National Security Council too big and large to carry out serious strategic defence review and decide upon security options. Will it be able to deliver goods as expected?
2. Will the bureaucratic set up allow strategic planning or will it (S.P.) be the first casualty with the main responsibility of formulating the review vested with Strategic Policy Group (SPG) comprising secretaries of key ministries of Defence, Home, Foreign Affairs and Finance among others, it is unlikely that they will get views of national security experts and other non-governmental professionals and even retired Generals?
3. Should Navy and Army be out of internal security duties as demanded by them?
4. How to implement the strategic policy decisions when there is lack of coordination between various agencies and there are conflicts of perspectives?
5. Why Kashmir issue has not been resolved so far in spite of our much superior weaponry and human resources?
6. How to bring awareness about various concepts of strategic security of national security and how to reconcile security with citizen's awareness and cooperative participation?
7. In your opinion, what are the factors which have been responsible for lack of effective strategic management of national security?

There should be an on going national dialogue on Television and mass media so that national security issues get the required attention of the people.

Concluding Remarks

Decision making and strategic management for national security call for not only managerial professionalism, adequacy of funds, vision and organisational support but strong political will is the most important factor. It is only after 53 years of Indian Independence that a holistic strategy for national security has been identified and recommended. But implementation of the recommendations of the ground will require strong political support, coordination between different agencies and political leadership. Strategic management of national security should be the concern of the entire nation and every citizen.

References

1. Kantilya—*Artha shastra*—English version-R.P. Kangle- Kautilya Artha shastra - Part II, Book 9, Ch.1.
2. Ghosal U.N. - A history of Indian Political Ideas p.153.
3. K.P Jog (Editor) *Perceptions in Kautilya Artha shastra* - Popular Prakashan. Mumbai 1999. Also Usha Thakkar - Morality in Kautilya Theory of Diplomacy.
4. Sudha Passi - National Security Council Big doesn't seem Beautiful - *The Times of India,* 30 May, 2001.
5. Lorsch - The invisible Barriers to Strategic Change.
6. Ari Guisberg - "Operationalising Organisational Strategy: Towards an integrative framework - Academy of Management Review, p. 3 July 1984.
7. James A.F. Stoner and Charles Wankel "*Management*" Practice Hall of India, 1987, p. 112.
8. Henry S. Truman - State of the Union - Address 6 January 1947.
9. For further details see Dr. Krishna Mohan Mathur - *Crime, Human Rights and National Security* - Gyan Publishing House, New Delhi, 1996, pp. 304-310.
10. For further details see Hatten Kenneth and Hatten Mary- *Effective Strategic Management: Analysis and Action,* Prentice Hall Engle Wood Cliffs 1988; Also Rue, Leslie, W. and Phyllis G Holland - *Strategic Management : concepts and Experience,* MC Graw Hill Book Com. Singapore, 1986.
11. Henry Muntzberg - "Strategy Making in Three Modes", *California Management Review,* 16 no 2 winter 1973, pp. 44-53.
12. Charles E. Lindblom "The Science of Muddling Through" *Public Administration Reviews* 19 no 2 Spring 1959, pp. 79-88.
13. Macridin Roy C (1980) Contemporary Political Ideologies—Movements and Regimes Cambridge Mass., Winthrop, p. 4.

13a Patrick J. Below, George L. Morrisey and Betty L. Acomb—The Executive Guide to Strategic Planning—Jossey Bass Publishers 1987. San Francises. p. 3.

14. Peter F. Drucker - *Managements Tasks, Responsibilities Practices,* Allied Publishers Ltd., New Delhi, 1996, p. 125.
15. D.C. Pathak - My Turn—Strategies have to be formed with Intelligence, *Hindustan Times,* 18 May 2001.
16. Narendra Gupta— India Must Rework its Security Plan - *The Times of India,* 12 December 1995.
17. Allex Miller—*Strategic Management,* Third edition Irwin MC Graw Hills, Boston, 1998, p. 41.
18. Henry Mintzberg - Rethinking Strategic Planning Part II New Role for Planners—Long Range Planning - 27 : 3 June 1994, p. 22-30. Also Mintzberg—The Rise and Fall of Strategic Planning, New York, 1994, p. 341.

19. James A.F. Stoner and Charles Wankel—*Management* - Prentice Hall of India, New Delhi, 1987, pp. 123-124.

20. K. Sunderji - National Security Management - systemic In-adequacies *Indian Express*, 27th June 1996.

20a. Subhash Sharma - Forward Engineering of Public Institutions in Market Economy - Towards a New Theory of Public Administrations - *Indian Journal of Public Administration* Oct.-December 1996, Vol. XLII, No. P. 639.

21. Gunnar Myrdal - *Asian Drama* Vol.II, London, Penguin Press pp. 715-22.

22. Dr. Subhash Sharma - Note 1. Forward Engineering for Strategic gearing - A Conceptual framework—*The Indian Journal of Public Administration,* Oct-December 2000, Vol. XLVII No. 4, p. 667. Also *Management in the New Age : Western Windows Eastern Doors,* New Age Publishers 1996, p. 221.

23. Dr. Subhash Sharma Note 1. Forward Engineering for Strategic Gearing - A conceptual frame. *Indian Journal of Public Administration* - Vol. XLVI No. 4 p. 672.

23a Report on defence rocks Lok Sabha opposition question Govt. Role—*Time of India,* 24 April 2003.

24. Gary Hamel and C.K. Prahalad "Seeing the future first" - Fortune 130;5 (September 5, 1994) pp. 64-70.

25. Dr. Krishna Mohan Mathur - *Crime, Human Rights and National Security*. Gyan Publishing House, New Delhi, 1996, p. 325.

26. Lt. Gen (Retd) V.K. Sood - Structuring National Security, *The Times of India,* 15 May 1998.

27. Executive Summary of U.S. Commission on National Security Report, 31 January 2001. U.S. Deptt. of State p. 2.

27a Subrahmanyam K. Patriot games: eating out of the foreign hand. Administrator 44 (1) July 2001. p. 44-46.

28. GOM (Group of Ministers) Report on National Security Revamp Released *The Times of India News Service* - May 24, 2001. Late Delhi Edition.

29. Manoj Joshi - Not by force Alone - Transparency best Counter to Insurgency. *The Times of India.* 28th August 2001, New Delhi, p. 10.

30. Inder Malhotra - The Safe Passage to Militants in Shopian Proves that the Centre has not learnt lessons from the past - Hazratbal to Shopian, Hindustan Times, 12 June, 2001.

31. Prakash Singh. Platform Advantage Maivaha - *Hindustan Times.*

32. Dr. Krishna Mohan Mathur - *Concerns and constraints in Administration,* R.B.S.A. Publishers, SMS Highway,s Jaipur, 1991.

33. Lt. Gen. S.K. Sinha - Punjab - Lessons from the past - *Indian Express,* May 27, 1987.

34. Dr. Krishna Mohan Mathur - *Police in India - Problems and perspectives*- Gyan Publishing House, New Delhi 1991, p. 90.

35. K.Sundarji - National Security Management - Systemic Inadequacies - *Indian Express,* 27th June 1996.
36. Dr. Krishna Mohan Mathur—*Towards effective management* - Pathways to excellence - Gyan Publishing House, New Delhi, 1999, p. 204.
37. Gen. K. Sundarji - National Security Management. Systemic Inadequacies, *Indian Express,* 27th June 1996.
38. Brahma Chellaney - " Defence and Security Policy "- India's Policy problems - Edited by V.A. Pai Panandikar, Konark New Delhi, 1996, Part - II.
39. Harrison Selig S. and Kemp Geoffrly - India and America - After the Cold War (Carnegie Endorwment for International Peace- Washington D.C, 1993, p. 3.
40. Matin Zuberi - Can we handle our nuclear waste? *The Sunday Times of India,* May 25, 1997.
40a Singh, Jasjit—India's nuclear policy: The year After-Strategic Analysis, 23(4) July 1999 p. 509-30, Also Udyay Bhaskar, C.- Nuclear Weapons and no first use, Strategic Analysis 22 (10) January 1999. p. 445-465.
41. Gen. K. Sundarji - National Security Managament - Systemic Inadequacies - *Indian Express,* 27 June 1996.
42. Suresh D. Sinha - *Security in the New World Order* - Chankya Publications, Delhi, 1993, p. 46.
43. N.N. Vohra - IB's way wardness Automous by Default - *Indian Expresss,* 30 January 1997.
44. N.N. Vohra - Internal Security Role of Police - *Indian Express,* 26 May 1995, Ahmedabad Edition.
45. J. N. Dixit - National security - The sources of Danger - *Indian Express,* 16th January 1996.
46. Refugees in India - *The Times of India,* 18th December 1997.
47. Dr. Krishna Mohan Mathur—*Crime, Human Rights and National Security,* Gyan Publishing House, New Delhi, 1996 p. 333.
48. Jasjit Singh - National Security - Internal and External Challenges. *The Times of India,* 26th July 1996.
49. J.N. Dixit - National Security The Sources of Danger - *Indian Express,* 16 January 1996.
50. Gen.K. Sundarij- National Security Management - Systemic Inadequacies - *Indian Express,* 27 June 1996.
51. T. Anathachari - National security - Plaything of politics - *Hindustan Times,* 20 January 1995.
52. Dr. Krishna Mohan Mathur - *Towards effective Management-Pathways to Excellence* -Gyan Publishing House, New Delhi, 1999, p. 206.

53. Editorial - *The Times of India,* 24 May 2001." Security Council"

54. J.N. Dixit - National security The source of Danger - *Indian Express* - 16 Januray 1996.

55. Amiya Kumar Ghosal - Spending on security - Modernisation. Not Money is the key - *The Times of India,* 13 July 1998.

56. T.V.R. Shenoy-Signs of Economic Mismanagement-*Indian Express,* May 30, 2001. New Delhi

57. K. Subrahmanyam any an - Public eye - It's the politician that we must guard against - *The Times of India* govt Business 7 Sept. 2001.

58. Ved Marwah - *Uncivil war - Pathology of Terrorism in India. Harper Collins,* New Delhi, India.

58.(a) Dr. K.M. Mathur - *Managing Human Resource Development.* An Indian Perspective - Gyan Publishing House, New Delhi, 2001, p. 223.

59. Regina Fazio Maruca - The Right way to go global - *Harvard Business Review* March - April 1944, p. 134-135.

60. Warren Bennis and Burt Nanus - *Leadership - The strategies for Taking charge,* New York - Harper-row 1985, pp. 6-10

60(a) K Subrahmanyam - Fostering Newer Panipats- Indias Lack of Strategics Planning - *The Times of India,* 4th January 1999.

61. D.C. Pathak : My Turn - Stategies have to be formed with intelligence - *Hindustan Times,* 18th May 2001.

62. Sweeping changes planned in Defence - *Hindustan Times,* 13th May 2001, PTI source.

63. Manoj Joshi - Wanted A Common Security goal - under scrutiny - Internal security - *The Times of India* - 3 August 2001.

64. Narendra Gupta. India Must Rework. Its Security Plan - 12 Dec 1995.

65. Jasjit Singh - National security, Internal and External challenges- *The Times of India,* 20th July 1996.

66. P.D. Malgavkar- Quality of Life and Governance - Trends, Options and Institutions - New Delhi - Centre for Policy Research- Konark Publishing House, 1996, pp. 315-324.

67. Praful Bidwai - New Security Mantra- Perils of a Paranoid—mentality - *The Times of India,* 2 July 1996.

68. Jasjit Singh - National Security - Internal and External Challenges - *The Times of India,* 25 July 1996.

69. Atal Behari Vajpayee - Indian Administration Today - Remedying Its weaknesses - Address delivered on Indian Institute of Public Administration's Founder's DAY on March 29, 1999 at New Delhi - *Indian Journal of Public Administration* January - March 1999 - Vol. XLV No. 1. (pp. 2-4).

Bibliography

1. Ali Aruna Asaf, Singh Darbar, *India's Unity and Security; Challenges*, Patriot Publishers, New Delhi, 1984.
2. Azar Bdward E. Chung-in Moon, *National Security in the Third World,* University of Maryland, England, 1988.
3. Agrawal, R.S., *Human Rights in the Modern World*, New Delhi, Cheetna Publications, 1979.
4. Beres Louis Reno, *Terrorism and Global Security. The Nuclear threat,* Westview Press/Boulder and London, 1987.
5. Batra T.S., *Human Rights, A Critique*, New Delhi Metropolitan Book Co. Pvt. Ltd., 1979.
6. Ali Asghar, *Communal Riots in Post Independence India,* Bombay, Sangam Books, 1984.
7. Barrier, N.G., *Roots of Communal Politics,* Delhi, Arnold, Heinemann, 1976.
8. Chakravartty Gargi, *Ganghi, A Challenge to Communalism*, New Delhi, Eastern Book, 1987.
9. Chibber Aditya, *National Security Doctrine*, Ed., New Delhi, Lancer International Pvt. Ltd, 1990.
10. Das S.T., *National Security in Perspective*. Gyan Publishing House, Delhi, 1987.
11. Dr. Subramanian S., *Human Rights and Police,* Hyderabad, Publishers Association for Advancement of Police and Security Science, 1993.
12. Das Veena, *Communities Riots and Survivors in South Asia,* Delhi, Oxford University Press, 1990.
13. Gupta Ranjit Singh, *Management of Internal Security,* Lancer Pub., New Delhi, 1994.
14. Ghosh S.K., *Communal Riots in India,* Ashish Publishing House, New Delhi, 1987.
15. Hingorani R.C., *Human Rights in India,* Oxford & IBH Publishing Co., New Delhi, 1985.
16. Iyer V.R. Krishna, *Human Rights and the Law,* Vedpal Law House, Indore, 1984.
17. Iyer V.R. Krishna, *Human Rights and in Human Wrongs*, B.R. Publishing Corp., Delhi, 1990.

18. Jayaramu P.S., *India's National Security and Foreign Policy,* ABC Publishing House, Delhi, 1987.
19. Kumar Ravindra, *Problem of Communalism in India,* Mittal Publications, New Delhi, 1990.
20. Kathpalia P.N., *National Security Perspectives*, Lancer International, New Delhi, 1986.
21. Kashyap Subhash, *Human Rights and the Parliament,* Metropolitan Book Co., New Delhi, 1978.
22. Mathur K.M. Dr., *Internal Security Challenges and Police in a Developing Society,* RBSA, Jaipur, 1989.
23. Mathur K.M. Dr., *Management of Internal Security,* Gyan Publishing House, New Delhi, 1995.
24. Mathur K.M. Dr., *Police, Law and Internal Security,* Gyan Publishing, New Delhi, 1994.
25. Mathur K.M. Dr., *Problems of Police in a Democratic Society.,* RBSA Publishers, Jaipur, 1987.
26. Mathur K.M. Dr., *Concern and Constraints in Administration,* RBSA Publishers, Jaipur, 1991.
27. Mathur K.M. Dr., *Police in India–Problems and Perspectives,* Gyan Pub. House, Delhi, 1991.
28. Mathur K.M. Dr., *Commentary on CRPF Act, 1949,* Published by CRPF Directorate General, 1976 Revised edition 1990.
29. Mathur K.M. Dr., *Vikassheed Samaj main Samsamyik Police ki Bhoomika* (Hindi), Gyan Publishing House, New Delhi.
30. Mathur K.M. Dr., *Swatantrottar Bharat mein Janta ka Uttardayatwa thatha police ki Bhoomika,* BRP & D, Published by Manager Govt. Printing Press Faridabad, New Delhi, 1992.
31. Mathur K.M. Dr., *Administration of Police Training in India–* Gyan Publishing House, Delhi, 1987.
32. Mathur K.M. Dr., *Indian Police Role and Challenges,* Gyan Pubhlishing House, New Delhi, 1994.
33. Mishra B.N., *International Social Security System,* Anmol Publications, New Delhi, 1993.
34. Nagar K.S., Charma G. Lt. Col., *India's Security Super Power Threat,* Reliance Publishing Co., New Delhi, 1991.
35. Nath Trilok, *National Security,* B.R. Publishing Corp., Delhi, 1986.
36. Nirmal Anjali, *Role and Functioning of Central Police Organisations,* Uppal Publishing House, New Delhi, 1992.

37. Nayar V.K. Lt. Genl., *Threat from within - Indias Internal Security Environment,* Lancer Pvt. Ltd., New Delhi, 1992.
38. P.N. Kathpalia, *National Security Perspectives*, Lancer International, New Delhi, 1986.
39. Pakem B., *Nationality Ethnicity and Cultural Identity in North-East India*, Omsons Pub., New Delhi, 1990.
40. Rajgopal P.R., *Communal Violence in India,* Uppal Publishing House, New Delhi, 1987.
41. Sharma P.D., *Police, Internal Security and Developmental Disorder in India,* Uppal Publishing, New Delhi, 1988.
42. Sarhadi, Ajit Singh, *India's Security in Resurgency Asia,* B.R. Chawala, New Delhi, 1979.
43. Sharma P.D., *Police and Criminal Justice Administration in India,* Uppal Pub House, Delhi, 1985.
44. Singh Jasjit, *Asian Security : Old Paradigms and New Challenges,* Lancer International, New Delhi, 1991.
45. Subrahmanyam K., *Indian Security Perspective,* ABC Publishing House, New Delhi, 1982.
46. Subrahmanyam K., *Grobal Security : Some Issues and Trends*, Lancer International, Delhi, 1987.
47. Saksena K.P., *Human Rights Perspective and Challenges,* Lancer Books, New Delhi, 1994.
48. Sharma P.D., *Police and Political Order in India,* Research, Pub. Delhi, 1984
49. Subramanian S. Dr., *Human Rights and Police,* Assn, For Adv. of Police, Hyderabad, 1992.
50. Vas E.A. Lt. Genl., *The Search for Security : Controlling Conflict and Terrorism,* Natraj Pub., Dehra Dun, 1989.
51. Shukla K.S., *Collective Violence Genesis and Response*, IIPA, New Delhi, 1988.
52. Tucker M.M., *Combating the Terrorists Democratic Responses to Political Violence,* Facts on File, New York, 1988.
53. Vasak, Karel The International Dimensions of Human Rights, UNESCO, 1982.
54. White Jonathan R., *International Security,* Vol. I, (IBH), 1986.
55. White Jonathan R., *International Security,* Vol. II, 1986.
56. *The Protection of Human Rights Act 1993.* New Delhi: Universal Book Traders, 1994.

Index